CW01249694

Equality, Citizenship, and Segregation

Equality, Citizenship, and Segregation

A Defense of Separation

Michael S. Merry

palgrave
macmillan

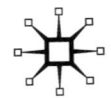

EQUALITY, CITIZENSHIP, AND SEGREGATION
Copyright © Michael S. Merry, 2013.

All rights reserved.

First published in 2013 by PALGRAVE MACMILLAN® in the United States—a division of St. Martin's Press LLC, 175 Fifth Avenue, New York, NY 10010.

Where this book is distributed in the UK, Europe and the rest of the world, this is by Palgrave Macmillan, a division of Macmillan Publishers Limited, registered in England, company number 785998, of Houndmills, Basingstoke, Hampshire RG21 6XS.

Palgrave Macmillan is the global academic imprint of the above companies and has companies and representatives throughout the world.

Palgrave® and Macmillan® are registered trademarks in the United States, the United Kingdom, Europe and other countries.

ISBN: 978-1-137-03370-3

Library of Congress Cataloging-in-Publication Data

Merry, Michael S.
  Equality, citizenship, and segregation : a defense of separation / Michael S. Merry.
    pages cm
    ISBN 978-1-137-03370-3 (hardcover : alk. paper)
    1. Cultural pluralism. 2. Segregation. 3. Minorities. 4. Citizenship. 5. Equality. I. Title.
  HM1271.M3974 2013
  305.8—dc23   2013002338

A catalogue record of the book is available from the British Library.

Design by Scribe Inc.

First edition: July 2013

10 9 8 7 6 5 4 3 2 1

To Nicholas, Sophia, and Peter
with all my love

Without [segregation], the American Negro will suffer evils greater than any possible evil of separation: we would suffer the loss of self-respect, the lack of faith in ourselves, the lack of knowledge about ourselves, the lack of ability to make a decent living by our own efforts and not by philanthropy.

W. E. B. Du Bois, *Writings*, p. 1263.

Many political and educational plans have failed because their authors designed them according to their own personal views of reality, never once taking into account (except as mere objects of their action) the *men-in-a-situation* to whom their program was ostensibly directed.

Paolo Freire, *Pedagogy of the Oppressed*, p. 83.

It is never a good enough excuse for refusing to think about something that you are afraid of where you might end up, or of the company you might end up in.

Matthew Cavanagh, *Against Equality of Opportunity*, p. 180.

Contents

Foreword		xi
Acknowledgments		xv
1	Introduction	1
2	Integration	21
3	Foundational Principles	47
4	Voluntary Separation	67
5	Religious Separation	93
6	Cultural Separation	117
7	Social Class Separation	139
Afterword		163
Notes		171
References		191
Index		213

Foreword

How ought a liberal society treat its racial, cultural, linguistic, and religious minorities, especially those that are geographically and institutionally concentrated and that labor under various kinds of disadvantage? For many political theorists, the answer depends crucially on the specific kind of minority one has in mind. If there is a consensus view, it is probably that some kinds of minorities (e.g., national minorities and indigenous groups) are entitled to have their separateness protected and even promoted while other kinds of groups (e.g., disadvantaged racial minorities and immigrants) ought to be integrated into the dominant culture and institutions of the society. On its face, this bimodal policy response to minority disadvantage is odd: Why is separateness appropriate for some but not for others? Why mandate integration for some but not for others? Some theorists have provided elaborate answers to these questions—in the North American context, for example, the work of Will Kymlicka is a prominent and influential attempt to provide such an account. But given the complexity of social reality and the variety of historical contexts and concrete situations faced by particular societies and particular groups within them, this "either/or" approach can't be the whole story. Yet the position that justice requires protecting separation for some but not others remains a dominant—perhaps *the* dominant—view in many societies.

Michael Merry has written a provocative book that confronts this view head on. He argues that integration is far from being a panacea for the minorities for whom it is often thought most appropriate. Attempts at integration often involve serious costs for its intended beneficiaries, and the promised benefits often fail to materialize. Indeed, given the record of failure of integration in many cases and the lack of political will to bring it about on fair terms, genuine integration is often not even a realistic possibility. The issue is not integration versus separation but rather the terms on which separation will be maintained. Furthermore, some forms of voluntary institutional separation are not antithetical to basic liberal values such as equality and citizenship. In many cases, separation is compatible with and may even promote these values.

A political theorist and an education scholar, Merry focuses on schools as the site of voluntary separation—and appropriately so given schools' role in advancing (or undermining) equality of opportunity and common citizenship. His argument proceeds in two steps. In the first few chapters, Merry provides a critique of integration and a prima facie defense of voluntary separation. The argument for separation, he suggests, must be prima facie, because so much depends upon the facts of the particular case. In the second half of the book, he fleshes out and applies the general argument to three cases: Hindu and Muslim schools in the Netherlands, African Americans in the United States, and (more speculatively and tentatively) working-class whites in England.

Merry's argument is partly principled and partly pragmatic. At the level of principle, Merry argues that integration cannot be, as Elizabeth Anderson (2010) has argued (at least in the case of African Americans), an imperative of justice. Even if segregation is often associated with injustice, it does not follow that the appropriate remedy is integration. The relation between segregation and disadvantage is too complex for that. Segregation and disadvantage are contingently, not necessarily, connected, so a justice-based approach to the disadvantage and inequality that often attends segregation must be attuned to that contingency. It must also be attentive to the costs of integration and potential benefits of voluntary segregation as well as to the political realities that restrict what is practicable. This argument clears the ground for the pragmatic one, which is that under certain conditions, and in certain cases, the most realistic and attractive approach will not be to insist on integration, however imperfectly realized and whatever the costs, but to explore voluntary separation as a way of pursuing equality and common citizenship. Often, the more promising approach will be to focus on the terms of separation rather than to continue to hope that one can eliminate it entirely.

One of the virtues of Merry's book is its ambitious scope, encompassing three very different cases from three national contexts. Too often, a whole literature grows up around a particular group, paying too little heed to other literatures that treat other groups that confront similar circumstances. A more fruitful approach, and the one that Merry takes, is informed by both the empirical evidence and the theoretical work that is related to a variety of groups. In drawing comparisons among the justice-based claims of segregated minorities across the Atlantic, Merry joins Iris Young (2000), whose treatment of segregation in North American and European cities has too seldom been followed up by other political theorists and philosophers. One can only hope that Merry's discussion will help contribute to a more international discourse on the issues that it considers.

Readers will find much to argue with here. Is Merry too sanguine about the compatibility of, say, Islamic schools and common and equal citizenship? Are predominantly black schools in the United States really a case of cultural separation, and must those schools be Afrocentric to have grounds to resist efforts at integration? Can working-class whites in England really make claims similar to those of cultural minorities? But these questions, and the worries and objections that they reflect, place the argument just where it should be—on the terrain of the specific cases in all of their complexity. This means that the arguments will necessarily be messy, and we should expect reasonable people to disagree on where the balance of reasons lies. But in clearing the ground to engage the debate at this level and providing exemplars of the kind of arguments that are needed, Michael Merry has provided a valuable service.

Andrew Valls
Oregon State University

Acknowledgments

People either with whom I have been privileged to discuss these ideas in person or from whom I have received written comments on some portion of the draft include Veit Bader, Louise Bamfield, Robin Celikates, Derrick Darby, Yuval Evri, Neil Ferguson, Özgür Gürel, Michael Halewood, Rich Harris, Yolande Jansen, Bart van Leeuwen, David Manley, Rinus Penninx, Roland Pierik, Anders Schinkel, Lucas Swaine, Andrew Valls, and Ben Vermeulen. Thanks also go to Tim Butler, David Gillborn, and Diane Reay for engaging conversations about social class. Special thanks to Bill New for his earlier work with me on African-centered schools and to Geert Driessen for his earlier work with me on Hindu schools. I am also grateful to Taylor & Francis for permission to reuse material from "Equality, Self Respect and Voluntary Separation," *Critical Review of International Social and Political Philosophy* 15, no. 1 (2012): 79–100; Sage for permission to reuse material from "Equality on Different Terms: The Case of Dutch Hindu Schools," *Education and Urban Society* 44, no. 5 (2012): 632–648; Blackwell for permission to reuse material from "Plural Societies and the Possibility of Shared Citizenship," *Educational Theory* 62, no. 4 (2012): 371–380 and "Segregation and Civic Virtue," *Educational Theory* 62, no. 4 (2012): 465–486; and University of Chicago Press for permission to reuse material from "Constructing an Authentic Self: The Challenges and Promise of African-Centered Pedagogy," *American Journal of Education* 115, no. 1 (2008): 35–64. Finally, my thanks go to members and audiences of symposia where some of these ideas have been presented, including Aarhus University (Copenhagen), Cambridge University, Eindhoven University of Technology, Loyola University (Chicago), Northeastern University (Boston), Oxford University, Roehampton University (London), University of Amsterdam, University of Bristol, University of Illinois at Urbana-Champaign, University of Karlsruhe, University of London, and the VU University Amsterdam.

1

Introduction

The provocative thesis I argue for in this book is that many forms of segregation are compatible with the liberal democratic ideals of equality and citizenship. More specifically, I aim to provide a philosophical justification for what I shall call *voluntary separation*. Many will stumble on this choice of words. Owing to the manner in which structural barriers often restrict what the members of some minority groups can do, many will be inclined to view separation as either a resignation to nonideal circumstances or, worse, a refusal to engage with the mainstream. I understand the reasons some have for holding this view. However, to the first point I will argue that there is far more agency involved in separation that cannot—indeed, should not—be explained merely in terms of resignation or defeat. To the second point I will show that separation does not preclude engagement with the mainstream, but in any case the terms and expression of that engagement do not hinge on integration.

Over the next several chapters, voluntary separation will refer to a pragmatic and only partially institutionalized response by certain minority groups to existing segregated conditions. The minority groups for whom my argument may have relevance are all stigmatized in some important way. By *stigmatized*, I suggest strong disapproval of some unspecified person or the group(s) they belong to by most members of the relevant majority group(s). Stigmas will vary from one context to another, and the meanings attached to them will evolve over time. Stigma may be attached to race, ethnicity/culture, religion, mental illness, speech patterns, social class, weight, disability, or sexual orientation. Notwithstanding the negative associations, even stigmatized groups nevertheless may manifest—or, at any rate, aim to cultivate—important forms of equality and citizenship. To build this case, I first identify relevant principles bearing on segregation and integration and then examine a number of sociological facts about each. I then scrutinize integrationist arguments before providing two prima facie justifications for voluntary separation. I then turn my attention to particular case studies.

Segregation

In its broadest sense, *segregation* refers to separation—or spatial concentration—as defined by some characteristic, such as race, ethnicity, socioeconomic status, political affiliation, gender, religion, employment status, or language.[1] Moreover, as a number of researchers observe, "social divisions based on religiosity, political ideology, family behaviours, and socioeconomic standing [in] some cases rival racial segregation in their intensity."[2] While I shall maintain that segregation per se does not augur harm, it almost inevitably will entail involuntary background conditions. That is, many of the opportunity structures, choice sets, and social networks at one's disposal are not of one's choosing; they are imposed or inherited.

But even in arguably mixed settings (e.g., malls, schools, neighborhoods, restaurants), it is often our segregated experience that shapes our expectations and behavior. This observation is so familiar and so common that it surprised no one when Beverly Tatum published a book called *Why Are All the Black Kids Sitting Together in the Cafeteria?*[3] The title would neatly capture a phenomenon mirrored throughout the world in both mixed and nonmixed environments. The same phenomenon is nicely captured in the ethnographic portrait provided by Gerd Bauman in south London: "There are pubs where Irish and Afro-Caribbeans, English and South Asians mix freely or even prop up the bar in daily cliquish companionship. Other pubs are favoured by some clienteles more than others. On the whole, an impression of segregation, or at least separateness, is inescapable in most pubs."[4] What can be said of London is of course also observable in Amsterdam, Buenos Aires, Cape Town, Delhi, and Jakarta. And what can be said of pubs can certainly be said of countless other environments. Of course, not all spatial concentrations are stigmatized; nor are the opportunity structures for all spatial concentrations the same. But irrespective of its manifold causes, in this book *segregation* will refer to the de facto situation of spatial concentration. It describes the situation *as it is*, the state of affairs into which many of us are born and grow up.

Separation

Conversely, and as its name suggests, *separation* entails a voluntary response to one's state of affairs. Now of course there is a sense in which all our voluntary actions are structured by involuntary forces. As Michael

Walzer puts it, the involuntary "is historically and biographically prior—the inevitable background of any social life, free or unfree. We move toward freedom when we make escape possible; divorce, conversion, withdrawal, opposition, resignation, and so on. But mass escape is never possible."[5] Notwithstanding this interplay of the voluntary and the involuntary, and a fortiori the many involuntary causes[6] of segregation, voluntary aspects often do simultaneously or subsequently occur. Even segregation, as Iris Marion Young points out, occurs "partly as a result of voluntary clustering and partly because of processes of exclusion."[7]

To illustrate the inextricable relationship between the voluntary and the involuntary, consider a number of middle-class examples: we may enthusiastically vote for our preferred political party, but most of us will have inherited ideas about politics from our parents, and in any case, the political options being offered are restricted; we may select courses from our university, but the credit structure necessary for graduating is predetermined; we may seek a job in our field of expertise, but the labor market is indifferent to our needs; we may recycle, but our habits are reinforced by laws, cultural norms, and others doing the same; we may use bicycles for transportation, but our choices are shaped by other factors, including the existence of bike lanes, the cost of gas, and the difficulties of finding parking in the city; we may want to live in the city, but our ability to do so is reduced by the price of rent; we may want our child in a Montessori school, but if there are no more spaces we are forced to choose another one.

The voluntary and the involuntary intertwine all the time in ways perceptible and imperceptible. Though its moral significance is highly variable, each of us unconsciously adapts our preferences according to myriad constraints. While those with more education and financial resources certainly have more options than those with less, we continue to recognize volition even when choices are restricted. Segregation and the choices that arise within segregated contexts are no different. So while real estate prices and realtor behavior may combine to restrict where I am able to live, I also may want to live near others with whom I share things in common or from whom I might expect some assistance. Living close to others with whom there is a shared cultural, linguistic, and even socioeconomic background provides a sense of familiarity and comfort. That is not to say that comfort is the overriding priority. As we will see soon enough, other things matter. The point here is simply that even when restricted or adapted to less-than-ideal circumstances, the choices we make do not count for naught.

Given the interplay between the voluntary and involuntary, some may be more comfortable with alternate labels: *pragmatic* or *responsive* separation come to mind. While I have no objection to either of these alternatives, I consciously employ *voluntary separation* (VS)—not only because choice is involved. More important, in my view, VS captures something that the other labels do not. As I explained earlier, segregation occurs for a variety of reasons, not only because members of particular groups have had to lower their expectations or "make do" with involuntary constraints. There is every reason to believe that most Sikhs, for example, actually *prefer* to live near other Sikhs (in Punjab or in the Diaspora) for the same reason that other groups[8] do, even if and when segregation is one of the consequences. It seems to me that this is a recognizable tendency applicable to any number of groups or group members defined by a shared set of characteristics or interests.

VS, as I will defend it, does not seek to camouflage or deny involuntary structural forces. Rather, it describes efforts to resist, reclaim, and rearrange the terms of one's segregation when those terms are counterproductive to equality and citizenship. To formulate my core argument succinctly, the end or purpose of VS is to make life more pleasant, but its justification hangs on its ability to enhance the conditions necessary for equality and citizenship. Empirically speaking, the forms VS might take will depend on the groups in question, the circumstances they face, the experiences or ideals that guide their separation, and the resources at their disposal. But normatively speaking, sometimes the most desirable and effective response to involuntary segregation is not to integrate neighborhoods or schools but to change the conditions under which one's segregated experience occurs.

I am certainly aware that some of these ideas, owing to their historical provenance and abuse, either resonate or fail to resonate with certain readers. Using separation and equality in the same sentence is a good example. In the Netherlands, where I live and work, the association to many has for decades seemed intuitively correct given the long history of institutional separation by political affiliation, social class, and religion. Under the Dutch pillarization (*verzuiling*) system, separate communities were governed by different social, religious, or ideological values, and with the exception of elites representing the respective groups, little interaction took place. Hence Catholics could grow up attending Catholic schools, participating in Catholic sport clubs, having only Catholic friends, listening to Catholic radio programming, and reading Catholic newspapers. Even as attitudes have begun to shift in recent decades, many continue to believe that separation can facilitate an important type of social and political emancipation.

Conversely, to many American readers the same association immediately evokes a strong emotional response—and for good reasons. Many will understandably associate the word *separation* with the 1896 *Plessy* decision (*Homer A. Plessy v. Ferguson* 163 US 537), in which all but one Supreme Court justice voted in favor of "separate but equal," effectively securing the de jure protection of institutional racism in all areas of public American life. Sixty years later, the *Brown* decision (*Brown v. Board of Education* 347 US 483) unanimously and effectively repudiated the logic of its predecessor. The finding that all-black schools were "inherently unequal"[9] in terms of material resources was beyond doubt, but the more far-reaching claim of inherent inequality associated with black space—a view with currency even today—rests on more dubious assumptions.[10] Even so, given this historical background, "equality under terms of segregation" will strike some readers as absurd if not offensive. Here I can only ask that the reader be willing to consider the argument and evidence on its own merits and bear in mind that the juxtaposition of *separate* and *equal* in other contexts does not necessarily evoke the same thing. Nor, in my view, must it mean what some of us take it to mean, even in the United States. In Chapter 4 I elucidate these matters in detail.

While there is a strong pragmatic element in my prima facie defense of VS, my arguments are situated against a broad theoretical framework of liberal democratic theory. Naturally, as an expansive and complex theory, it contains many—often conflicting—elements. Among its more passive elements we find respect for the rule of law, toleration, equal liberties, a willingness to reciprocate with fellow citizens, and at least a minimal level of loyalty to the political community. But liberal democratic theory also contains elements less focused on shared values and interests—among them, associative membership (in its many forms), contestation, and dissent. A healthy democracy will not merely replicate that which came before but will actively and consciously reproduce it.

As is well known, two of its core principles—liberty and equality—are distinct yet intertwined. Each complements one another in the sense that many forms of political and moral equality imply liberty. Or to put it the other way around, there is equality based on the extent to which liberties that should be available to all *are* available to all. Citizenship, too, is fundamental. As a liberal democratic principle, citizenship captures something important about liberty and equality. The relationship might be captured in the following way: liberal democratic citizenship entails equal liberty entitlements. More will be said about each of these principles in Chapter 3.

But because this book is not about these concepts per se but rather about the ways in which segregation facilitates or fails to facilitate equality and citizenship, I distinguish them in the following way: I assign both equality and citizenship a principled role with respect to integration. Moreover, I will use these same principles in framing the prima facie case for VS. Accordingly, both equality and citizenship will serve as the framing principles. Liberty, too, plays a principled role in liberal democratic societies and has a complimentary relationship to both equality and citizenship. Equality without liberty is little more than uniformity. Nor is citizenship without liberty much more than rhetoric. Either of these in the absence of liberty implies the renunciation of much of what it means to be human.[11]

However, with respect to the focus of this book, liberty—of conscience, movement, and association—conspires with partiality to produce and maintain segregation. That is to say, unless restricted or steered in certain directions, its exercise does not generally facilitate integration. In short, liberty is a *nonfacilitative* principle. So rather than setting up a predictable opposition between liberty and equality in which integration relies on equal citizenship while separation relies on liberty, both the case for integration that I examine and the prima facie argument for VS will focus on the role that the two framing principles play.

Integration

As I suggested earlier, many of us understandably associate segregation with inequality, particularly as this relates to inequality of resources and opportunities. Yet despite the clear linkage between some forms of segregation and social inequality, most scholarly accounts remain notably one sided, some going so far as attributing both the presence of discrimination and the structural causes of inequality to segregation itself. After providing detailed and lurid—but also rather selective—accounts of the harms of segregation, many scholars who write on the subject implicitly or explicitly embrace the belief that in order to remedy problems associated with social inequality, stigma, and discrimination, society must become more integrated.[12] Integration becomes a proxy for justice in the kingdom of liberal ends—if not an end in itself. While I also believe that integration under certain conditions can promote equality and citizenship, it is not integration that I defend but rather the best—and most realistic—means of fostering and realizing equality and citizenship under nonideal conditions. So while I do not repudiate integration, I also do not accept the belief that integration is always or even often the most sensible or effective strategy to achieve equality and citizenship. I call that belief *integrationism*.

To illustrate, consider an educational application. An integrationist will argue, for example, that segregated schools are bad for a society that values citizenship and opportunity on equal terms. Rather, it is far better for children of different backgrounds to come together and focus on what they share in common. But this belief is fraught with inestimable obstacles and difficulties. For starters, neighborhoods and cities on every continent are segregated (to be sure, some more than others) along many lines, and schools typically reflect this. In part due to the nonfacilitative role that liberty plays—in choosing both where to live and which schools to attend—both voluntary and involuntary features of segregation persist. Second, even if we all were to agree on the integrationist ideal, integration invariably entails far less sacrifice for members of majority groups whose backgrounds more closely correspond to the institutionalized habits, norms, and values of the mainstream. Unsurprisingly, as we will see in more detail in later chapters, even so-called integrated schools in fact are asymmetrically organized to benefit members of the majority group.

Integrationists remain blithely optimistic about the good that integrated school environments can or will accomplish. But very often this is a comforting illusion. For the integrationist ideal in the education example to be compellingly true, its proponents at a minimum must demonstrate (1) that integrated schools supply important goods unavailable in segregated schools and, further, (2) that they are more important than children being educated where they feel welcome, which is often within their own communities. Of course, being educated within one's own community is not a guarantee of feeling welcome or receiving an appropriately challenging education, but the point here is simply that in the absence of relevant enabling conditions integrated schools may only perpetuate inequality when its organizational features and hidden curricula function to perpetuate the status quo.

An integrated school will perpetuate inequality, for example, if unarticulated assumptions serve to reinforce stereotypes of certain pupils; if teachers continue to be ill equipped to handle the cultural and social class differences children bring with them into the classroom; and if sorting and selecting mechanisms remain—as they typically do—the normal state of affairs. So while I share many of the concerns that integrationists have about segregation, I contend that it is the *features* of segregation—and not segregation itself—that should matter. Contrary to the integrationist creed, I espouse the view that both equality and citizenship can be fostered and realized in segregated communities, even under nonideal conditions. Some integrated environments may indeed accomplish the same aims. However, the fact that some communities fail to foster these automatically hangs not on the environment being segregated but rather on the absence of relevant enabling conditions.

Consider by way of analogy the ideal of *inclusion*, which is a distinctive way of understanding integration. Whether all children with disabilities should sit alongside their nondisabled peers remains a practical as well as a moral question. One child with, say, emotional disturbance disorder or autism may function reasonably well in a mainstream classroom, while many, or even most, will not. Among other things, we will need to assess the nature and severity of the disability, whether pull-out instruction benefits or alienates, how inclusion affects the pupil in question (but also how it affects his or her classmates), how "reasonable accommodation" in the classroom should take place, and so on. To be sure, when de jure policies separate children by disability—emulating analogous policies on the basis of gender, ethnicity, or race—they should be challenged as discriminatory. But it is doubtful whether doing away with all separate instruction is beneficial. The point here is simply that there are analogous ways in which a belief in inclusion operates as an ideal rather in the same way that a belief in integration does.[13] But with respect to either belief we will want to articulate a defensible theoretical conception, one that might be used to frame how we understand the particularities of specific cases.

Even if we strip away the more fanciful ideals of integrationism, as a concept, *integration*[14] remains an abstract and underspecified notion. One may speak of spatial, sociocultural, socioeconomic, civic, and psychological aspects. *Spatial integration* very simply refers to the mixing of populations in a specific context, even when the mixing may be rather superficial. *Sociocultural integration* refers to the adoption of language, habits, and expectations of a host society. *Socioeconomic integration* indicates access to labor market opportunities, including the skills and capacities needed to take up specific vocational pursuits. *Civic integration* will include legal residency as well as a disposition to engage with fellow citizens on matters of mutual concern. Finally, *psychological integration* denotes a feeling of belonging. Others think of integration in terms of progressive stages ranging from formal rules guaranteeing basic freedoms and access irrespective of background to more informal and voluntary mixing of persons of different backgrounds in the private sphere.

Rather than getting bogged down in stage theories of integration or quibbling with idiosyncratic definitions, I will employ a broad definition. By *integration* I refer to spatial as well as both formal and informal social mixing of members belonging to different groups without specification as to the degree or quality of interaction between them. However, in some cases it will be helpful to distinguish different uses of the term. For example, we can distinguish between the ideal and its policy expressions. As an ideal, integration may be linked either to equality or to citizenship. With respect to equality, as a policy we may recognize integration in attempts to mix the workplaces, neighborhoods, and schools to, say, facilitate opportunities crucial for upward mobility. With respect to citizenship, as a policy we may recognize integration in citizenship tests, labor market participation, and a variety of other social, cultural, and political expectations associated with (typically) national membership. Regardless, both interpretations share the conviction that more social life ought to be shared rather than maintained as separate. Both equality and citizenship, then, operate as framing principles and accordingly are central ideals in this book. On either account, the overriding goal of integration is to promote more favorable outcomes for disadvantaged groups and their members by diminishing the harms associated with segregation.

Parsing Separation

On virtually every continent, the notion of separation predictably conjures negative associations: societal fragmentation; a corrosive alternative to shared citizenship; an ever-widening achievement gap; harmful ethnocentrism and mutual distrust; and, finally, deepening inequalities between the haves and have-nots. To link separation and violence we need only think of the Balkans, Kashmir, Nigeria, and Northern Ireland. Elsewhere, in Aceh, Tibet, Bosnia, Sri Lanka, Palestine, and Egypt but also in the Basque region of Spain or the Kurdish regions of Turkey and Iraq, dozens of countries remain mired in tribal, ethnic, and religious hatred, political conflict, and violence with no clear resolution in sight. Cities, too, remain infamously segregated, including Beirut, Nicosia, Jerusalem, and Mostar, to take only a few examples. In deeply plural societies rent by strife and inequality, separation appears to militate against what integration purports to guarantee. Indeed, given the need to coexist, respect, deliberate, and work toward solutions with others whose backgrounds, experiences, and beliefs are different from our own, integration—and not separation—seems to many of us the only sensible strategy in terms of both socioeconomic justice and lasting peace and stability.

With so many negative associations of separation at our fingertips, why even entertain the idea? Here are four reasons. First, to suggest that separation along linguistic, cultural, religious, ethnic, and social class lines is fundamentally untenable is both demographically naive and morally presumptuous. Empirically speaking, both segregation and separation have been with us for millennia,[15] and both are here to stay. Second, to disapprove of separation is to underestimate and undervalue the reasons for spatial clustering and communal attachments, particularly as these apply to minority groups. Third, conceptually speaking, separation does not entail a repudiation of integration. Indeed, most groups who benefit from separation are already integrated in important ways, as Will Kymlicka points out with respect to ethnic enclaves: "Many aspects of public policy affect [immigrant / ethnic minority] groups, including policies relating to naturalization, education, job training and professional accreditation, human rights and anti-discrimination law, civil service employment, health and safety, even national defence. It is these [policies] which are the major engines of integration."[16] Separation, then, can and should be seen as a form of integration by other means. Fourth, contrary to many of the examples mentioned in the previous paragraph, separation is not synonymous with hatred and violence. Nor does coming to terms with certain facts about separation entail pessimistic resignation to the status quo. But it is important to distinguish between different types of separation; they are not all the same. Separation comes in many forms, many of them both morally and politically benign.

Separation as Inclination

In perhaps its most innocuous expression, then, separation broadly describes the habit of preferring to be with others like ourselves. Any of us who examine our social networks, our neighborhood, and our close friends will recognize this to be true, even if it is truer of some than others. Though we may cross borders throughout our lives, the need may not be pressing, and its absence does not herald moral apathy or prejudice. Owing to a bewilderingly complex and diverse world in which each of us must adapt and find our place, the quest for meaning, belonging, and purpose inclines us toward coherence: coherence of cultural backgrounds, tastes, preferences, lifestyles, hobbies, and so forth.

Evidence for separation is in abundance throughout the world. Long before European settlers arrived on American or African shores, tribes were separated by territory, language, and custom. European cultures themselves were—and to a large extent remain—separated by politics, language, and culture. Around the world today, but especially in the West, most large cities have a wide array of ethnic neighborhoods. For some, these spaces provide refuge from social exclusion; for others, they simply provide a place of belonging for its members. Or they may be both. Paradoxically, too, they also may provide a bit of cosmopolitan spice to other locals, tourists, and travelers. To be sure, not every member of every group feels at home in their "own" community. Any of us may feel as though we were born into the wrong family or tribe. Some will experience not safety or belonging but disapproval and discrimination from their own group.[17] And of course few of us limit our interactions to specific groups. We mix in the market and the workplace; we may travel, live abroad, learn new languages, and embrace cultural diversity.

Be that as it may, an honest appraisal of personal habits and behaviors will consistently show that most persons, irrespective of background, socialize[18] and interact principally with others who share similar traits (e.g., language, ethnicity, social class, culture, religion). Indeed, location, social class, language, and cultural background determine much of what we do and with whom we do it. Even more common are interactions on the basis of shared interests, such as recreation preferences, artistic tastes, and so forth. That is, most persons naturally gravitate toward those with whom they share a great deal in common. Sociologists refer to this as the homophily principle.

Correspondingly, to one degree or another, anarchists, athletes, musicians, environmentalists, and Unitarians separate with others with whom they share more interests or concerns. Secular academics do not typically socialize with the religiously devout, and vice versa. Ukrainian speakers seek out other Ukrainian speakers. On some level Muslims bond with other Muslims. Backpackers and cyclists meet up with others like themselves. Yoga, gardening, and Sanskrit enthusiasts do the same. Our need for coherence and our need for belonging go together. Coherence does not mean that identities are fixed or noncomplex; nor does it mean that there are not potential risks. But even if we can imagine a society in which segregation is not the problem that many of us think it is, there will continue to be reasons to support many forms of separation if only to provide important goods—such as belonging or membership—to the persons for whom such membership matters.

Institutional Separation

All forms of separation in one way or another are institutionalized. Institutionalized separation may come in the form of community centers, places of worship, neighborhood associations, ethnic businesses, media, and schools. In its institutional expression, separation also may involve special rights and dispensations. In the former case public or private institutions may be permitted as either an expression of equal treatment or a right to freedom of association—or both. In the latter case the aim may be to provide special dispensation to some minority communities. For example, orthodox Jews and Muslims have won the right to appeal to religious law in some countries as it applies to marriage, divorce, and other personal matters.[19] Other instances involve more substantial institutional change. For example, devolution has made it possible for both Scotland and Wales to have their own legislatures, though each remains within the United Kingdom. American Indian tribes in the United States have autonomous governance over their reservations and territories and manage their own internal affairs, though their members remain American citizens. To be sure, each of these gestures by the respective governments came very late indeed, after centuries of cultural and political repression, land-grabbing, and even genocide. But separatist impulses have been present both before and after colonial interference.

Separation as Strategy

Other more radical forms of institutional separation can be named. Perhaps the most radical form of separation involves an attempt by one group to separate from the authority of the state with the aim of achieving political autonomy.[20] Here *separation* refers to secession and explicitly involves nation building. Nation building entails the reproduction of a societal culture via separate forms of government, laws, and customs as well as schools whose purpose is to inculcate culturally and linguistically distinctive institutions and norms. There are many examples of groups who viewed secession as the only way to secure equal recognition and political autonomy, including in recent years various post-Soviet and postcolonial states, the birth of Southern Sudan, and, not long ago, the declaration of a separate Azawad state within Mali. Meanwhile, identifiable nation-building institutions exist in Flanders, Catalonia, Quebec, and Scotland; moreover, each political entity (region, province, or country) contains secessionist tendencies. However, for the time being, each remains an integral part of Belgium, Spain, Canada, and the United Kingdom, respectively.

Another unusual form of separation involves willful and permanent withdrawal by minority groups from the mainstream society. Examples may include religious settler communities (e.g., Canadian Hutterites) or indigenous cultural minorities (e.g., the Inuit in Nunavut). In cases where coercion, abuse, or compromised well-being of group members has been demonstrated (e.g., the Children of God cult), separation has precipitated state interference.[21] In most cases, however, exemptions (e.g., from jury duty, military service, even schooling beyond a certain age) have been made for certain minority groups to govern their own affairs and perpetuate their own way of life. Even so, a number of cases continue to elicit concern and perplex experts. The European Court of Justice, for example, has repeatedly expressed grave concern that the Roma be given their full rights as citizens, while most Roma prefer to remain outside of mainstream institutions and norms. Though poverty and illiteracy rates among the Roma remain extremely high, a majority do not want their children to attend state schools.[22]

The foregoing discussion hints at different ways of thinking about separation, but directly engaging with all of them is quite superfluous to my task. To begin with, I do not incorporate either secessionist or withdrawal cases into my argument in this book for a number of reasons. First, both secession and total withdrawal from the mainstream represent a small number of cases. Secession in particular involves a degree of political and military action either irrelevant or simply not available to most segregated groups. As for total withdrawal from mainstream society, apart from monasteries and extremely small or marginal groups, separation in most liberal democracies only rarely takes this form, almost certainly because the institutions necessary for reproducing a societal culture are more than most can manage.[23] Further, both secession and withdrawal categorically repudiate integration to any social or political norms outside of their own self-imposed standards. Conversely, I would argue that VS can be reconciled with many interpretations of integration.

Separation: When and Where?

The time period I have in mind is the here and now. The here and now is of course shaped by what came before. Hence current levels of segregation have a historical narrative that helps to explain it. But the here and now refers to the ways groups and their members respond to the conditions that they not only face but also *create*. How long VS should occur will also depend on many factors, among them the realistic opportunity structures available to those living in segregated environments, the feasibility of realistic alternatives in integrated environments, and certainly the wishes of those whose lives are shaped by one or the other.

With respect to the context, the argument in this book will be informed by the broad empirical literature in both North America and Europe, where segregation has been the most studied. So, specifically, the context is the United Kingdom, Continental Europe, and North America (excluding Mexico). Because these are the contexts I know best, I intentionally restrict the purview and leave it to others to decide whether the arguments contained in this book can be extrapolated to other contexts. With respect to the institutional character of VS, in the next three chapters I focus on both neighborhoods and schools and not, for instance, the workplace, where interactions between persons of different backgrounds are most commonly found.[24] The subsequent three chapters will take up the institutional dimension by examining specific school contexts. Of course, the institutional scope of schools is broader than this; neighborhood associations, local government, and business also play a part. But apart from an expansive portrait of the organizational features of schools, I will not detail the precise institutional arrangements necessary for facilitating VS in the community, labor market, or political sphere.

A focus on education in no way ignores or downplays the relevance of VS in other spheres of human existence. It is certainly likely that VS as expressed, say, within a neighborhood association or through a citizen action group can and does produce many of the positive outcomes in which I am interested. Equality and citizenship, too, can be fostered and expressed in many different ways. Be that as it may, I will focus chiefly on the educational sphere for five reasons.

1. What the precise institutional and political arrangements of VS should be will very much depend on a number of variables that pertain to a particular time and place and may not translate very easily to other contexts for a variety of historical, economic, and demographic reasons. Moreover, the plurality and variability of communal life makes it difficult to make reliable comparisons. Schools, on the other hand, are chiefly a compulsory social institution and span many years of a child's life.
2. As a frequent site of segregation, schools are often the focus of policy debates, and this is not surprising, for it is arguably here that voluntary, coordinated, and effective institutional responses to the harms of segregation can best be organized. With respect to the problem of stigma—and its school-related concomitants, low expectations, discipline, and bullying—this is significant.
3. A majority of school-aged children in industrialized states continue to attend schools, and most adults already will have attended them. No other institutional alternative (e.g., religious institutions, neighborhood associations) comes close; nor are they as consistently well funded, attended, and monitored. In many countries, private schools are also funded and monitored.
4. Much ink has been spilled documenting the ways schools structure and reproduce various types of inequality. Yet perhaps more than any other social institution, at the level of rhetoric, schools continue to be seen as the great "equalizer" in the sense of offering all children a free education with a view to supplying opportunities to learn and successfully enter the labor market. Hence schools serve to promote some notion of equality.
5. An educated public remains a central goal of most governments. All industrialized countries have school systems at a minimum designed to promote literacy and numeracy but also knowledge of laws and institutions in the respective country. Further, one of the central aims of public education in most countries is to promote some notion of citizenship.

Education does not unseat the urgency of creating and sustaining fair and accessible structural opportunities; nor does it replace political mobilization necessary to challenge injustice. However, education does serve as the seedbed necessary for, and conducive to, accessing opportunities and pursuing reforms within the broader political structures. So while I provide a number of normative arguments that can be used to support a prima facie case for VS, the school is but one focus. VS can and does take many forms and assumes different guises, and the precise site and scope of separation will remain somewhat unsettled as long as the details of particular cases remain unknown. In short, what specific shape VS will take, or how it will look in its institutional design, will hang on the details of specific contexts and the interests of particular groups.

Separation for Whom?

Even if it were possible to reach a broad consensus on the importance of VS, we will not settle once and for all the following contentious question: *to and for whom does the argument for VS apply?* Earlier I mentioned that I will focus on stigmatized minorities. But some will inevitably ask who determines whether a group is stigmatized. Is stigma always visible? Further, will every member of a stigmatized group know or experience stigma? Because I cannot tackle each and every example of stigma and am unable to take up each and every possible candidate for VS, the answer to this question will remain contested. And well it should. After all, stigma may attach more to some members of stigmatized groups than others: lighter-skinned blacks who may or may not pass for white; gays and lesbians who may or may not adopt more heterosexual behavioral norms; the religiously devout who either practice their faith discretely or embrace ecumenism; disabled persons whose disability either is not known to others or garners more sympathy, and so on. Any and all of these defy easily identifiable markers of stigma.

Consider three complicating factors. First, some social factors and identity markers can mediate or attenuate the harms of stigma. For example, gender, social class, language, or sexuality may compensate for a stigma like skin color; conversely, skin color may compensate for gender, social class, language, or sexuality. Some groups and individuals experience stigma across all categories, but stigma typically comes in degrees. Nor is stigma necessarily permanent; it may be either temporary or enduring. It may abate over time as social and economic conditions and language proficiencies improve, academic and professional interactions and achievements increase, and public attitudes change. But consider a contrasting case:

outside of a few areas of spatial concentration, North American Muslims were largely an invisible minority prior to September 11, 2001, owing to their higher educated and middle-class status and their tendency to assimilate to mainstream cultural norms. Obviously the events of that fateful day changed what it meant to be Muslim in North America. But with respect to stigma, different groups for different reasons will come to mind for different readers.

Second, stigma is not always visible. For instance, persons with significant hearing loss are unable to function fully in many environments without the help of hearing aids, FM systems, and interpreters. But notice several things about this example. First, stigmas that once quite strongly impacted the deaf community have diminished considerably in most industrialized societies. Enrollment in deaf schools has fallen off dramatically in North America, even as deaf culture and deaf rights have gathered strength and increased in visibility within the American mainstream and elsewhere. None of this is to say, however, that the deaf community faces no stigma at all—or even that its reasons for separation (into neighborhoods, community groups, and schools[25]) are no longer valid. To the contrary, notwithstanding strong antidiscrimination legislation protecting the rights and interests of deaf persons, many places either are ill equipped to make good on those rights (e.g., rural communities) or simply remain uncommitted to changing the environment to accommodate special needs. Further, important cultural and experiential commonalities are shared by members of the deaf community that contribute to a flourishing life. Moreover, I would argue, these forms of separation among members of the deaf community are conducive to important forms of equality and citizenship.

Third, what should we say about those who are stigmatized while in other respects belonging to the numerical majority? What indeed do we say about groups for whom public ridicule and condescension are routine occurrences in their experience while having other characteristics that in important ways match those of the mainstream? Here we may think of significantly overweight persons as well as many white persons who are poor. Unlike some groups for whom stigmas have been reclaimed as a sign of pride (e.g., queer pride, black pride), it is far less obvious how stigmas of this sort would lend themselves to the arguments I later present for VS. Even many stigmatized ethnic minority groups in Europe can appeal to the Islamic *ummah* to regain a sense of belonging, which plays an important compensatory role. Are similar resources available to overweight people? Well, they might be, notwithstanding the known health risks associated with obesity. *Fat pride* and even *fat rights* have now entered political discourse.[26]

The foregoing comments serve to illustrate the complexities of establishing not only a clear case for stigma but also the appropriate response to it. Why, then, use a concept that is itself ambiguous or contested? In part, because similar problems attend the alternatives (e.g., disadvantaged, underprivileged, marginalized, excluded). Moreover, I believe that stigma captures something important about the way persons are treated because of some marker or attribute they have, though of course it is the significance *others* ascribe to those markers that produces the stigma in the first place. As each of the case studies in later chapters will demonstrate, disadvantage and exclusion are at least partly explained by the prior existence of stigma.

The Structure of the Book

Over the next few chapters I present a series of arguments and case studies that, I hope, will challenge some of the standard ways that many of us typically think about segregation and integration without ignoring or downplaying the seriousness of segregation's dark side. The pivotal argument will appear in Chapter 4, where I aim to show that VS, under the right conditions, can and often does supply important personal and social goods: ones that should be valued in pluralist societies that care about equality and citizenship. Neither equality nor citizenship is dependent on integration. In fact, I argue, they often thrive in its absence. Further, at the risk of repeating what I have already said, the institutional focus for much of the argument will take place in the educational sphere. Education in fact will resurface in one form or another in each of the chapters.

In Chapter 2, I consider both the facts about segregation and the case for integration as framed by equality and citizenship. The thrust of the integration-for-equality argument is that integration combats social disadvantage by distributing resources more equitably to children in need. I then examine a second argument—namely, integration for citizenship. Here the argument entails the notion of "shared fate," involving certain capacities of citizens to see themselves as bound up in relations of interdependence with others. I then interrogate integrationist arguments and examine the role that liberty, in particular liberty as partiality, plays. Finally, more empirical evidence for integration is scrutinized.

In Chapter 3, I take a step back from the integration argument to more closely examine the core principles. We can all agree that equality, citizenship, and liberty are important, but why are they so? I show that all three principles are mutually reinforcing but also that only the first two are purportedly facilitated by integration. I begin with liberty. While it cannot be divorced from how we think of equality or citizenship—indeed they are interlocking concepts—I show not only that integration does not aim to foster liberty but, more important, that the exercise of liberty does not facilitate integration. Conversely, integration is believed to assist in fostering and realizing both equality and citizenship. Both principles indicate different types of status, but they also operate as ideals. Equality captures something important about equal recognition, status, and opportunity. Meanwhile, citizenship points to shared civic ideals as well as different kinds of civic virtue possible within a pluralist conception of citizenship.

In Chapter 4, I provide a prima facie defense of VS, again as framed by equality and citizenship. The first argument is integration for equality. Here I argue that VS is defensible when equality—meaning equal status and treatment—is not an option under the terms of either integration or involuntary segregation. I then argue that under conditions of inequality-producing segregation, VS may be more likely to provide the resources necessary for self-respect for members of stigmatized minority groups. The second argument is integration for citizenship. I refine the principle of citizenship by focusing on civic virtue. I argue that civic virtue entails promoting the good of the community but that this is not dependent on integration, nor must it reduce to political virtue. Later, I show that civic virtue in the form of VS offers an important space for public deliberation. My goal is to show that civic virtue can and does take place under conditions of involuntary segregation but that VS is a more effective way to facilitate it. Both arguments provide only a prima facie justification, for while some forms of separation may offer a necessary condition for the achievement of equality and civic virtue, they cannot offer a sufficient condition. Further, both arguments for VS must be read against the background of highly nonideal conditions. Accordingly neither the cultivation of self-respect nor the fostering of civic virtue need wait for ideal conditions of equality under integration to arrive. I then respond to three criticisms that may be brought against my argument.

Chapter 5 entails an examination of VS on religious grounds. Institutionally the focus is schools. While the existence of religious schools is nothing new, including their role in supplying community and support to vulnerable immigrant groups, the rise of Islamic and Hindu schools in Western countries is. I focus on the Dutch context for reasons that I explain. Though religious in orientation, I will examine the extent to which these schools also serve the purpose of supporting vulnerable ethnic minority groups as well as criticisms directed at these schools—in particular, worries about parental partiality and the interests of the child.

Chapter 6 offers a defense of separation on cultural grounds. Again the institutional focus is schools. African-centered schools represent an undeniably provocative response to the stubborn problem of urban segregation. These are a uniquely North American phenomenon, and their existence has been very controversial, even within the black community. In this chapter I explore both the characteristics and aims of African-centered education and will consider the contributions they make as well as the various risks they undertake in achieving them. I then examine and respond to the charge of cultural essentialism.

In Chapter 7, I tackle a particularly vexing case involving stigma on the one hand and racial privilege on the other. I focus on the poor white working class of northern English cities. To the extent that the features of this group match the characteristics of stigma and exclusion that define other groups, a prima facie case for VS may also apply. However, with respect to this group, the case for VS is less clear for at least two reasons. First, the cultural resources once available to this group have been severely eroded. Second, it is doubtful whether the relevant enabling conditions needed for VS to produce desirable effects are available within the English context. I also address a number of worries about white separation. In light of these and other concerns I offer only a tentative case for VS.

Conclusions

While this book aims to provide a philosophical account of VS, it would not be possible were it not for the abundance of available empirical research on segregation, including research about which I am somewhat critical. Facts about segregation are therefore crucial to this book. Yet however we think about these matters, even a judicious look at the empirical evidence will not do all the work; moral arguments are also needed. Combining moral arguments with empirical research may push some of us to think about segregation in a manner to which we previously have not been accustomed. Just as important, moral arguments alone are also not enough. As I demonstrate with my critique of integrationism, a general moral argument will not suffice. Not only do nonideal background conditions matter, but a general moral argument also will not go very far in helping us determine what is best for *specific* persons and their *specific* needs in *specific* contexts.

Because its implementation varies widely, nowhere do I fill in the details for how VS ought to work or which expressions it ought to take apart from those that promote self-respect and civic virtue, as I will later demonstrate. Hence readers looking for detailed policy recommendations will be disappointed. Nowhere do I adumbrate financing or supervisory schemes; nor, apart from schools, do I specify a list of institutions needed to facilitate or enable VS. Those will need to be decided on a case-by-case basis and in light of relevant historical and circumstantial variables. However, what I do make clear is this: if the prima facie case for VS is to be justified, it must meet a number of necessary and sufficient conditions. It must enable and enhance equality and citizenship in ways that matter not only to the groups in question but also to the host societies.

So in one sense the justification for, and application of, VS will hang on the details of particular cases. But in another sense the argument stands on its own. And if I succeed in that endeavor, only then can it be applied to other contexts and specific case studies to see whether and how well it succeeds—hence the prima facie argument. Being a prima facie argument means that the argument holds to the extent that a number of conditions prevail. In the absence of those conditions, a prima facie argument is considerably weaker. Because it is simply not possible to consider each and every empirical case study, I limit myself to only a handful of examples.

Along the way, I remind the reader that VS need not supplant integration. When integrated environments are able to supply the conditions necessary for the fostering of equality and citizenship, they should be applauded, studied, and emulated. But two things must be remembered. First, integration is not a proxy for justice. Both equality and citizenship can be cultivated and maintained under conditions of segregation. Indeed, spatial concentrations may help facilitate them. Second, even if everyone shares the moral beliefs supporting the ideal of integration, these will not suffice to usurp important freedoms of association and movement. Nor will they suffice to establish the details of housing or education policy needed for integration to bear fruit.

Which forms should VS take, and for how long must it occur? As I argued by analogy with reference to inclusion, much will depend on the specific features of the groups and environments in question. Given the need to examine innumerable specific cases, no definitive answers are available beyond the arguments I provide. Yet, as I argue in Chapter 4, so long as integrated environments fail to supply the conditions necessary for self-respect and civic virtue, then perhaps for that long, VS will be needed.

2

Integration

In this chapter I look squarely at segregation and the integrationist response to it. We might formulate the integrationist imperative in this way: one inescapable feature of segregation is that persons of different ethnic, religious, and socioeconomic backgrounds have limited interaction with, and understanding of, each other. Such limited interaction, the standard argument runs, fortifies stereotypes and discrimination, undermines social trust, and restricts economic opportunities to those already in positions of social advantage. If these things are true, integration offers a real alternative.

On both accounts—namely, integration for equality and for citizenship—a democratic society will presumably function more fairly and effectively when persons or groups are not segregated from one another but instead meaningfully interact across their respective differences. It appears to follow from this that mixed neighborhoods and school environments will do more to ensure equality and good citizenship. The case for integration operates with these ideas in mind. I will proceed as follows. First I examine segregation and its harms. Some forms of segregation are harmful both to individual persons and to society generally. Using the principles of equality and citizenship, I then examine the case for integration, whose purpose is to redress the harms of segregation. The first argument is framed by the equality principle. The second argument is framed by the citizenship principle. Rather than postpone it until the end, I offer a critical response to each as the argument progresses.

To avoid misunderstanding I want to be clear about my aims. Though I will not hesitate to criticize the naiveté of integrationism—namely, the belief that integration is a proxy for justice—we should never take integrationist ideals lightly. Ideals of all sorts serve an important purpose in facilitating moral progress, and this can have a profound effect on how persons are viewed and treated. In many cases ideals, rigorously pursued, have brought about radical changes in both thinking and legislation that now ensure equal rights and protection. Consequently attitudes toward, and treatment of,—previously stigmatized—minority groups in a number of societies have overturned centuries of oppression and violence. These accomplishments, many of which have occurred within my lifetime, are not trivial; they represent a gargantuan leap forward in realizing justice to a palpable degree. Many of these accomplishments suggest that integration may serve the same purpose—namely, the pursuit of integrationist ideals will reduce levels of segregation and, with them, the harms that segregation may produce.

However, though I never suggest that we should jettison integrationist ideals, I do argue that integration is not a proxy for justice. In holding this view it is my aim neither to minimize the injustice some forms of segregation undoubtedly occasion nor to discredit the ideals of integration inasmuch as these inspire us to break down structural barriers to equality and citizenship. Instead, the aim is to carefully assess the strength of integrationist arguments as they are couched by theorists against the actual choices people make as well as the background conditions in which integrationist policies are enacted. Even when striving for more just institutional and structural background conditions we can afford neither to ignore the less-than-ideal circumstances in which everyday decisions are made nor to assume that integration is the only strategy capable of producing equality or good citizenship.

Segregation

As we saw in Chapter 1, *segregation* refers to spatial concentrations on the basis of some characteristic, such as ethnicity, socioeconomic status, political affiliation, gender, religion, employment status, or language. The reasons for segregation are not reducible to one cause, such as racism, class privilege, or housing policy. In most societies, entire regions, cities, and neighborhoods remain deeply segregated for a complex set of reasons, usually combining both voluntary and involuntary mechanisms. Most accounts of segregation understandably focus on residential segregation—often tied to school attendance—and the persistence of prejudice toward specific minority groups. There are well-known and longstanding discriminatory realities attending segregation in many societies—realities in which various dominant groups have determined whether others could enjoy equal civil status or exercise freedoms, such as choosing where to live or attend school. Meanwhile, even when circumstances may be institutionally unequal, there also are unmistakable patterns of voluntary separation reflecting a preference to be with others who share common traits.

Be that as it may, egalitarian critics of segregation point to the structured ways in which certain communities are advantaged or disadvantaged because of how they are positioned in society relative to others. For example, some children are advantaged, much evidence shows, because they often attend schools with better resources, have more educated and involved parents, sit next to more motivated peers, or attend schools with higher retention rates of principals and teachers, and so on. Moreover, children from wealthier and more educated family backgrounds on average perform better than those from poorer and less educated family backgrounds. I shall have more to say about education in due course, but for now we can summarize this view as follows: when environments are segregated—(whether by institutional design or demographic composition is not particularly relevant)—poorer citizens concentrated in neighborhoods or schools without the presence of middle-class citizens suffer acute disadvantages. Whether this is so in the majority of cases requires case-by-case analysis, but it certainly is true enough of the time that few of us will impugn the basic claim. Indeed, these are allegations many of us now take for granted.

So it is understandable that the very word *segregation* for most people summons decidedly negative connotations and that responses from scholars and policymakers are predictably downbeat. Accordingly, in a number of societies segregation has long been seen as a problem to be solved, a societal ill whose time for a cure is long overdue.[1] Yet while segregation, for many, explicitly refers to social inequalities that result from the isolation of certain groups from society's basic resources, it continues to be a standard historical feature of multicultural and class-based societies. Segregation is salient in the housing market, the labor market, and the education market. Indeed, while there is arguably more boundary crossing and mixing of persons of different backgrounds than ever before, neighborhood and school segregation indices in most Western societies remain quite high,[2] and in many sectors segregation worsens as countries cumbersomely wrestle with the challenges posed by immigration, migration, and asylum.[3]

Even when sharing a similar vocabulary, not all societies frame segregation in the same way.[4] In the United States, for example, the word continues to conjure a legacy of slavery and de jure discrimination against blacks. A number of factors, however, makes this facile association increasingly misleading—among them, the considerable socioeconomic and cultural variation within the black community, a sizable population that identifies as mixed, and a panoply of ethnicities in American society that more and more renders the black-white dyad obsolete. Because school segregation in the United States generally has followed neighborhood segregation, various initiatives, whether by incentive or court order, have been implemented in neighborhoods and schools over the past 45 years to try to reverse the effects of institutionalized racism.

Elsewhere segregation is also clearly visible; neighborhood segregation in places like the Netherlands and the United Kingdom conspires with a school system that allows for admissions criteria that give priority to a particular religion or pedagogical preference.[5] Meanwhile, as debates about immigration continue to unfurl in various European states, segregation is widely believed to militate against social cohesion and a shared sense of national identity. In light of these concerns, the death of multiculturalism has been heralded, and renewed calls for integration and shared national identification top the political agenda.

Here integration more often than not refers to a complex and dynamic social process of being grafted into a set of practices, ideas, and norms assumed and practiced by majority populations. Proponents of integration in most European countries typically are found politically on the Right and Center Left for reasons having to do with negative feelings toward non-Western immigration in general or Muslim immigrants in particular. Though its meaning remains unclear, *integration* normally is directed toward visible—and stigmatized—minority groups with the aim of their adopting specific cultural values, habits, and norms.[6]

To illustrate the attitudes and dispositions driving these concerns, consider a recent example from the United Kingdom. Early in 2011 Prime Minister David Cameron gave a speech at the Munich Security Conference in which he highlighted the urgency of combating homegrown radicalization. Setting his sights in particular on extremist versions of Islam, Cameron invoked the idea of integration to address the threat from within. In his speech, the presence of segregation—in opposition to integration—was depicted as a threat to both social cohesion and national security. Among other things, Cameron had this to say: "Under the doctrine of state multiculturalism, we have encouraged different cultures to live separate lives, apart from each other and apart from the mainstream. We've failed to provide a vision of society to which they feel they want to belong. We've even tolerated these segregated communities behaving in ways that run completely counter to our values."[7] Cameron was particularly critical of two positions—first, that of those on the "soft left" who focus on poverty as the cause of extremism. That position, he argued, maintains that the real problem with homegrown terrorism is social inequality: tackle poverty in poor ethnic minority neighborhoods and extremism will go away. Such claims were voiced again following the riots in the summer of 2011. The second position Cameron criticized holds that grievances against British foreign policies explain the turn to extremism. Rejecting both, the prime minister argued that both of these are symptomatic of a much deeper problem—namely, an ideology that repudiates democratic values. Here the citizenship ideal comes plainly into view. It is not particularly relevant right now whether Cameron is right; what is interesting is not only the repeated reference to "we" in the cited passage of his speech but also the prime minister's implied reference to *integration*.[8] Elsewhere in Europe, politicians and ordinary citizens continue to defend some form of segregation for its ability to facilitate the pursuit of shared interests, while others decry segregation in any form as a travesty of constitutional freedom that both exacerbates social inequality and undermines national solidarity.

Integration

As we also saw in Chapter 1, integration means different things to different people. One may speak of spatial, civic, sociocultural, socioeconomic, and psychological aspects. For the most part, however, I use *integration* to refer to spatial as well as both formal and informal social mixing of groups without specification as to the degree or quality of interaction between them. With respect to the framing principles of equality and citizenship, I specifically use integration in the following way: *integration for equality* will refer principally to status and treatment, but also to socioeconomic resources, promising a more fair distribution of goods and opportunities; *integration for citizenship*, on the other hand, holds out the promise of more democratic access to persons saddled with disadvantage and marginalized through the mechanisms of social exclusion and stigma.

In what follows I examine the case for integration by focusing on two arguments that correspond to the framing principles. The first argument explicitly addresses segregation as a source of inequality, particularly for stigmatized minorities unable to access opportunities in education and the labor market. Here the thrust of the argument maintains that integration combats social disadvantage by distributing resources more equitably to the socially excluded. The second argument tackles many of the concerns mentioned in the previous paragraph. It entails both political stability and social harmony on the one hand and the terms of equal recognition needed for deliberation on the other. Here integration promises the resources of communally shared values and social cooperation, and these supply the basis for a healthier democratic society.

Integration for Equality

Few seriously dispute that serious harms sometimes coincide with segregation. These harms may include inferior educational and employment opportunities, less access to public goods and services, and seemingly indelible forms of stigma and discrimination. Elizabeth Anderson observes, "[Segregation] isolates disadvantaged groups from access to public and private resources, from sources of human and cultural capital, and from the social networks that govern access to jobs, business connections, and political influence. It depresses their ability to accumulate wealth and gain access to credit. It reinforces stigmatizing stereotypes about the disadvantaged and thus causes discrimination."[9] Many empirical studies have corroborated the view that many types of involuntary segregation do indeed compromise opportunities for those occupying a less favorable group status. When spatial concentrations coincide with poverty, high unemployment, limited health care, lower school quality, poor housing infrastructure, and restricted social networks, the effects of segregation on inequality can be dire indeed.[10] For example, the average quality of involuntarily segregated schools continues to lag far behind that of schools predominately populated by the white middle class irrespective of per-pupil spending amounts.[11] Many who live in involuntarily segregated neighborhoods also attend schools in which fewer resources, higher incidents of violence, or regular teacher turnover are the norm. Indeed, research has suggested time and again that schools that serve high concentrations of poor and minority children are simply inferior. Specifically, they are more likely to have teachers with less experience and fewer qualifications, high student mobility, high teacher and principal attrition, less family support, lower literacy rates and test scores, and students with poorer health.[12]

Segregation is arguably more harmful to poor and stigmatized minorities, whose self-respect is damaged and whose educational and career opportunities may be restricted when they are separated from more privileged children, their parents, and the social capital to which such contact might ostensibly give access.[13] Taken together, stigma and disadvantage take a toll on a child's sense of self-respect. Self-respect describes a sense of being in charge of one's destiny—that is, having a reasonable sense of self-determination with respect to choices and the ability to act meaningfully on those choices. But of course the psychological and social conditions that make self-respect possible vary widely, with genes and the environment continually in interaction. The presence of self-respect may therefore fluctuate according to circumstance. For example, the experience of sudden (or chronic) failure or relational loss may induce a sense of crisis. But the fact that one is a member of a stigmatized minority group in itself presents special challenges to self-respect. Indeed, self-respect may have an inverse relationship to stigma.

I shall have more to say about self-respect—particularly in relation to resilience—in Chapter 3. The point I wish to make here is simply this: integration aims to rectify socioeconomic injustice by spatially integrating environments. The basic idea is that by mixing neighborhoods and schools, careful to avoid concentrations of one ethnic group or social class, the prospects of the less advantaged will improve without harming the prospects of the more advantaged. Integration on this understanding entails the transfer of social capital to the least advantaged so that routes of opportunity and social networks are expanded, enabling informed choices and better outcomes.

Taking a comprehensive view of integration, Anderson sets her sights on exhaustive reforms within mainstream social and political institutions, in particular a forward-looking interpretation of affirmative action as an effective tool to get us there. She writes, "just institutions must be designed to block, work around, or cancel out our motivational and cognitive deficiencies, to harness our non-moral motives to moral ends [and] to make up for each other's limitations by pooling our knowledge and wills."[14] Integration in her view envisions a "restructuring of intergroup relations, from alienation, anxiety, awkwardness, and hostility to relaxed, competent civil association and even intimacy; from domination and subordination to cooperation as equals."[15] An increasingly integrated school and workplace, she argues, will lead to persons relaxing around each other, having fewer stereotypical views of others different from themselves, and sharing information and networking strategies that make power sharing possible. What most urgently needs to change, she continues, "are people's unconscious habits of interracial interaction and perception. Such *practical* learning can take place only in integrated settings."[16] Indeed, it is primarily through "practical experience" that opposition to integration will be overcome. In the final analysis integration will remove barriers to social mobility.

Equality and Education

In order to demonstrate that segregation undermines democracy itself, Anderson contends that a diverse political elite is necessary in order to combat the social inequalities caused by segregation.[17] Integrated schools can offer more fairly distributed opportunities that will lead to a larger pool of candidates who can more effectively do the bidding of those with whom they share a similar background. They can do this because they supposedly better understand the circumstances, needs, and concerns of their less fortunate group members. But to cultivate the necessary civic capacities in that elite, education must be integrated. Anderson submits, "[D]iverse members [of society] must be educated together, so that they can develop competence in respectful intergroup interaction. A democratically qualified elite must be an elite that is integrated across all the major lines of social inequality and division that characterize it . . . A just K–12 educational system must prepare students from all sectors of society, and especially those disadvantaged along any dimensions, with sufficient skills to be able to succeed in higher education and thereby join the elite."[18] To buttress this claim further, Anderson observes that "the black-white achievement test score gap is largest in states with the most highly segregated schools, and smallest in states with the most integrated schools."[19] Without developing her argument in full, I simply want to stress that her notion of "sufficient" is pretty robust. Her notion of democratic equality aims to promote freedoms "sufficient for functioning as an equal in society";[20] more specifically, her goal is to more fairly distribute opportunities to those who may be denied them simply by virtue of attending a "bad" school. Moreover, even if we might challenge—as I intend to—her use of empirical data to make her point, this in itself does not weaken or disqualify the normative claim. Indeed, any progress toward justice requires an imaginary beyond what for the moment seems politically unfeasible. Hence her call to integrate schools "at all levels" is admirable for what it seeks to accomplish.

Even so, there are a number of conceptual and practical difficulties. Putting aside the fact that sufficientarian arguments do little to eliminate problems of vagueness about what a "sufficient" education entails, there are unavoidable tensions between *sufficient* and *equal* that Anderson does not resolve.[21] Certainly equality can motivate and frame a sufficientarian account, and Anderson certainly knows that considerations other than equality matter. I understand Anderson to be saying that a sufficiently equal education is one that aims to provide everyone with the social capital necessary "to function as an equal in civil society." Even so, it remains unclear just what the justificatory role of equality is supposed to be with respect to distributive arrangements. Moreover, as we have seen, her notion of "equal" rests on question-begging integrationist assumptions.

With respect to the empirical difficulties of her argument, three things can be said. First, the arguments for an integrated elite tend to downplay sharp cultural, political, and social class divisions among minority groups. It is likely true that members of marginalized groups generally exhibit different legislative priorities than members of historically privileged groups. It is also true that minorities in positions of power play an important symbolic role. Even so, there is little reason to believe that elites from marginalized groups will be more responsive than others to the concerns of its more vulnerable and politically disenfranchised members.[22] Second, Anderson seems to assume that integrated schools are the only type of educational institution capable of equality, by which she means that they are the only institutions capable of supplying the forms of social and cultural capital necessary for living fruitful lives in a multicultural society. We can draw no other inference from her argument but that nonintegrated schools don't—or worse, can't—supply these goods. It is difficult to escape the inference that most schools with high minority concentrations are ipso facto inferior.[23]

Third, her selective use of the available demographic and educational research insinuates a causal relationship that is extremely difficult to determine. We will want to know more about other features in these school systems than can possibly be derived from the minority-majority student ratio. In contrast to her compelling evidence for the benefits of mixed juries, police forces, and the military,[24] Anderson's hypotheses about mixed schools rely on heavily contested data. Integrated schools *might* remove prejudice and barriers to social mobility, and they *might* increase participation and deliberation across social class boundaries among concerned citizens. But when market forces, a scarcity of resources, middle-class advocacy, high student and staff turnover rates, and weak teacher training programs define our social and political reality, such outcomes are far from obvious. More hangs on effective democracy than merely integrating voting districts or schools.

Integration for Citizenship

As we will see in Chapter 3, citizenship may reflect either robust or pluralist expressions. Both, however, imply modes of interaction on terms of equality, without which we have very little basis for political participation and deliberation. The citizenship argument is framed by these concerns. While there are legitimate concerns about language acquisition or labor market participation, worries are perhaps most frequently expressed about the fostering of tolerance of persons with whom we have little contact. Segregation bears upon this discussion because it is believed to facilitate prejudice and stereotyping of others; it also is believed to increase out-group distrust. Such dispositions augur poorly for democratic deliberation, where the importance of engagement with others who espouse different views is extremely important. Segregation is further thought to undermine the possibilities of fostering common ground on which citizens from disparate backgrounds can deliberate about issues of social and political import. The argument for integration here is that persons cannot come to understand and respect others whose beliefs, cultural differences, or other personal traits are manifestly different if there is an absence of interaction in the first place.

Melissa Williams has endeavored to surmount the tensions caused by pluralism in democratic societies by describing citizenship as "shared fate," by which she means that persons come to "see themselves as enmeshed in relationships which they may or may not have chosen, with individuals who may be very different from themselves."[25] She refers to this realization as shared fate because unlike the various voluntary associations we choose, fate describes the copious ways in which our lives are involuntarily intertwined with others by virtue of our shared human characteristics and mutual interdependence. The core virtues necessary for shared fate are as follows:

- the capacity for enlarged thought
- the imaginative capacity to see oneself as bound up with others through relations of interdependence as well as through shared history and institutions
- the capacity to reshape the shared practices and institutions of one's environment through direct participation

Taken together the first two require persons to realize that others adhere to different customs or habits of thought and that conflicting perspectives need not be cause for alarm. In order for plural societies to function smoothly but also fairly, there should be some kind of meaningful interaction with persons whose backgrounds, core assumptions, beliefs, or group affiliations one does not share. That, at least, is the ideal, and as an ideal it serves an important purpose.

The absence of regular contact with others who occupy different social or cultural positions certainly challenges our capacity for enlarged thought. But while our ability to identify with what others actually feel, think, and experience (the elements of empathy) is at times overwhelming and difficult, this does not prevent us from trying. We hear firsthand accounts from others; we immigrate or encounter the immigrant; and we vicariously enter into another's life through media, novels, and film. Unable to lead anyone's life but our own, we rely on an empathic imagination to provide us with counterexamples of a life we *might* have lived. But here empathy is simply another way of saying a capacity for enlarged thought.

A capacity for enlarged thought also means that we learn the importance of listening to others and hearing what they have to say with a view to arriving at a deeper and more complex understanding of the situation or issue being discussed. Further, in theory the "open mindedness" such encounters encourage will help to avert dogmatic thinking and simplistic solutions and also likely facilitate more cooperation with others with whom one may not agree. All of this captures what Williams surely means by the ability to see oneself as bound up with others through relations of interdependence. After all, our lives are not as disconnected from others as we may think, no matter how different their political views, religious beliefs, or cultural practices may seem.

Finally, the capacity to reshape the shared practices and institutions through direct participation means that whatever our differences with others may be, at the end of the day we must have ways of communicating with each other as well as the willingness to submit (but also appeal) to the same laws and institutions for settling disputes as well as for advancing the good of the community by forging new paths of social cooperation. Social cooperation is but another way of expressing the substance of citizenship.

Against this backdrop, integration—in neighborhoods, schools, and workplaces—purportedly will improve social cohesion in pluralist societies because it offers persons of different backgrounds opportunities to learn from each other and to respectfully interact. In particular, power sharing and respectful interaction will reduce prejudice, stereotyping, and distrust. Socially excluded and stigmatized groups over time will become less stigmatized. Respectful interaction also will improve possibilities for mutual cooperation. Integration for citizenship aims to curb the distorting effects of stigma that lead to civic inequality through discrimination. With its emphasis on equal recognition and treatment, we again see the manner in which the framing principles complement one another.

Citizenship and Education

Because persons normally socialize with others who share similar interests and background traits, encounters with diversity are believed to work in the following way: they are important for disadvantaged children who often lack important knowledge and skills as well as norms and values necessary to thrive in mainstream society. But such encounters also are believed to be important for broadening the empathies of more privileged children, whose lack of contact with stigmatized minorities or marginalized citizens prevents them from seeing minorities as equals. Under certain conditions[26] such interactions can be enormously positive and conducive to a reduction in prejudice and generally to a more civilized society. Of course, interactions need to be supplemented by accurate information (to combat stereotypes) as well as legislation (to combat discrimination).

Schools are very often the focal point of these discussions, because they arguably present the best chance for children from different backgrounds to cross those seemingly naturally occurring divides. Indeed, schools continue to be places where policy discussions and initiatives to counter segregation most persistently occur. Attempts to correct segregation found in the workplace or the neighborhood often begin with attempts to facilitate school integration. Integrated schools, the argument runs, promise a better future for disadvantaged minorities by curbing harmful stereotyping and discriminatory behaviors among their more advantaged peers. For example, Anderson opines, "studies consistently confirm the integrationist hypothesis. Students who attend more racially integrated schools lead more racially integrated lives after graduation: they have more racially diverse co-workers, neighbours, and friends than do students who attend less diverse schools."[27] This view is buoyed by the optimistic idea that "public schools play an important role in promoting norms of respectful discourse and undermining prejudice."[28]

But of course integrated public schools as such are not only loci of enlightened tolerance, equity, and power sharing; they are also sites of bullying, interethnic tension, and differential treatment. Anderson would presumably argue that this is all the more reason to improve the conditions of integrated schools. I agree. But we should not forget the nonideal conditions of this contact. As she surely knows, much hangs on the conditions of the interaction as well as on the nonshared experiences of the participants. Veit Bader astutely observes, "Whether the effects of interaction are beneficial depends partly on the voluntariness of interaction and on contextual variables such as (the absence of) threats, (patterns of) discrimination, socio-economic inequalities and negative-sum games. Everyday interaction in global cities or mixed neighbourhoods, for example, certainly involves contacts among strangers and fosters conscious awareness of the 'other,' but it does not automatically encourage toleration and political openness to the stranger's views and claims."[29] Even when prejudice reduction may result from integrated workplaces, neighborhoods, and classrooms, this may not always generalize beyond those one knows on a personal basis. Indeed, integrated settings may be just as likely to confirm stereotypes of others as they are to remove them. Further, peer group preferences, a form of self-segregation, means that meaningful interaction between children of different backgrounds is rather limited.[30] Finally, even in schools that are highly diverse, structural features within schools, such as tracking systems and ability grouping, unsurprisingly contribute to internal segregation.[31]

That interactions in school between children of different ethnic, religious, or social class backgrounds produce the elements of good citizenship—that is, tolerance, social trust, and mutual cooperation—reliably and across many contexts, is certainly an attractive hypothesis. But it is a hypothesis for which compelling evidence remains woefully deficient, not least because both the conditions as well as the quality and duration of interactions generally dilute the significance of that contact.[32] In short, the integration-for-citizenship argument, entailing the widespread integration of neighborhoods or schools, is one that too often eludes reality.

While it is true that Williams's notion of shared fate offers us a creative and optimistic way of surmounting differences that divide us by focusing on our common experience, shared fate tends to ignore two things. First, much of what defines our experience is simply not shared. Racism and stigma, for example, in both their institutional and personal causes and effects, are not shared by all or even most groups. Even within specific groups that may be stigmatized, the effects of stigma are highly variable. For example, not all darker-skinned persons will be stigmatized equally or in the same way. Much depends on the context, immigration history, demographic concentration, social class, religion, tribal affiliation, and so on. In some societies many of these variables converge to multiply the harms stigma brings, while in others the opposite occurs. Second, shared fate downplays (or ignores) the various and sundry ways in which the nonfacilitative principle operates. In Chapter 4 I will argue that one of its effects—namely, segregation—can itself facilitate the possibilities not only for communal solidarity but also for equality as self-respect and civic virtue. But for now it suffices to point out the impact of liberty as a nonfacilitative principle on concerns about shared fate. In the absence of draconian policies that override parental prerogatives, the cherished right to choose the place one wants to live or the school one feels is appropriate for his or her own child makes segregation—to a significant degree—inevitable.[33]

Integration Interrogated

Wherever we land on the question of integration, to some extent we must rely on both experience and empirical research. Sociologists, geographers, and public policy analysts have provided us with an abundance of research and data on segregation. Their studies detail in various ways the manner in which certain groups are concentrated by ethnicity, gender, socioeconomic status, religion, or political creed. Many of these studies describe the pace and effects of segregation, shedding light on both the reasons for and the effects of segregation. Yet for all the strengths of these studies, they do not yield the conclusive outcome many assume they do—namely, that integration is a proxy for justice. There is always a danger of making data say what we want them to say, and that certainly applies in this case as well. For example, implicit (if not explicit) in most of these studies is the assumption that *any* form of segregation is exclusionary and therefore harmful—both to the unfortunate individuals "trapped" by it and to the society as a whole for permitting it.

We see this, for example, in the literature on school segregation and desegregation during the past forty years. For the most part, scholarship has operated on the assumption that any kind of separate education for poor and minority children is bad for them.[34] It would not be difficult to adduce enormous amounts of data to make this case. As I demonstrated earlier in this chapter, we can certainly expect to find many kinds of harm resulting from some forms of segregation. Even so, I am convinced that many unexamined assumptions, combined with a selective use of evidence, have framed the research in such a way that it now passes for unassailable dogma. Notwithstanding the many valid concerns raised by segregation studies, integration arguments are built on a selective use of evidence and a set of flawed assumptions.

The first flawed assumption is to hold that segregation ipso facto instantiates disadvantage or harm. No doubt much harm coincides with some forms of segregation, and certainly some types of segregation are unable to produce equality or civic virtue. But this is clearly not always the case: spatial concentrations may produce hope or despair; much will depend on the background conditions—opportunity structures, choice sets, and social networks—attending the segregation. To be sure, some spatial concentrations are doubtless marked by poverty, substance abuse, and gang violence. Without efforts to interrupt the downward spiral, social disadvantage and moral despair become endemic to certain neighborhoods. But many other spatial concentrations supply resources of solidarity unavailable in more integrated settings.

The second and closely related flaw is to argue after the fact from worst cases. To be sure, where segregation takes the form of concentrated poverty, or coincides with violent and hopeless ghettos, shanty towns, and barrios, we should not be complacent. But to argue that segregation as such is harmful cannot bear up under scrutiny. Many segregation accounts fail to give sufficient attention to any or all of the following: (1) the cultural, ethnic, and social class differences between and within minority groups; (2) consideration for the preferences of the groups and individuals themselves; (3) a sober account of the terrific harms incurred under the banner of integration; (4) an acknowledgment of the positive features that often coincide with spatial concentrations; and, finally, (5) the recognition that other modes of empowerment not dependent on integration can and should be pursued under nonideal circumstances.

Taken together, these flaws and omissions inexorably lead to a faulty conclusion—namely, in order to counter discrimination and disadvantage neighborhoods and schools must be fully integrated (i.e., mixed). Indeed liberals routinely genuflect before the ideal of an integrated public school while conveniently ignoring many of its well-documented structural realities. I look at some of this evidence shortly, but first I examine some of the philosophical tensions that arise when we factor in the nonfacilitative principle of liberty as partiality. To do that, I consider the matter of school choice.

School Choice and Parental Partiality

The context is the United Kingdom, and the issue is school choice and social justice. Here we come face-to-face with a dilemma confronting any conscientious parent struggling with a justification of whether or not to opt out of a local school in order to access better educational options. The dilemma might be formulated in the following way: When is the education available to my child below an adequate standard such that I am justified in opting out? "Opting out" is one way of expressing the decision to avoid a school one thinks is less than adequate. Opting out also expresses an important—but by no means the only—mechanism that contributes to segregation.

Adam Swift has offered a thoughtful account of this dilemma. He is not unmindful of the risks such choices have for others; nor does he neglect the rationalizations that often attend such middle-class dilemmas. He argues that "allowing relatively advantaged parents to opt out of state education has an *absolute* depressing effect on the quality of education provided for the great majority of the population who attend state schools."[35] Given the hyperlevels of inequality between state comprehensives and expensive private schools—and hence segregation along socioeconomic lines—Swift argues that elite private schools, in principle, should be abolished.

However, under nonideal conditions it may be reasonable for parents to opt out of a local school; they may in fact be justified in attending the very schools that Swift would otherwise abolish, because this may be the only way parents can secure an adequate education for their children. Here partiality takes center stage, and for Swift it is the right kind of partiality, because it expresses something fundamental to the parent-child relationship. Partiality means that parents have moral obligations to their own children that they simply do not have to others and moreover that these obligations arise from the special regard one has for his or her own children.[36] In order for parental partiality for one's own child to trump more abstract demands of justice, a number of conditions must exist. Among these are the following: consideration for the costs to one's child of bearing more than one's fair share; considerations for how badly others may be affected by one's choices; and, finally, the burdens that parents have *only if* they can reasonably expect others to do their fair share (i.e., comply with the demands of justice).

Matthew Clayton and David Stevens have offered an egalitarian critique of Swift's view. They agree with Swift that under ideal conditions a great deal more partiality is permitted by parents for their own children. Yet they repudiate his view that parental partiality under nonideal conditions must trump more abstract demands of justice, even if this means exacerbating inequality for others. Of course, determining the precise meaning of "adequate" or an education that is "good enough" will be fraught with subjectivity and in any case interpreted relative to a particular context where other options are available. Clayton and Stevens also rightly point out that determining "fair share" or even "legitimate partiality" will not be an exact metric. Yet in order to buttress the egalitarian position, they argue that under nonideal conditions, the burdens of justice demand that we accept more than our fair share of inconvenience, even if this means our child receives *less* than an adequate education. They write, "We also have a duty to share the burdens that injustice inflicts upon us. It is surely wrong to add to the burden shouldered by those who are already more unjustly treated."[37] They continue, "It is *pro tanto* unjust for an individual to act in a way that worsens the position of others who are already more unjustly treated than he or she is."[38] I quote them at length:

> Those who opt out [of the local school] cause the position of those who remain in the comprehensive system to be worsened. Moreover, if anything, their conduct is morally worse because there is the added factor that those who are made worse off are comparatively already suffering more injustice ... And, surely, if they refuse to opt out, parents would be condemning their own child to an unjust level of educational opportunity. However, if we are egalitarians, our thoughts about permissible conduct in non-ideal circumstances must be sensitive to the *extent* to which different individuals suffer injustice. In lessening the degree to which their own children suffer from injustice, parents who opt out are not merely worsening the position of others' children who are already unjustly treated. They are worsening the position of children who are *more* unjustly treated than their own children. That must be a cause for egalitarian concern.[39]

In order to demonstrate why doing more than one's fair share is consistent with an egalitarian outlook, Clayton and Stevens compare solidarity in school attendance with a rescue attempt at sea, with rationing schemes in times of war, and also with private health insurance schemes. The "duty of solidarity," they argue, demands that we restrain certain forms of partiality in terms of the choices we make. Why? Because justice demands that we refuse to exercise our liberties in ways that will harm others. The fact that others refuse to cooperate should not diminish our long-term goal of eradicating injustice. Sharing the burdens of justice, pace Swift, means that we often must do far more than our fair share precisely because others are not willing to make similar sacrifices. Hence if egalitarians are to be faithful to their ideals, then they will gladly do more than their fair share so that justice may be advanced.

It is important to bear in mind that their dispute focuses on the British, and particularly the English, context. And when the school choices really are that stark—namely, between public comprehensives and elite privates—partiality arguments justifying the latter do look untenable. It seems intuitively correct that justice is compromised when the opportunities available are partly determined by the size of one's bank account.[40] Accordingly, the argument Clayton and Stevens offer against Swift's partiality position appears to have some moral bite. Notice, too, that both their concern for solidarity and their worries about misapplied partiality have implications for both of our framing principles.

Take equality first. If fewer low-income families can access an education that approximates the quality of education available to those better off, inequalities are not only constant, owing to various (genetic or socioeconomic) inherited advantages; rather, as Clayton and Stevens argue, they are exacerbated. Or consider the implications for citizenship. If persons from different backgrounds lack the opportunities to interact and engage with those whose ideas, experience, and beliefs they do not share, then surely any robust notion of citizenship will be compromised. What is more, the importance of a shared-fate vision of citizenship, enabling us to see ourselves as mutually interdependent with others, seems to be lost. Remember that a shared-fate perspective stresses the importance of mutually reshaping the social and political practices and institutions through direct participation; without this, those with more social and economic capital will access positions of power, excluding the less advantaged from decision making. (We saw this earlier with Anderson's appeal for an integrated elite.) So both equality and citizenship ostensibly are imperiled by segregation.

Now even if we share with Clayton and Stevens the importance of solidarity and the worries about misapplied partiality, many things remain rather unsettled. Their position in fact rests on a number of questionable assumptions that I want to scrutinize more closely.

First, take the food rationing and health care examples, where the principle of fairness means that there is a prospect of a desirable outcome achieved through mutual cooperation. Here solidarity means that certain options are off limits so that everyone has immediate access to an important good. But this clearly is not straightforward in the case of school choice. Simply remaining in the same school with the less advantaged does not get us very far. Clayton and Stevens concede this point but then simply leave it at that. A central problem with their argument, however, is their belief that all children attending the same schools will somehow further the cause of educational justice. The belief is based on the thesis I expounded earlier—namely, that the social capital middle-class children bring with them will yield positive peer effects on others less fortunate. Further, the belief is propped up by the idea that middle-class parents will become more involved in their children's school in such a way that also redounds to the less fortunate. In short, Clayton and Stevens's argument against school choice is but another way of defending integration, one that assumes that mixed school environments—particularly those mixed by social class—will improve the overall quality of the school.

One place where we might expect tangible effects from integration is in the retention of more experienced and better qualified teachers. Schools with more qualified and experienced teachers generally do offer a better quality education. (I return to the question of teacher incentives in Chapter 6.) But of course this is only half the picture. In terms of actual parent behavior and institutional practices (e.g., ability grouping, discipline referrals, teacher seniority), the idea of doing one's "fair share" does not suffice to explain how the mere presence of middle-class children improves the prospects of the less fortunate. Moreover, the idea that restricting parental choice will somehow more closely approximate justice is unhelpfully vague. It will not do simply to point to inequality-exacerbating benefits that may arise in some less integrated environments. Instead, one will need to demonstrate a causal relationship (and this depends crucially on the real gains and harms occasioned by opting out) as well as an epistemologically sound case for justifying solidarity in a way that takes legitimate expressions of partiality seriously.

To be sure, abolishing elite private schools is one way to eliminate egregiously unfair advantages for those who are already privileged. But I hardly need to point out that denying one's own child an adequate education, even when dressed up in the name of justice, raises a number of other difficulties. Remaining in a failing school in the name of solidarity while allowing one's own child to suffer for those ideals hardly counts as a moral imperative, and the comparison of remaining in an inadequate school with a rescue attempt at sea simply defies credulity. As we will see in more detail in the next section, integration hardly begins to solve the problem of inequality for at least two reasons: (1) most inequalities are transmitted and cultivated *outside* of school, and (2) mixed school environments are organized in ways that perpetuate inequality. Believing that the presence of middle-class children will somehow augment equality is simply naive for reasons that I trust will become increasingly clear. But integration also hardly solves the problem of citizenship, often for the very same reasons. We should not expect better outcomes for equality or citizenship simply by spatially integrating *any* environment.

The Empirical Evidence: A Closer Look

As we have seen, stratification studies accurately underscore a significant injustice—namely, an unequal access to critical resources by society's more vulnerable members. Efforts to combat inequality resulting from segregation have assumed different forms. Yet while urban planners continue to debate both the theoretical and empirical benefits of integrated neighborhoods, it is integrated schools that are the crucible of the democratic dream. Indeed, to the extent that segregation coincides with poverty concentration, particularly when this overlaps with ethnicity and race, many continue to believe that the single most effective strategy for improving equality is the integration of schools. Those who have documented the harmful effects of involuntary segregation[41] suggest that school integration will promote equality for disadvantaged students by providing access to better resources. These resources include better course offerings, more experienced teachers, and social networks that ostensibly arise from interaction with the social capital that middle-class children and their parents bring to school. Through the availability of said resources to the less advantaged, one can expect the doors of opportunity to open. So more than simply a chance to interact with those of a different background, integrated schools are believed to supply crucial social and economic opportunities—through the availability of more resources—to the less advantaged.

More recently arguments have been marshaled for socioeconomic integration as the solution to educational inequality.[42] The basic idea is to mix the right percentage of poor with middle-class students in order to raise the achievement levels of those left behind. Socioeconomic disparities between schools and classrooms are especially germane to the concern for equality, for arguably the most significant disadvantage for poor children is a lack of exposure to, and interaction with, others whose cumulative cultural or social capital positions them more favorably to both the intrinsic and instrumental benefits of education. Both forms of capital broadly describe the possession of assets—knowledge and skills—that have purchase power vis-à-vis the institutionalized norms of the dominant society.

Take language. Mastery of the dominant language, which correlates very strongly with social class, enables one to navigate one's environment more effectively and to access opportunities not available in the absence of the requisite knowledge and skills. For those—say, recent immigrants—not lucky enough to be born to parents with large and fluent vocabularies in the dominant language, access to and interaction with fluent others can make a crucial difference. Such exposure can mean opportunities to receive more interesting and challenging coursework, better advice from school counselors, higher test scores, and, ultimately, better employment opportunities. I will return to the socioeconomic argument in Chapter 4, as some recent evidence suggests that integration under very particular circumstances can have fruitful results for children from poorer backgrounds. For now it will suffice to say this: tackling segregation is understandable given the levels of inequality many children face, particularly if poverty corresponds to some morally irrelevant aspect of their identity such as ethnicity.

Yet even allowing for widespread agreement about the harms of segregation, the empirical evidence suggests that efforts to turn back the tide of segregation have made little progress. Efforts to desegregate or compensate for segregation include but are not limited to the following: bussing, quotas, transfer programs, and teacher incentives. Yet more than a decade into the twenty-first century, all but a handful of desegregation experiments have yielded few substantive results, and many have been repealed or are in retreat.[44] Desegregation orders have been removed over the past twenty to thirty years; urban restructuring policies disrupt but do not generally augment substantive contact between groups in mixed neighborhoods; the middle-class members of all colors flee from areas of urban decay at the same time that gentrification of neighborhoods across the urban landscape continues at unprecedented speed; and of course many continue to concentrate in specific neighborhoods by choice in order to benefit from the support systems more homogenous communities provide.

But whatever the actual disappointments and setbacks, to date there has been no diminution of rhetoric championing integrated schools as perhaps the best possibility for the disadvantaged growing up in stratified societies to access equal treatment. As we have seen, some admirably insist that privileged groups must shoulder their portion of the burden in order for integration to occur, because whatever the actual costs of integration are, the benefits will be worthwhile.[45] Yet however admirable, the idea assumes, without evidence, that the benefits of integration—again, often defined only in the vaguest of terms—will be forthcoming without reckoning with more than half a century of failed desegregation efforts or tallying up the costs that until now have disproportionately landed squarely on the shoulders of minority groups. Zvi Bekerman's remarks are relevant here: "At times, [integrationist] agendas strive sincerely to promote the interests of minority groups and confront mainstream hegemonies. At other times, such agendas are just paying lip service to political correctness. For whatever reasons, these initiatives [to consciously integrate schools] seem, in the best of cases, not to be attaining their goals and, in the worst of cases, oblivious to the reasons for their failure."[46]

Let us return to the idea of an ideal mix of pupils, which I briefly mentioned earlier. Here the idea is that integrated neighborhoods and schools will provide poorer students direct access to the social capital their middle-class peers possess. But we should be skeptical of this position. Why? Because the difficult-to-admit fact of the matter is this: most middle-class parents who pride themselves on living in "diverse" environments[47] or who talk up the importance of integration nevertheless maintain social networks almost entirely composed of others exactly like themselves.[48] These same parents tightly control not only the schools their children attend but also the teachers they have and the activities in which they participate. There is little evidence to support the claim that the presence of middle-class parents in mixed schools raises the academic performance of less advantaged pupils[49] or benefits the overall quality of the school.[50] To be sure, a concentration of middle-class parents can vote on a referendum to raise their taxes or sign petitions to keep their schools functioning reasonably well. Yet in daily affairs most middle-class parents are particularly adept at calling attention to the needs of their own children.[51]

The result is that most integrated schools remain deeply stratified within. Not only is there overwhelming evidence that many poor minorities face tremendous risks (of special education assignment, low track assignment, discipline referrals, expulsion, etc.) in mixed schools;[52] it is an open secret that few teachers have the skills to manage diverse classrooms very effectively. Capturing the challenges facing school districts in numerous countries across Europe and North America, researchers from France report, "While underprivileged students [in mixed schools] may benefit from their peers' cultural capital, the fact that they face more severe academic competition, and thus are at a higher risk of being among the lowest performing students, tends to limit the positive effect of social integration in a system in which teachers naturally adapt their expectations and teaching methods to the 'better' students."[53] Proposals to counter segregation using weighted pupil funding (or *pupil premiums* as they are known in the United Kingdom) also are not a panacea. No doubt money supplies important resources and relevant disparities between states and even districts should and can be minimized. But the argument remains a red herring insofar as it fails to consider other variables that are difficult to evaluate purely in fiscal terms.

More egalitarian societies do no better at preventing segregation—between ethnic groups or between rich and poor people—from occurring than less egalitarian ones, as the following excerpts make abundantly clear. Anderson reports of Denmark, "Even though we have succeeded in starting up classes in schools with a 50/50 mix, many of them fall apart during the first four years . . . Many children and parents find that it is difficult and very hard work to make the children get along and develop friendships after school, and quite a few give up after the first three to four years. The difficulties cannot be explained in simple terms, but [are] a complex field of social, linguistic, cultural and ethnic differences and the challenges must equally be met with a set of various contributions."[54] Similar results are reported from Sweden: "Without active participation from the local community, parents, and students in setting up extracurricular activities . . . and without any serious implementation of urban governance, no long-lasting changes can be imposed and no enduring trust in multicultural urban schools will be fostered among parents and students. Thus, the strongest students will carry on leaving the schools, while the newly arrived refugees will be directed to them. This is how the pattern of social and ethnic segregation is being perpetuated."[55] Both countries spend on average far more money on schools with high concentrations of poor minorities, yet the achievement of these schools lags predictably far behind that of middle-class schools. The same is true in the Netherlands, where the segregation problem is so visible that schools are labeled either "white" or "black." In fact, the phenomenon begins much sooner than that, for even a large percentage of childcare centers are segregated.[56]

Again, there can be no question that money matters; without it there are no buildings, qualified personnel, curricular materials, and so on. But of course the issue often is not whether schools with high concentrations of stigmatized minorities have fewer material resources. As illustrated earlier, many schools in fact receive far more per-pupil spending than others precisely *because* they have higher concentrations of poor children.[57] The issue that matters, to integrationists like Anderson, is not only fiscal resources but also access to the resources of social capital that schools with larger percentages of white, middle-class pupils ostensibly provide. There is no question that access to social networks is both advantageous and desirable. But four things should be remembered.

First, the argument assumes that resources from middle-class children and their parents are equally available and fairly distributed, or that power sharing will organically evolve in so-called integrated schools. Yet this is a claim for which there is a dearth of corroborating evidence. Anne Newman partly explains why:

> The emerging picture of deliberative policy-making in the education arena [is] often rather grim: those citizens best equipped and most likely to deliberate about education policy are least bound by the outcomes, while those most dependent on the outcomes are likely to be least well-prepared for, and most marginalized in, the policy process. In theory, deliberation is an attractive ideal for its ability to counter much of what is wrong with the politics of public education—atomistic, self interested maneuvering to secure private advantages, with costs to the collective good. Yet, as deliberation proceeds on the ground, these very ills are more likely to be reinforced than reversed.[58]

Second, access to social capital from others is not the only consideration, certainly not when it cannot compensate for an absence of self-respect. Indeed, so-called integrated settings may prove to be rather disruptive to the social networks stigmatized minorities need. We need a broader conception of *resources*, including the following: organizational features, strong leadership, school climate, shared values, caring teachers, involved parents, role modeling and career guidance, consensus on academic goals, and appropriate discipline. These have proven far more reliable resources in producing educational equality for underserved minorities, even under conditions of segregation.[59] I return to some of these in Chapter 4.

Third, even when we find integrated successes here and there, most research demonstrates that the outcomes are extremely modest. Take transfer programs. In theory they make it possible for disadvantaged (read: poor, minority) youth to attend schools with more abundant social capital. Parents who have pursued this option believe that their children will be exposed to a more rigorous curriculum and be able to tap into social networks needed to gain access to better career opportunities. Transfer programs certainly have enjoyed modest success, and the potential benefits to both minority and majority children should not be downplayed. Nevertheless, beyond a vaguely defined tipping point, many middle-class parents express anxiety about a sizable influx of disadvantaged youth.

For reasons that perhaps are best explained by both social desirability bias and implicit bias,[60] these assumptions are rarely articulated out loud. Instead, parents who "favor diversity" (but evidently don't like *too much* of it) are likely to argue that money that follows students to middle-class schools should instead be used to improve urban schools, or they complain that children bussed in from other school districts lower academic expectations and disrupt school norms. Schools eager to abstain from alienating their middle-class parents of course respond to these concerns, finding ways (e.g., "voluntary fees," advanced placement differentiation) to discourage lower-class and minority children from either enrolling in the first place or sitting in the same classes with middle-class children. Meanwhile, from minority communities the criticisms against transfer programs are directed at the physical and psychological costs children must bear either to travel such long distances to receive a quality education or to join a school community in which their presence is not welcome. Even advocates of integration through transfer programs admit that the obstacles that must be overcome with these programs are immense.[61] Unsurprisingly many have by now ceased to operate.

Fourth, the academic effects of mixed schools also are modest at best. A number of studies across Europe and North America consistently show that mixed classrooms produce only slightly modest gains for disadvantaged pupils, in part because the overwhelming majority of schools engage in some form of ability grouping and tracking.[62] Indeed, most schools must offer advanced placement electives, gifted and talented options, and accelerated programs if they are to succeed in placating and retaining their middle-class parents. Even if we could imagine some system of equalized schooling (say, by abolishing elite private schools—for example, gymnasia or grammar schools), the educational advantages of individual families would simply become more significant.[63] Indeed, most inequalities are in fact transmitted *outside* the school.

In order to level the playing field, we might consider restricting what more advantaged parents are able to do. Yet even when parental choices are restricted, the intuitions of middle-class parents to do what they think is best for their own children coincide with the basic liberties and rights liberal democratic constitutions guarantee. To be sure, the way that many middle-class parents access informational networks and navigate school systems can sometimes border on exploitative.[64] It is tempting to vilify those who flee bad school environments as overly ambitious or simply racist. But Sally Power puts this in perspective. She writes, "Changing individuals' decisions without challenging the deeper structuring of class differences will make little, if any, difference. Nor probably will even changing 'the rules.' *Middle-class parents have always proved remarkably adept at colonizing even those educational reforms designed to promote the opportunities of disadvantaged parents* . . . This is not because they have bad intentions, but because they have the resources and desire to protect their privileges for their children."[65] As Power's remarks indicate, in the real world legitimate forms of partiality manifest in various ways; among them, the desires to access limited resources, to improve the prospects of one's own child's future, and to optimize one's social position certainly count. Fears of downward mobility are real.

And while the middle class and affluent certainly have more resources at their disposal, parental advocacy is not restricted to them. Parents with lower levels of education also exercise their choices on the basis of preferences, even if their preferences on average are less well informed. "Less affluent and less well-educated parents," one British study reminds us, "are different but not deficient choosers."[66] From another British study, the authors observe that for poor parents, kinship and cultural and infrastructural ties may be "more important in choosing a neighborhood than the desire to live in less deprived neighborhoods."[67] Tilting the playing field in favor of the less educated—through public information campaigns, priority in school registration, and the like—may very well produce a number of salutary outcomes, and in many instances it may be morally negligent not to do so. But it is far from obvious whether restricting the liberties of the middle class will lead to more integration or that integration will produce greater equality.[68]

Conclusions

In this chapter I examined integrationist arguments using the framing principles and offered a number of philosophically and empirically based responses to each. Along the way I have challenged a number of integrationist assumptions. In particular I have argued against the idea that by integrating neighborhoods and schools, poor students gain direct access to the social capital their middle-class peers possess. This is because middle-class parents are particularly adept at securing advantages for their own children. Here we saw clearly how the exercise of liberty frustrates integration. Whether that is a terrible thing or not will partly depend on the factors attending segregated environments as well as our reasons for believing that integration better approximates justice than other alternatives.

As policy initiatives fail and political will to counter segregation falters, many continue to decry what they see as a retreat from noble integrationist ideals. There may in fact be much to lament, but it is a flaw in logic and an absence of imagination to suggest that justice must wait for inclusionary zoning policies or ideal socioeconomic "balances" in neighborhoods and schools to take effect before other alternatives should be made available or before parents can pursue a quality education for their own children on their own terms. To think otherwise is to make a fetish of integration. For

W. E. B. Du Bois, the blind pursuit of integrationist ideals was tantamount to "a fatal surrender to principle." Indeed, he wrote, to endure bad schools simply because they are "mixed" is a "costly if not fatal mistake."[69] If integration is an attractive symbol of justice and is to translate into real moral progress, the relevant resources must be equally available and fairly distributed. To the extent that integrationist ideals can deliver on these promises, neither the attending efforts nor the modest successes should be spurned.

But we also should not pass too quickly over the fact that for a great number of stigmatized minorities today, the promise of equality through school integration rings hollow. Indeed, owing to both an absence of diversity in many neighborhoods and the merely rhetorical commitment to integration among middle-class parents, the prospect of integration is not even an option. Where we do find integrated settings, much of the time there continue to be forces at work that erode the social bases of self-respect among society's most vulnerable groups. Confronted with low expectations, labeling patterns, cultural stereotypes, bad school reputations, and run-of-the-mill substandard education, parents increasingly look for alternatives in order to find equality of treatment and opportunity. As I will argue in Chapter 4, alternatives need not be integrated ones. But before we get there I think it worthwhile to step back from the foregoing empirical emphasis and reflect more deeply on our framing principles. What does each of these concepts entail, and why do they matter? Chapter 3 represents an effort to better appreciate how equality, citizenship, and liberty complement each other and to properly frame the concerns surrounding integration and segregation. It also will provide the foundations for the prima facie case for voluntary separation.

3

Foundational Principles

One of the tasks of social and political philosophy is to critically examine concepts that define the moral landscape and also are used to shape public policy. In this chapter I take a step back from the sociologically informed discussion about integration in Chapter 2 in order to examine the principles—normative ideas—that guide the integration argument and also frame the discussion in the chapters to follow. For my framing principles in the last chapter, I focused on two concepts: equality and citizenship. I used these principles to frame the integration discussion because in the literature there is a strong correlation between them. Indeed, some of that literature even assumes a causal relationship—namely, that integration will foster more equality and better citizenship. Meanwhile, other important principles make the realization of integration elusive and difficult. Here I refer to the role of liberty. But first consider the ways in which all three principles inform and reinforce each other.

Take equality and citizenship first. To the extent that equality indicates a particular status or set of opportunities, a notion of shared citizenship is implied. Likewise, citizenship implies a certain kind of equality—for example, of rights and responsibilities—even when inequalities of all sorts outline the terms on which both the promises and demands of equality and citizenship occur. Moreover, both citizenship and equality serve to indicate specific types of legal and moral status; citizens of a particular city, province, or nation in principle share equal entitlements to the privileges and obligations attending that citizenship. Citizenship indicates a particular status to the extent that we can rely on indicators like legal residency, constitutional rights, or perhaps even language proficiency. Similarly, while equality need not be tied to national contexts (it can, for instance, supply the basis for transnational rights), it indicates a particular status to the extent that we can demonstrate equal treatment before the law or equal opportunities in the labor market between similarly talented and motivated individuals.

Meanwhile, liberty also serves a supremely important function in free and democratic societies: as both a political principle and a legal right. It also operates in tandem with equality and citizenship. For example, equality involves securing equal liberty for all. Inequality entails decreased liberty, especially for the disadvantaged. Similarly, various kinds of liberty (e.g., of conscience, of expression) are integral to citizenship and support the kinds of society in which equal rights for all citizens can exist. But at the same time liberty also describes certain conditions and capacities for taking up and pursuing those things that matter to us—including, as we will see, justifiable partialities we express toward intimate others—and forms of membership with others with whom we share important things in common. However, given the way that liberty as a principle facilitates both freedom of movement and association, it is fair to say that it is not conducive to integration. So with respect to integration, liberty is a kind of nonfacilitative principle, and most efforts to promote integration will clash with liberty. For that reason I framed the integration argument in Chapter 2 around equality and citizenship and will do likewise in Chapter 4 in outlining the case for voluntary separation (VS).

All three principles are fundamental to our understanding of democratic ideals and institutions. An absence of consensus as to their meaning and application in no way diminishes their importance. Notwithstanding sharp disagreement from disparate philosophical or political viewpoints, persons from all walks of life recognize their significance, even if the ranking between them varies or their aims and purposes occasionally work at cross-purposes. Further, the important relationship between these principles on the one hand and segregation and integration on the other cannot be overstated.

What follows is by no means a comprehensive examination of these concepts; nor do any of these concepts exhaust the ways one might talk about integration or segregation. Instead, the purpose is simply to flesh out what these concepts entail and to highlight their relevance to our subject. In the first section I examine liberty and, again, I dub it a nonfacilitative principle given the way its exercise hinders the actualization of integration. I also will show how one fundamental expression of it—namely, partiality—while perhaps obstructive to integration is nevertheless something we cannot do without. In the second half of the chapter I focus on the framing principles and their relationship to integration. I begin with equality, outlining its basic features without delving into the contested nuances of egalitarian theory. One aspect of equality—namely, equality of self-respect—plays an important role, and it resurfaces again in Chapter 4. I also give considerable attention to the role that education can play in promoting and facilitating equality. I then turn my attention to citizenship, mapping its broad contours and characteristics, distinguishing between robust and pluralist accounts before examining its relationship to education. My own argument, spelled out more clearly in Chapter 4, takes its cue from a pluralist account.

Liberty

Many of us are accustomed to thinking of liberty as an absence of coercive interference. We imagine that it is law—custom and legal obligation—that hampers it and prevents us from doing what we want to do. But this rather Hobbesian view (repeated inter alia by Bentham) is flawed in at least two ways. First, it fails to differentiate between different kinds of interference. Interference of a legitimate paternalist sort, for instance, does not constrain liberty but rather enhances it. Countless examples of paternalist interference with liberty (e.g., interference with liberty to prevent one from consuming harmful and addictive drugs or from playing in busy streets) illustrate this very well. Good laws and good governance actually make liberty possible; they protect people against arbitrary power and domination.[1] Laws therefore represent a kind of nonarbitrary interference whose aim is not to constrain but rather to further liberty.

The second problem with a strict noninterference view is this: in order for liberty to get any traction there first must be enabling conditions and reasonable choice sets. As Hume observes, we cannot seriously claim "that a poor [person] has a free choice to leave his country, when he knows no foreign language or manners, and lives, from day to day, by the small wages which he [earns]."[2] As the quotation vividly illustrates, the range and type of structural constraints matter for the exercise of liberty. Nor can liberty be ensured merely by the presence of a choice set or evaluated on the basis of a crude form of preference satisfaction. Absent the relevant opportunity structures, choice sets, and social networks that facilitate the effective use of liberty, only the vapors of liberty remain. In other words, liberty must be constituted not only by capabilities and attributes but also by social arrangements that make its exercise possible in the first place. Capabilities and attributes will include things like financial resources, decent health, and a strong work ethic. Among the social arrangements that enable liberty we find transportation, institutions of higher learning, health care services, and a judiciary system that can facilitate and ensure basic conditions of fairness. Broadly construed, capabilities refers to the freedom to choose how to live and the actual ability of persons to choose different lives within their reach.[3] Many capabilities will not differ from one culture or political context to another, yet the exact capabilities, attributes, and social arrangements that are critical to the exercise of liberty in the final analysis must be deliberated on relative to context and necessity.

In order to provide and maintain the conditions necessary for the exercise of liberty, states play an important role. The liberal democratic state is called upon to arrange and facilitate the liberties of persons in the public as well as the private sphere. It does this in at least two ways. First, it subsidizes or provides public services without which many citizens would be less free to take up other, arguably worthwhile pursuits. Further, laws governing public health and safety as well as compulsory military service may be enacted for the legitimate purpose of promoting human liberty, social order, and justice. This constitutes the state's legitimate paternalist role. So more than merely protecting or regulating liberty through the ratification of laws, the state's facilitative role is that of enabler.

Second, and paradoxically, the state also enables liberty by constraining it. Constraints on liberty operate to safeguard the interests of others. For instance, liberal democratic states can organize and regulate liberty through progressive taxation or antitrust legislation so that persons (or corporations) with more resources are less able to exploit those without them. Indeed, the state is generally recognized as the guarantor of last resort in arranging the equal liberties of coequal citizens and specifically in seeing to it that children receive at least a minimum of basic care. A robust conception of basic care will include provisions for decent health and an education suitable for gainful employment.

Further, freedom of expression is famously subject to incitement constraints, just as freedom of association is subject to mutuality constraints. That is, persons may not say whatever they wish irrespective of the consequences of what they say. I may not slander, threaten, or provoke others to violence with impunity; nor may persons associate with others however and wherever they wish irrespective of intent and effect. Hate groups may be justifiably monitored and even banned when their pernicious designs come to light. Moreover, a group's involuntary members—children in particular—fall under the ambit of legitimate moral concern in liberal democratic states. Of course, some constraints are more trivial than others—being unable to play tennis because there are no available tennis courts is not of the same order as being undernourished—but this doesn't alter the basic point.

The idea that liberty must be coercively restrained normally demands some kind of justification. But here we can recall Mill's harm principle, which stipulates that liberty may be restrained when it interferes with or prevents someone else from being free.[4] Even principled libertarians, who place considerable stock in their liberty to dispose of their property as they choose, nevertheless recognize important side constraints.[5] Incentives and mild forms of coercion may be justified both for the purposes of preventing harm[6] and for steering choices in directions favorable to well-being. For example, health insurance can be mandated for all citizens, and providers can be regulated so that affordable care is available to all, and traffic and weapon laws legitimately restrict what persons can do with their liberty in order to ensure relative order and security. Indeed, we might say that law and security are prerequisites for the exercise of liberty.

In modern liberal democratic states we typically parse liberty into a number of different articulations, but there are three that are familiar: (1) freedom of conscience, (2) freedom of association, and (3) freedom of expression. Freedom of conscience involves the right to choose one's own moral viewpoint and to follow its directives. Freedom of association permits me to make common cause with others who in one degree or another share my convictions or at any rate share my interests in some relevant sense. Lastly, freedom of expression involves the right to express in a variety of ways the beliefs and ideas I consider important. All of these normally dovetail with one another and normally may be pursued to permissible ends. Whichever expression it takes, liberty is not boundless. Yet so long as our liberties do not inappropriately interfere with identical liberties for others, liberal democratic societies for the most part permit adults to both think and associate with others as they like as well as to act on the dictates of their conscience.

When it comes to regulating and ordering liberty, liberal democratic states generally do a minimally respectable job of supplying and distributing valuable social goods. (Of course, some liberal states do a much better job than others.)[7] Yet while there is basic consensus on the importance of liberty, and moreover concerning the various ways that the state may legitimately use its authority to regulate the uses of that liberty, the state's role continues to be controversial in its regulating of liberty in two areas: (1) its distribution of resources through coercive taxation,[8] and (2) its infringement on the liberties of parents to direct the lives of their own children. Here the constitutional right to choose the school one's child attends—even when one's choices are restricted—is an important expression of liberty. In the following section I take up the latter of these.

Liberty and Education

In all liberal democracies the freedoms to raise one's child and to select the type of education one wishes to have—provided it is both available and affordable—are generally considered extensions of basic liberty rights. Freedom of educational choice for parents is also viewed as an entitlement in all liberal democracies, even if the scope of choice varies widely from place to place[9] and parents possess disparate means of exercising it. Article 26.3 of the Universal Declaration of Human Rights states this as follows: "Parents have a prior right to choose the kind of education that shall be given to their children." Article 2 of the first protocol of the European Convention on Human Rights has its own version: "The State shall respect the right of parents to ensure such education and teaching in conformity with their own religious and philosophical convictions." Even in Article 7 of the Universal Declaration of the Rights of the Child it is plainly stated that the best interests of the child "shall be the guiding principle of those responsible for his education and guidance; that responsibility lies in the first place with his parents."

Most liberal democratic institutions also secure these fundamental rights through constitutional guarantees. Indeed, apart from cases warranting paternalistic interference on the grounds of abuse or neglect, parents enjoy very wide latitude in decisions to have and bring up their own children, including the sharing of beliefs and interests. This of course extends to education. The liberty of parents to select an education they deem suitable for their own children, provided that parents' own liberties do not unduly or improperly infringe on the liberty of their children (which is rather difficult to assess outside extreme cases) is one that is consistent with a liberal democratic state aiming to facilitate a plurality of choices as well as the exercise of individual liberty.[10] Here we face what I later call the problem of pluralism.

In sum, while parents may not freely exercise their liberties however they like (e.g., they are not justified in abusing their children), they are generally entitled to give priority to their own children. Where basic educational opportunities exist and rudimentary political freedoms are secured, parents enjoy strong prerogatives in raising their children as they see fit and in selecting an education for their own child. That brings us to a particular way liberty is expressed.

Partiality Revisited

As an expression of liberty, partiality broadly describes a justifiable special regard persons show for another. Usually this special regard is based on a unique relationship such as parent to child or sibling to sibling, but it also may be community resident to community resident. Just as often partiality arises out of shared interests and preferences and the fact that we gravitate toward others like ourselves. We not only seek out others with whom we share things in common; on the basis of those commonalities we also construct and sustain "memberships." Those memberships partly define who we are and provide us with meaning and purpose. All these are intrinsically and irreplaceably worthwhile goods borne of relationships defined by partiality. Indeed our partiality toward some of those with whom we share our lives actually defines the particular relationship in question and makes it special. This is the case with respect not only to how, and with whom, we freely associate but, more specifically, to how we express our love and concern for our children.

Parenting is in fact *the* quintessential partial relationship, and the favoritism parents display toward their own children involves unique loyalties, responsibilities, and duties that in most cases they do not display toward other children.[11] That is to say, while the intrinsic value of one child is equal to the intrinsic value of another, one's obligations to all children are not equal; nor would we reasonably expect them to be. Should parents feel obligated impartially to allocate their love, attention, and fiscal and emotional support equally to all children, we would rightly observe this as an abdication of a duty to regard one's own child in a partial way. Being entirely dependent on their guardians or parents for emotional and material support, children justifiably *deserve* many forms of partiality as a basis for their own well-being.

Here we potentially are confronted with some of the sharpest tensions between equality and citizenship on the one hand and liberty on the other—namely, in the realm of family intimacy. Even if all or most parents demonstrate partiality toward their own children in matchless ways, it will not be done on a level playing field. Even when the same disposition—in this case, partiality—is being expressed, its inputs and outputs will themselves produce more inequalities. Hence what it means for person x to express partiality toward his own child will likely have an indirect (though unintended) impact on person y. While egregious forms of partiality can be averted by the state through constraints on liberty, the garden variety of preferential treatment that parents display toward their own children produces, or at any rate sustains, innumerable forms of inequality.[12]

Similar challenges confront more demanding conceptions of citizenship. Later we will see how in a pluralist conception of citizenship both toleration and liberty play a crucial role. Citizens enjoy fairly broad discretion over the choices they make and the associations they pursue and maintain. This at least partly entails that citizens develop and pursue different conceptions of a life worth having, and regarding a pluralist conception of citizenship, we cannot reasonably expect these to conform to one model. Second, we are justified in seeking out memberships and support from a variety of social networks; social networks nourish and sustain us through community solidarity. Further, they provide us with a sense of belonging and attachment essential for personal happiness and well-being.

Partiality for others who share our group status may also be legitimate. Members of a neighborhood or town understandably will prioritize their own needs over those of distant others. Notwithstanding the universalizability of moral responsibility in the abstract, real-world constraints on moral action render obligations to distant others supererogatory. Citizens of a particular country may legitimately express partiality for fellow citizens on the understanding that citizens of other nations will do the same in theirs. To not do so is to compromise justice at the local level and further risk undermining the political stability of the society one inhabits. Of course difficulties arise when conditions unfavorable to benign forms of partiality are absent. Military regimes that fortify their armies while allowing their citizens to starve may warrant exceptional interference. Natural disasters may warrant similar paternalist interventions. In cases like these a cosmopolitan ethic emerges on the basis of our shared humanity, which places certain (reasonable) demands on our attention and resources.[13]

But notice that the more particular our networks are (i.e., the closer they come to meeting personal needs and preferences—and these are related to partiality), the more likely they are to be ranked over other kinds of interests—for example, the comparatively remote attachments I may feel toward fellow citizens with whom I may share very little in common. Notice, too, that the prioritizing of associations or attachments with specific social networks means that some unavoidably may be favored over others. Some of these attachments will be innocuous; others will likely bear adversely upon both equality and citizenship. That certainly appears to be the case when we recognize a strong correlation between partiality and what I later call the threat of ethnocentrism.

Of course, expressions of partiality are not always legitimate; both its motives and its effects can be scrutinized. Partialities that traduce the ingredients from which both equality and citizenship are built can be justifiably constrained. Where unavoidable conflicts continue to arise, priorities must be hammered out in the messy details of everyday life. I return to some of these concerns about partiality and citizenship in Chapter 4, but for now it should be noted that the expression of many forms of partiality appear to be legitimate. But liberty as partiality is not the only game in town. Whether making the case for integration or for VS, other principles are needed. To see how, I now examine what I call its framing principles. I begin with equality, focusing on equality of self-respect before turning my attention to citizenship.

Framing Principles

Equality

There are two ways we might speak of equality. One is of a more natural or embodied sort: persons are not endowed with equal genetic potential or equal physical attributes. Some are more talented in certain respects than others, just as some are taller or shorter. But there is also a moral or political sense in which we may speak of equality. In the more formal sense equality denotes equal rights and responsibilities and, in principle, roughly fair opportunities offered to all citizens. One core purpose of equality is to secure liberty for all on terms of equal recognition and treatment. Equality under a system of natural liberty describes a fair starting point with respect to careers open to talents. That is to say, within a just political system persons of similar aptitude and motivation ought to enjoy roughly the same prospects. Such a system naturally would include formal prohibitions against discrimination. Political philosophers have dubbed this approach the natural aristocracy, though it is now widely accepted that even the possession of talents or disabilities is undeserved. How, or whether, to correct these remains hotly contested terrain among egalitarians, who also continue to debate among themselves the extent to which talents, effort, and choices are morally relevant.[14]

It is neither fruitful nor necessary to get bogged down in these arcane disputes. It will suffice to point out that the main liberal versions of equality require first a recognition aspect—namely, the state treats its citizens as moral equals—and then an opportunity aspect—namely, fellow citizens have roughly equal rights and opportunities. In other words, liberal equality entails equal status in both the moral sense and the political sense. In the moral sense, then, it corresponds with an equality of self-respect. Self-respect is fundamental to any acceptable notion of social and moral equality. While the content and requirements of self-respect are imprecise, it undoubtedly suggests having a positive regard for oneself. Positive regard for oneself entails a natural sense of self-importance that can be either cultivated or crushed by circumstance and experience. More ontological versions of self-respect are based on the concept of human dignity, the notion that persons have intrinsic worth as members of the human community.[15] In the *Groundwork of the Metaphysics of Morals*[16] Kant considered human dignity to be an unconditional good. It describes the basic value persons have irrespective of their individual characteristics. Indeed this is equality in the moral sense. The absence of a regard for human dignity—whether precipitated, say, through a denial of public recognition or conditions of social deprivation—not only dramatically lessens the possibilities of self-respect; the probability of humiliation also dramatically increases.[17] It is therefore not misleading to say that dignity corresponds closely to self-respect.

I do not want to overstate the point here. In Chapter 4 I show that even stigmatized persons are often resilient, even under highly unfavorable conditions. But because self-respect constitutes a fundamental value, one of the best ways to promote this value is to ensure that individuals can take up and pursue those things that matter to them. For John Rawls it entails the ability, so far as it is within one's power, "to advance [one's] ends with self confidence."[18] Provided that the enabling conditions of liberty are met, this means not only that persons possess a conviction about their conception of good but also that they are capable of pursuing it. Here we see the connection between the intrinsic and instrumental benefits of self-respect, for self-respect is the psychological antecedent to self-reliance, and the more equally distributed the notion of self-respect is, the more possible it is to speak of justice.[19]

With respect to the political sense, societies generally are more equitably structured when their major institutions are framed by these convictions. But of course one must take seriously a number of socially contingent background characteristics that to a large extent shape if not determine the opportunities people enjoy. Where and when one is born, to which parents, in which neighborhood, and whether during an economic boom or a downturn all are significant contributing factors. So are one's nationality, religion, ethnicity, gender, peer group, employment status, and level of physical and cognitive ability. Each of these plays an important role in the lottery that produces profoundly unequal opportunities. Therefore equality of opportunity in its broadest sense means that one's prospects should not be determined, or unduly influenced, by any of the aforementioned morally irrelevant factors. Instead, it requires certain distributive arrangements that level the playing field for those whose genetic endowment or environmental hazards ensure fewer opportunities to pursue a life they consider worth living. While antidiscrimination laws may succeed in restraining inequality, an absence of (overt forms of) discrimination in itself does not constitute equality; it is but a necessary though insufficient condition of equality.

But efforts to promote equality do not require equalization in the sense of leveling up or down to identical points of input or output; nor need they entail identical treatment. Further, liberal notions of equality ostensibly allow for inequalities where these result from genetically inherited—and thus undeserved—talent, effort, and choices and further recognizes that these are largely immune to equalization. For example, even if it was possible, say, to generally equalize income and wealth, we would expect that differing levels of talent, motivation, and effort—certainly in very heterogeneous societies—will severely complicate efforts to promote equality. Indeed, efforts to equalize are difficult if not impossible to achieve given the range of variables (e.g., talent, effort, resources) that elude equalization. Many inequalities, including the preferences we have, result from a mixture of inheritance and environment that profoundly shape the options in life that we pursue and our chances of happiness and success. Amartya Sen observes, "Equality in terms of one variable may not coincide with equality in the scale of another. For example, equal opportunities can lead to very unequal incomes. Equal incomes can go with significant differences in wealth. Equal wealth can coexist with very unequal happiness. Equal happiness can do with widely divergent fulfillment of needs. Equal fulfillment of needs can be associated with very different freedoms of choice. And so on."[20]

But the difficulties do not stop there. Consider, for instance, that many persons espouse equality as a value yet believe that charity, rather than state-managed (read: coercive) wealth distribution, is the best way to assist the poor. So even if it were possible to settle the conceptual difficulties and consensus could be reached regarding efforts to mitigate injustice, we would continue to face challenges at the implementation stage: Are policies fiscally and logistically feasible? How likely will they produce the effects they promise? How will the pursuit of egalitarian policies affect important liberties (e.g., partiality toward one's children)? And most importantly, will state actions that aim to promote certain outcomes be perceived as legitimate?

Equality and Education

Most of us recognize the importance of equality of opportunity, particularly in the educational sphere. States typically assume the responsibility for providing and regulating the education of children. They ensure legal entitlement of all children to a minimally adequate education, including among their aims the promotion of literacy and numeracy skills sufficient for basic functioning. Some egalitarians argue that adequacy standards will not suffice and that competences necessary for public reasonableness and political participation also must be fostered.[21] More on that later. But at least in principle, equality of opportunity means that everyone, irrespective of income and wealth, religious or nonreligious affiliation, ethnicity or gender, and ability or disability, has the right to a free education and the opportunity to make social advances as a direct result of that educational benefit.[22] Of course these benefits tend to be both scarce and variable, so they are by definition not attainable by everyone. Even so, the availability of a quality state-provided education to all children typically is viewed as a public good worth defending, even by those who opt out of the system.

In theory, states provide a public education to their citizens on the equality-promoting view that persons should have the right to make social advances without regard to morally irrelevant characteristics. Irrespective of the form in which it is offered, education plays a key role in the distribution of equality, for it entails access to different kinds of goods. Suitably prepared and delivered education supplies intrinsic goods that can contribute to one's ability to flourish. Learning to read or paint, for example, can be its own reward. But one's ability to flourish also depends crucially on the capacity for economic self-reliance. For this, persons must have information, choices, skills, and opportunities for remunerated labor acquired through either apprenticeships or formal schooling. Educational equality thus describes instrumental goods for one's qualifications. However, achievements always stand in relation to others with whom one must compete for scarce resources. That is, the value of my education is at least partly determined by the education that others receive.[23] So a quality education will supply crucially important goods, and educational equality means that access to, and the quality of, my education should not hang on something as arbitrary as my school's postal code or the size of my parents' income.

Educational policies built on egalitarian principles can take many forms. For example, consider its policy implications in relation to poverty and disability. In order to compensate for a poor distribution in the choice lottery, schools with higher concentrations of poverty often require more resources to compensate for disadvantage; the same goes for many children with disabilities. Similarly, children saddled with disabilities or social disadvantage are eligible if not entitled to receive additional support, and considerably more financial resources should be earmarked for that purpose. In many countries, this explains targeted funding for schools servicing children with extra needs. While the policies are crafted differently according to context, they now generally receive broad support, because arguments for equal consideration and treatment have been extended to include many previously marginalized groups of persons.

Other equality-motivated policies, enacted at both local and national levels, include the following: spending caps on wealthier districts, restricted parental choice, incentives to attract more talented teachers to high-need schools, class-size reduction, the rotation of effective school principals, means-tested vouchers, and weighted pupil funding. The same egalitarian logic extends beyond the educational realm. Efforts to promote equal treatment, for example, include many forms of public assistance available to all (e.g., fire protection, disaster relief, unemployment and disability protection, social security) as well as institutions and services (e.g., museums, libraries, parks) whose benefits are public in the best sense of the word. Each of these goes some distance in leveling the playing field for all irrespective of one's background characteristics.[24]

Of course, while it is certainly the case that a free elementary and secondary education serves to promote equality of opportunity, neither that ideal nor the policies believed to instantiate it will have much effect in the absence of enabling conditions, which is to say specific relational, environmental, and institutional supports. Examples of the relevant conditions will include any of the following: attentive and loving parents, affordable health care and child care, a satisfactory income, the presence of highly qualified and inspirational teachers, meaningful employment opportunities in the labor market, and equitable recruiting strategies to ensure fair consideration of qualified candidates. Each of these, and many others besides, effectively works in tandem to improve the opportunities of children born into relative disadvantage, and without them, schools—integrated or not—do very little indeed to promote equality of opportunity. When combined, however, these supports can help level the playing field for those who by no fault of their own begin life dramatically behind their more advantaged peers.

Yet notwithstanding the important gains of universal education, educational equality, owing to the breadth of its application, is an ideal that consistently garners unanimous agreement but about which there continues to be no consensus concerning how best to interpret and implement it.[25] Perhaps short of radically improbable and draconian measures, such as abolishing the family or massively overhauling capitalist economies, the social and economic circumstances into which persons are born similarly are largely impervious to overly demanding versions of equality. It is for this reason that we might regard certain versions of egalitarianism as utopian.

That is not to say that efforts to promote equality should be abandoned. To the contrary, even in the absence of such consensus, much can be done to mitigate the undesirable causes and effects of inequality. For instance, any robust conception of equality will demand that economic inequalities do not spill over into noneconomic areas such as political influence and legal protections. Both litigation and political campaigns, for example, will yield less unfair advantage for a few if allowable expenditures are fixed and enforced or if a fairly designed lottery determines who receives what. Life as we know it, however, does indeed suggest that overly demanding forms of social equality are utopian: even under regimes of progressive taxation and stiff government regulation, the wealthy continue to enjoy considerably more access to resources and power.

Yet the basic point remains: whether inherited or not, unfair advantages do not absolve us from the moral imperative to equalize (1) where inequalities clearly result from injustice or bad luck or (2) where it is legitimately possible to do so. But as a matter of policy, how best to achieve equality between persons with unequal prospects remains an open question. We seem to do better approximating a more modest conception of equality—one that both corrects for more egregious abuses and compensates for various types of disadvantage but also one that allows for the fostering of equality under nonideal circumstances. Such a conception, I argue, is consistent with equality for self-respect. In Chapter 4, equality for self-respect will serve as the basis of one argument as it applies to separation. That, however, must wait. Next I turn my attention to the second framing principle—namely, citizenship.

Citizenship

Beyond the particulars that define legal residency, citizenship arguably consists of shared membership in a political space on the basis of mutual moral and legal rights and responsibilities broadly understood. This is basically where the agreement ends. Most political theorists who write about citizenship are prepared to defend some variant of Aristotle's view—namely, that the citizen "should be moulded to suit the form of government under which he lives"[26] without endorsing his more demanding conviction that the general aims and purposes of individual lives invariably dovetail with those of the state. Meanwhile, answers to any of the following questions remain largely unsettled, even by those who routinely debate them: How should the elements of citizenship be fostered? Can this be done without violating the state's legitimacy? Are there nonnegotiable dispositions and behaviors that must manifest in the lives of all citizens? Might our voluntary attachments and obligations justifiably trump memberships that we inherit or that others wish to impose on us?

Robust accounts of citizenship describe the reciprocal and informed engagement of citizens with their respective political institutions and with each other. Robust accounts may also include the capacity to challenge authority, to reasonably disagree with other points of view, and to dissent on principled grounds from positions sanctioned by the majority. Further, robust accounts normally require that one imaginatively engage with others whose perspectives and experiences are different from one's own and work together to sustain or reform the political institutions to bring about positive change. More demanding accounts, such as those of Stephen Macedo, even maintain that the health of our democracy is to be found in "its ability to turn people's deepest convictions—including their religious beliefs—in directions that are congruent with the ways of a liberal regime."[27] The question is whether robust accounts are sufficiently responsive to how most citizens are inclined and entitled to exercise their liberties and organize their lives, particularly when these correspond to other modes of voluntary association.

Meanwhile, less robust—or what I henceforth call pluralist—accounts remind us that while some lives are perhaps defined by politics or political activism, most of us subscribe to a less explicitly political version of civic virtue. William Galston avers that "we cannot rightly assess the importance of politics without acknowledging the limits of politics,"[28] driving home the point that citizenship entails many types of expression—and not only those pertaining to overtly political action. In other words, *civic* virtue—consisting of dispositions and actions that promote the good of the community—does not collapse into *political* virtue. Moreover, pluralist accounts stress the range of choices that free citizens are entitled to make provided they meet their basic civic responsibilities and obligations. That is to say, while one might be duty bound to operate within the parameters of the law, citizenship also entails fairly broad discretion concerning how one expresses liberty—for example, with respect to the choices one makes and the associations one wishes to pursue and maintain. Here both toleration and liberty come to the fore, and most persons recognize that the best way to facilitate civic liberty is to allow persons to pursue their individual or group interests according to their own principled beliefs so long as they do not unduly interfere with or limit the liberty of others.

With respect to political virtue, pluralist accounts concede the importance of cultivating important skills and dispositions but normally require only that persons understand their basic rights and adhere to their legal obligations. This is because there is a variety of ways that persons can fulfill the requirements of "good citizenship." To be sure, moments of direct political engagement have their place. But unlike some varieties of liberal republicanism, demanding uninterrupted and explicitly political forms of civic engagement (something ordinary citizens would find difficult to sustain in any event), advocates of pluralist citizenship stress the importance of toleration. Framed as civic virtue, toleration entails the recognition that people's lives go better when they are free to pursue those things that matter to them, provided these pursuits do not overtly harm others.

The distinction I make between robust and pluralist accounts is, of course, rather artificial. Neither account is monolithic. Both accounts stress the importance of rights and responsibilities; both also value pluralism, social networks, and the need to protect the private sphere. Further, both accounts stress the importance of civic engagement, though pluralist accounts impose fewer imperatives on how or when it ought to be expressed. So long as a critical mass of concerned citizens consciously reproduces the laws and institutions necessary for the healthy functioning of a democracy, considerable discretion can be left to the private sphere, and a range of legitimate nonpolitical pursuits can be tolerated irrespective of whether or not they promote civic virtue. Certainly robust accounts have a narrower scope of permissibility on both fronts, but pluralist accounts do not ignore basic rules of decency or duties that apply to everyone irrespective of their personal habits or convictions. The private sphere, for instance, is not immune to criticism on any account of citizenship that takes shared responsibilities or egalitarian concerns seriously. In any case, the distinction I have drawn serves mainly to emphasize different understandings—but also to enunciate the scope of requirement citizenship imposes on us.

Whether the conception of citizenship is demanding or not, many challenges are associated with reconciling the centralized aims of states with the diverse array of beliefs and practices among society's members. These form a loose collection of memberships out of which the diffuse tapestry of citizenship arises. Call this the problem of pluralism. Pluralism describes the condition of multiple interests inhabiting the same political space. While the fundamentals of differing value systems may not vary, in the details they often do.

The pressures of pluralism are nothing new in the realm of political theory, and they present certain challenges for citizenship. How much pluralism can states accommodate and still retain the social cohesion necessary to function as a state? Should states concern themselves with internal cohesion by actively promoting a common national identity? What would those features be? What does recognition of minority groups entail, and how far should it go? In aiming to promote equality of treatment, which institutional supports are necessary? Should there be special exemptions from collective responsibility when these conflict with internal group interests? Will the institutionalization of group rights help or harm its members? How important are national borders for fostering common citizenship?

We need not settle these questions here; for the moment, it will suffice to point out their routine occurrence. The point is simply that many challenges commonly arise within pluralist societies, some of them problematic and others not. Whichever civic dispositions and skills are requisite, we can agree that the acceptance of pluralism does not entail that all forms of belonging are salutary or that individual conscience always is a reliable guide. All societies, liberal democratic ones perhaps especially, host a wide assortment of specific memberships coherently possible in both the private and public domains. I say "coherently possible" because memberships that intentionally or unintentionally aim to undermine the possibility of cooperation across difference generally are viewed as undesirable given the threat they pose to both equality and citizenship in general and to other forms of belonging in particular. To ignore the importance of cultivating the dispositions and behaviors associated with citizenship—such as respectful engagement—is to neglect virtues that matter.

Given the perceived or real threat of "balkanization," liberal theorists seem especially preoccupied with memberships that potentially pose a challenge to what is coherently possible under a liberal democratic social contract. Even in the absence of violence, some memberships may also be undesirable (though tolerated) if such forms of belonging repress the liberties of some members or discourage all contact with the outside world. Call this the threat of ethnocentrism. But even ethnocentrism has its benign varieties. Preferring one's own group to another on the basis of shared interests and experiences is something we all do. Yet when memberships are taken to mean concern for one's own group at the expense of others, this is no trivial matter. In Chapter 4 I return to some of these concerns.

But the basic point here is that there are principled limits to what can and should be tolerated, and these standards can be defended and enforced. Even when certain behaviors are defended on cultural or religious grounds, prohibitions on rape, usury, and honor killings not only delineate basic human decency; each can also be shown to violate the norms of citizenship inasmuch as they each involve the violation of other citizens' fundamental rights. Robust or pluralist, all liberal variants of citizenship will draw a distinction between multiple conceptions of a good life on the one hand and clear violations of basic human dignity on the other. Where those distinctions should be drawn, however, remains a matter of intense discussion within the walls of liberalism itself.[29]

And here again we see clearly the problem of pluralism as well as the threat of ethnocentrism. These remain seemingly insuperable challenges to societies that are both liberal and democratic on the one hand and deeply segregated on the other. Keeping the potential harms of pluralist accounts (e.g., ethnocentrism) at bay while avoiding untenably robust accounts that downplay the "social matrices of personal flourishing"[30] remains a central challenge for political theory. Implausible amalgamations of robust and pluralist accounts do not move us closer to resolving these tensions. Robust or not, the requirements of citizenship normally encompass both voluntary and involuntary memberships within nation-states and beyond, for as global citizens our lives are often imperceptibly tangled with dissimilar cultural others. And robust or not, most versions of citizenship are coupled with integration and cohesion as important policy goals. As we will see in Chapter 4, however, the political demands of citizenship take on strident and contentious forms in countries grappling with immigration, segregation, and alarming levels of social and economic inequality.

Citizenship and Education

As we saw earlier in this chapter, a number of relevant purposes and benefits underwrite the aims of education, principal among them the fostering of civic equality. In most countries where states play the leading role in educational provision, citizenship education in one form of another is compulsory. Basic to an understanding of citizenship are the knowledge and skills necessary to function and participate in democratic societies. Citizenship must begin with the basics—literacy and numeracy—and expand outward to knowledge of basic rights and political institutions as well as a minimum threshold of respect for others with whom one does not agree. It will inculcate knowledge of constitutional rights and liberties as well as an awareness of the obligations we have toward others on the basis of our shared citizenship if not our common humanity.

Robust versions may also include developing one's capacity to identify with and reflect on a set of judgments and beliefs about what constitutes a good life. Either way, most political theorists argue that citizenship cannot be left to chance. Specific civic virtues must be cultivated. For instance, Amy Gutmann looks to the contribution that schools can make and argues that the details of any citizenship education cannot merely settle on minimal requirements but instead must cultivate capacities to reflect critically on one's (or one's parents') core commitments. Moreover, she argues that civic virtues must include "the ability to articulate and the courage to stand up for one's publicly defensible convictions, the ability to deliberate with others and therefore to be open-minded about the politically relevant issues, and the ability to evaluate the performance of officeholders."[31]

But given both the problem of pluralism and the threat of ethnocentrism we just encountered, the worries about balkanization are real. Any serious account of citizenship must devote considerable attention to what is shared among citizens from disparate backgrounds, which means that any shared notion of citizenship is an articulation of equality—of recognition, status, and treatment—and must include the cultivation of dispositions and habits necessary for promoting the good of the community. Of course, what that good entails and how the community should be defined will in large part depend on the context in which these discussions take place. Even so, and elusive though it may be, little dispute exists about the need for a commons, a place where agreements can be reached and disagreements can be discussed and negotiated by citizens on basic terms of equality.

Irrespective of whether civic education occurs in a school or not, legitimate civic education will refrain from inculcating uncritical loyalty toward the state; it will accommodate both plurality and dissent.[32] And whatever the details of civic education should be, elevated ideals are not enough. Irrespective of whether persons extol the virtues of the nation-state or wax nostalgic about a glorious past—its common ideals, shared norms, and values—ordinary citizens are far more likely to attach themselves to some *concrete* and specific understanding of what those shared elements entail. Some may feel themselves to be proud Scots, Argentinians, or Japanese, yet except in moments of profound national crisis (e.g., militaristic threats, natural disasters), these identifications for most remain rather abstract. Consequently, absent an intentional cultivation of, say, patriotic sentiment, the tug of republican virtue on our more immediate and local priorities will likely remain relatively weak. Indeed, our civic virtues, as I argue in Chapter 4, often arise from attachments facilitated by our spatial concentrations and voluntary memberships with others like ourselves. These attachments, more often than not, fundamentally define who we are and what we care about.

Conclusions

In this chapter I elaborated the features of the framing principles. The purpose was to better understand not only how these principles relate to each other but also how each bears upon both integration and segregation. In demonstrating their interdependence, I argued that one of the main respects in which citizens are supposed to be equal is their liberty. Where there is more equality, there should be more liberty. Conversely, many kinds of inequality entail less liberty for the disadvantaged. Additionally, various kinds of liberty (e.g., of conscience or expression) are integral to what we understand citizenship to mean. In short, liberty sustains the kind of society in which equal rights for citizens can exist. At the same time, there are tensions. We saw this in particular with the principle of liberty—especially when expressed as partiality. We might ask, for instance, why citizenship aligned to some particular but partial view of nationhood should be assumed, a priori, to be of more importance than other associations and groupings to which someone may belong. And here we are reminded of how liberty functions as a nonfacilitative principle vis-à-vis integration, for partiality expresses, in many ways, what we care most about and why.

And we should not forget that some expressions of partiality inevitably will coincide with segregation.

What one is permitted to do with his or her own time and resources remains a significant challenge not only for both moral and political theory but also for ordinary citizens living in pluralist societies. Which choices are we permitted to make for ourselves and for those who matter to us? Are others affected by what I do, and if so, how badly? How much solidarity is one obliged to show, by what means, and for how long? With each of these questions, we feel both the pull of egalitarian concern and the tug of civic requirement. Resolving these tensions cannot be settled objectively. The prioritizing or ranking of ideals must be examined and justified against the varying backdrops of deeply plural societies that contain innumerable inequalities. Some steps can certainly be taken to restrain one principle so that others may prevail. As we have seen, various justifiable restrictions may be imposed on the exercise of liberty for the purpose of protecting and promoting that of others. However, certain expressions of liberty will be morally problematic for integration if its arguments exclusively rely—as they do—on the principles of equality and citizenship. Partiality in particular appears to operate at cross-purposes with both. That, however, is something I intend to dispute.

In Chapter 4 I argue that while some integrated environments may be able to provide important goods and resources, we should not expect them to be the *only* environments in which they are available or can be distributed, perhaps especially to those who need them the most. To show this, in what follows I will use the framing principles and argue a prima facie case for voluntary separation.

4

Voluntary Separation

In Chapter 2 I examined a number of harms that correlate strongly with some types of segregation. In response, I analyzed and critiqued arguments in favor of integration using the framing principles: equality and citizenship. In this chapter I defend a prima facie case for voluntary separation (VS). I will defend the view that involuntary forms of segregation can and often do co-occur with organized responses to resist, rearrange, and reclaim the terms of one's segregation. This response best captures the fundamental difference between segregation and separation. In developing the argument in this chapter I outline its components using the framing principles exclusively. Like the arguments for integration in Chapter 2, those based on liberty will play no role. The prima facie defense of VS will consist of two main arguments.

The first argument is that VS is defendable when equality—meaning equal status and treatment—is not an option under the terms of either integration or involuntary segregation. To that end I briefly revisit the argument in Chapter 3—namely, that self-respect constitutes a fundamental value and, further, an important basis for equality. I then argue that under conditions of inequality-producing segregation, VS may be more likely to provide the resources necessary for self-respect for members of stigmatized minority groups.[1] Here I focus in particular on VS in education, largely because concerns about equality routinely occur in this arena. The upshot of the first argument is that VS may more successfully supply the bases for equality by cultivating self-respect, but that separation must be accompanied by other relevant conditions that must be satisfied if equality is to be achieved.

The second argument rests on a pluralist reading of citizenship. I argue that civic virtue entails promoting the good of the community, but it does not reduce to political virtue, nor is it dependent on integration. While segregation and disadvantage commonly coexist, many forms of segregation actually facilitate the occurrence of civic virtue. In other words, it may not be in spite of but rather *because* there are spatial concentrations that civic virtue can be more effectively fostered. Accordingly, so long as segregation provides facilitative conditions for the fostering of civic virtue, integration is not an irreducible good. To that end I explicate and defend voluntary forms of separation consistent with civic virtue. I further argue that while civic virtue typically begins with the local, this need not limit one's capacity to think beyond the local. Local attachments need not foreclose fostering other modes of belonging or restrict the scope of moral concern. Later in the chapter I show that civic virtue in the form of VS offers an important space for public deliberation. Contrary to the integration-for-citizenship arguments discussed in Chapter 2, I will show that integrated settings are not the only fertile ground on which the harvest of civic virtue depends. In the second half of the chapter I respond to specific challenges to my argument: ethnocentrism, deliberation, and stratification.

Caveats

Before proceeding any further, three caveats must be broached. First, my arguments for VS must be read against the background of highly nonideal conditions, but neither the cultivation of self-respect nor the fostering of civic virtue need wait for ideal conditions of equality under integration to arrive. Both equality and civic virtue can and often do take place under conditions of involuntary segregation, but VS is a more effective way to facilitate it. Of course, the negative features of segregation can and often do outweigh many of the positive sides to separation that I consider in this chapter, such as those that coincide with and result from our preferences: to be near family and friends, to select a local school for one's child, and to have access to culturally useful facilities, services, and products that may be in limited supply if not absent in other neighborhoods. So if segregation is causally linked to an absence of critical resources and social capital, and if possibilities for equality and civic virtue are drowned out by despair, then it is indeed an affront to basic moral principles to suggest that all is well.

Second, I will defend a prima facie justification of VS, because while VS may be warranted and necessary, it is not a sufficient condition of equality, nor will it suffice to foster civic virtue. Other conditions must exist in order for a sufficiency threshold to be met. However, determining precisely what a sufficiency threshold entails will require deliberation about relevant stakeholders on a case-by-case basis. But the main point is simple: VS should not be pursued in the absence of other considerations. For example, no credible portrait of self-respect can be sketched in the absence of other important conditions (e.g., decent health, safety, reasonable work opportunities) favorable to well-being. That goes for group membership as well. The importance of shared interests or belonging does not guarantee the innocence of VS. Separation according to shared tastes and preferences in music, for instance, does not carry the same moral force as intentional separation by, say, race or social class (though it must be said that these all too frequently overlap). Moreover, separation that demonizes outsiders is unacceptable. We can all think of harmful forms of separation—gangs, militant nationalists, and cults, for instance—and when these violate the requirements of civic virtue they are without defense. Hence separation must be accompanied by other relevant conditions that must be satisfied if the demands of civic virtue and equality are to be met.

Third, by describing these actions as "voluntary," I do not ignore the structural background conditions against which choice sets operate. All of our choices occur against a background of institutionalized realities. Persons are positioned differently; many are saddled with significant disadvantage. Citizens must adapt to less-than-ideal personal attitudes and behaviors as well as nonpersonal social, technological, and economic forces already at work.[2] So like liberty and autonomy, voluntariness is exercised relative to various contextual constraints, including the very shaping of one's preferences by external circumstances. In other words, the voluntary choices of individuals or benign forms of ethnocentrism alone cannot explain segregation. But then again, neither can structural elements. Spatial concentrations occur for a host of complex reasons.

Now we come to the first of two framing principles in establishing the argument for VS. In proceeding with this argument I focus on a particular aspect of equality: equality as self-respect.

Voluntary Separation for Equality

VS entails cultivating the means to self-respect. As we saw in Chapter 3, *self-respect* refers to a positive regard for oneself—a natural sense of self-importance. Ontologically, self-respect is based on the idea of human dignity—a sense of intrinsic worth. Dignity denotes the basic value that all persons possess by virtue of their humanity. For the purposes of my argument I will assume human dignity to be a priori and therefore will provide no further argument for it here beyond what I have already said in Chapter 3.[3] But self-respect also provides an important basis for self-determination inasmuch as it contributes to the ability to take up and pursue things that matter to individuals. Self-respect describes having a reasonable sense of self-determination with respect to choices and the ability to act meaningfully on those choices. But, of course, the psychological and social conditions that make self-respect possible vary widely. A sense of self-respect may therefore fluctuate according to circumstance. For example, the experience of sudden (or chronic) failure or relational loss may induce a sense of crisis. Further, certain facts about segregation may affect self-respect, particularly if one is a member of a stigmatized minority group. That status in itself presents a number of challenges for self-respect. Indeed, self-respect may have an inverse relationship to stigma.

In Chapter 2 we first encountered a correlation between segregation and stigma. Being a member of a stigmatized group significantly increases the chances of disaffection, exclusion, and risk. Risk factors include economic instability, compromised family structure (e.g., through migration, incarceration, or death), poor health, exposure to violence, school failure, and negative media attention. Indeed, for members of stigmatized minority groups, visible differences are themselves risk factors, and when there is external pressure to conform to societal norms and a cultural gap divides two dramatically different worlds, risk increases.

Despite these risk factors, many show great resilience—that is, they possess or acquire the tools necessary to rise above adversity and challenge, the conditions that induce risk. In some instances resilience is attributable to personal characteristics such as temperament, IQ, or coping strategies employed to offset the worst effects of stigma. Yet in most studies there appear to be important mediating effects attributable to other, enabling factors. These include teacher effects, peer relationships, parental intimacy, neighborhood safety, and community support. Indeed, resources such as these are crucial to the cultivation and nourishment of self-respect and for stigmatized minorities may be the only practical means of reducing inequality. In many cases these enabling factors are simply unavailable in integrated settings.

Given the gravity of these risk factors, separation will not suffice as a prima facie justification—certainly not if equality is the overriding concern. It would be folly to reject inequality under terms of involuntary segregation only to embrace inequality on one's own terms. Prima facie justification for VS at a minimum rests in part on attending to the conditions necessary for the cultivation of self-respect. Further, the possibilities for stigmatized minorities to acquire self-respect should be roughly equal to those that more privileged children have. But without self-respect all references to equality collapse. To be sure, there are different ways of nurturing self-respect, and not all stigmatized minority groups or advocates of separation agree on the method. But one thing on which all advocates of VS agree is that equality set on terms by others may actually serve to undermine self-respect rather than nurture it.

It is important here to notice the conditions under which this equality for stigmatized minorities must be procured. The social bases of self-respect first need to be arranged in ways that are conducive to its actualization. Equality entails, first, the recognition one receives as an equal member within one's own community. Not everyone will rank their memberships in the same way, of course, but the efficacy of VS lies in the social networks that nourish and sustain a sense of belonging and attachment. Nurturing these attachments can prove decisive for one's capacity for self-respect and self-determination. The purported benefits of exposure to cultural, racial, or religious difference and of sustained contact with the "other" are secondary concerns.

There can be no doubt that some forms of segregation negatively influence self-respect, particularly when there is stigma. But when self-respect is compromised or diminished by the absence of enabling conditions or reasonable choice sets outside one's own community, its cultivation may crucially depend on fostering it by other means. In what follows I will concentrate on the school environment, as this is both the site where stigmas for children are first encountered and where stigmas arguably can most effectively be combated.

Establishing the foundations of self-respect in schools can play an important role in securing a strong sense of self in young people. Education enacted as VS will address pervasive academic deficiencies, but it will also strengthen individual well-being. The means for fostering self-respect will differ according to the philosophy and personalities of each school, but in nearly every case it will involve building a positive organizational climate and school ethos. Here W. E. B. Du Bois describes the conditions of VS that facilitate equality: "The proper education of any people includes sympathetic touch between teacher and pupil, knowledge on the part of the teacher, not simply of the individual taught, but of his surroundings and background, and the history of his class and group; such contact between pupils, and between teacher and pupil, on the basis of perfect social equality, as will increase this sympathy and knowledge."[4]

These teacher-pupil relations certainly buttress self-respect as the basis for equality; however, for VS to supply the basis for equality it will not suffice for a school with high needs to simply have a few good teachers. Other critical resources, often not in abundance for stigmatized minorities in so-called integrated schools, include high expectations, a caring ethos, shared values, cultural recognition, and a sense of belonging. These can be further strengthened through a committed school leadership, positive role modeling, camaraderie among ethnic peers, parental intimacy and involvement, and communal support. And of course enabling conditions external to the school are also critical; decent housing, affordable health care, nutrition, nurturing relationships, and economic opportunities are also needed to ensure desirable outcomes.[5] Taken together, these all represent crucial resources with intrinsic benefits favorable to self-respect; these, in turn, are likely to buttress academic achievement and its instrumental benefits beyond the school environment.

Paradoxically, having these resources at one's disposal in a separate environment will be of vital importance to successfully functioning in a multicultural society. Why in a separate environment? Remember that integrated environments for many are not even an option. In any case, the knowledge and dispositions needed to function in a multicultural society need not be learned in mixed settings.[6] The requisite dispositions, knowledge, and skills required for multicultural citizenship, including informed participation and mutual goodwill, can be learned by attending first to the bases of self-respect. While it may be ideal to learn these skills in mixed environments, it is important to stress, again, that segregation is not a situation any one group has created itself; nor have stigmatized minorities invented the stigmas with which they are forced to live.

Self-respect, which serves as a basic foundation for equality, is an indispensible foundation without which other resources will fail to have an effect. VS facilitates educational opportunities for equality by rearranging the conditions of existing segregation. Thus, insofar as VS does a better job of supplying self-respect, it is plausible to say that it also more effectively enhances equality. Whatever the specifics of each case, the aim is to control and determine, within limitations set by the state (e.g., teacher certification, graduation requirements), the staff, values, curricula, and instructional design of the school with a view to promoting equality. As Du Bois put it, "Instead of our schools being simply separate schools, forced on us by grim necessity, they can become centres of a new and beautiful effort at human education, which may easily lead and guide the world in many important and valuable aspects. It is for this reason that when our schools are separate, the control of the teaching force, the expenditure of money, the choice of textbooks, the discipline and other administrative matters of this sort ought also, to come into our hands, and be incessantly demanded and guarded."[7] Notice, too, that equality is not dependent on integration. Integration imposes its own "grim necessities"—those that can be significantly attenuated in environments in which equality is delivered on more favorable terms. I now move to the second argument. Here the discussion is informed by the second framing principle, but I focus in particular on the importance of civic virtue.

Voluntary Separation for Civic Virtue

In Chapter 3 I distinguished between robust and pluralist accounts of citizenship, with the former being more demanding than the latter with respect to informed participation in the public sphere and the capacity to reasonably disagree with others and with the latter allowing for considerable latitude with respect to one's associations and pursuits so long as citizens meet their basic civic responsibilities and obligations. The distinction between these accounts, again, is somewhat contrived. Robust accounts occur across a panoply of choices and pursuits, while pluralist accounts do not exclude principled disagreement or shared beliefs and practices with those outside of one's group. Nor do most pluralist accounts dismiss norms of decency that apply equally to the public as well as the private sphere. But I develop the conception of civic virtue within a pluralist account because the broad outlines of VS are more consistent with its features.

Virtue refers to dispositions, habits, and actions whose excellence promotes individual and collective well-being. These may include things such as kindness, honesty, mutual respect, self-discipline, compassion, loyalty, toleration, and generosity. Virtues are civic to the extent that they contribute to, and strengthen, the communal good. Civic virtues are rooted in the character of an individual and have a positive impact on society; they do not merely indicate social cooperation for self-interest.[8] Obvious examples include the building and maintenance of parks, schools, community centers, and libraries. Literacy campaigns, job services, and drug rehabilitation centers produce similarly positive civic outcomes. The cultivation of civic virtue is often facilitated by local and fairly homogeneous networks where social trust is strongest.[9]

Critics worry that these virtues will be self-contained—that what may work for a community will not facilitate the knowledge and skills needed to engage with those *outside* of one's community. Yet hearty civic virtues are neither contained nor restricted to specific locations; they have what economists call powerful externalities. To paraphrase Robert Putnam, inward-looking (bonding) virtues do not exclude outward-looking (bridging) virtues. So the benefits of a neighborhood watch program that shares the responsibility for safe and congenial relations among community members may very well move outward to adjoining neighborhoods, where the relevant virtues also can be emulated by others. Accordingly, the local and communal may significantly overlap with the national or global. How "civic" the relevant virtues are will depend, in part, on their efficacy and reach; how broad the scope of common good is will arguably depend on the good being promoted. Whatever the case, the effects of civic virtue will be felt first and foremost near their source: the family, neighborhood, region, or nation-state in which the relevant virtues and activities are cultivated and flourish.

Meanwhile the correspondence between civic and political virtues is less obvious.[10] Civic virtue may include political acts such as lobbying, town meetings, and voting, but it need not. Instead, it might include coaching little league baseball, good parenting, volunteering one's time at a homeless shelter, or planting trees. What gives these activities civic import is their impact on the lives of others. Here, *civic* draws attention to people's roles as citizens and their relation to the state and to others within the same country, most of whom they do not know.[11] If and when conditions change, persons may choose to participate in overtly political acts; consider, for example, the stunning events of 2011 across North Africa and the Middle East. But civic virtues need not be overtly political; indeed, nonpolitical actions often contribute more to the common good within a particular community.

Nor should civic virtue be conflated with republican notions of citizenship that accentuate national over communal attachments and their attendant expressions of common good. Civic virtue does not reduce to a political conception that subsumes all that persons think and do. Certain political obligations—basic rights and responsibilities—may exist, and the way we identify ourselves may include membership in a polity, but attachments to a particular family, ethnic group, religion, or neighborhood for most of us assume greater importance and priority. It is within these communities that the possibility of civic virtue arises. Indeed, particular interests, concerns, and values usually guide the practices and concerns specific to one's group. In their particularity our attachments express what matters most to us; they are capable of describing our deepest concerns and passions as well as capturing our imagination about what is most meaningful. They even may most effectively galvanize our efforts in responding to others in need. Indeed, attachments to specific groups often supply persons with the substance of belonging that makes more expansive notions of cooperation both possible and meaningful.

Hence long before we are able to reflect on its significance, the very possibility of civic virtue begins with attachments nourished by those with whom we have daily interaction—that is, those whom we already know. Its elements likely will include a history, language, and a broader cultural context, and its expression may or may not be political, but these strong attachments to one's community of choice or inheritance need not be in conflict with the obligations of a shared political membership. The point is simply this: all of us rank our attachments according to both proximity of interest and obligation, and where these conflict, we must sort out our priorities.

Of course, community-centered civic virtues facilitated by local attachments need not eclipse more remote concerns. Indeed, our links to strangers are rarely as remote as we may think. Local communities also function within broader polities, and even nations operate within broader alliances. Nor are markets delineated by strict regional or national boundaries; migration and immigration, too, occur across increasingly porous borders, and natural and manmade disasters also have very real human and environmental effects on all of us. In moments of crisis it is our humanity—and not, say, our national identity—that is paramount. Suffering and deprivation expose our frailty and helplessness in the face of forces beyond our control; the best moments of civic virtue are those that make possible the bonding necessary for mutual assistance and goodwill.

Indubitably, when there is familiarity with one's community members, psychologically we feel those bonds even more. But morally speaking, a tragedy that befalls one group is no less devastating because they speak a different language, possess a different skin color, or adhere to a different religion. One's local communal attachments do not foreclose moral concern and responsiveness to others unlike ourselves.[12] Again, "bonding" does not preclude "bridging." Should our specific group memberships inhibit us from responding to the needs of others or from acting in concert with others irrespective of shared beliefs and habits, the value of our civic virtue is rendered inept.

But neither the cultivation nor the presence of civic virtue is dependent on integration. To the contrary, integration often occasions assimilation that inhibits civic virtue. That is to say, integration often entails bracketing of differences in social status and preemptively determining acceptable forms of civic virtue. Rarely is the cultural, economic, and political integration that occurs within one's own community seen as valuable in itself.[13] While nonagent relative factors cannot be overlooked, structural barriers to opportunity are not the only relevant features to consider vis-à-vis segregation; there are also cultural and individual processes at work. Members of particular groups also gravitate toward neighborhoods where they feel more comfortable, where they are with others like themselves, where communication and cultural norms are understood, and where they may profit from living with others who share similar lifestyles, social networks, and cultural needs. To suggest that segregation chiefly transpires, say, as a reaction to racism is to willfully ignore these other elements.

Many spatial concentrations open up opportunities for entrepreneurship and other forms of service provision, such as clothing and grocery stores, newspapers, community centers, and job networks. These lead to an institutionalization of networks and services that not only increases the attractiveness of the neighborhood in question (whatever its drawbacks and liabilities) but also contributes to the maintenance of a subculture many find attractive. Moreover, not only do its members find these features attractive; others outside these communities seek out separate enclaves for their own purposes.[14] Hence while it is certainly true that some types of segregation are irredeemably harmful, this is not always the case. Indeed, many positive features of segregation have been observed.[15]

In many neighborhoods segregation can have a direct and positive impact both on community solidarity and on local politics; associational membership[16] often is an antecedent if not the impetus to other forms of civic virtue. Cities and neighborhoods with spatial concentrations also have better facilitated political inroads for aspiring politicians, who in turn can be more responsive to the concerns of the local citizenry.[17] The denser the associational network is, the more civic virtue and political trust one often can expect.[18] This trend cuts across demographic lines and exists in neighborhoods across many societies.[19]

None of the foregoing romanticizes poverty or discounts the role of structural barriers and discrimination that persist even for relatively successful minority groups. But contrary to much moral and political rhetoric, segregation need not cause alarm; much depends on the specific features—voluntary or involuntary—of the segregated space. If segregation undermines the possibility of equality or civic virtue, then something else must be done, but neither the fostering of equality nor the cultivation of civic virtue depends on integration, and in fact they often thrive in its absence.

Voluntary Separation

Underlying the foregoing arguments for VS is the recognition that many forms of separation have provided an alternative to failed attempts at integration. Whether in the neighborhood or in the school, VS partly describes an attempt to provide a safe haven. This includes the fortification of fragile identities and expansion of the limited opportunities of those who, under less favorable conditions of integration or involuntary segregation, are far more likely to experience stigma and discrimination. Combining the associative preferences of community members with the cohesion their particular attachments provide, VS plays a protective role partly by rectifying a situation of alienation and exclusion its often stigmatized members routinely experience.

But protection is not the only way to describe the aims of VS. Another is the promotion and maintenance of social networks of caring and attachment that give meaning to people's lives. As we have seen, an honest appraisal of personal habits and behaviors will consistently show that most persons, irrespective of background, socialize[20] and interact principally with others who share similar traits (e.g., language, ethnicity, social class, culture, religion). Even more common are forms of separation that transpire due to shared interests, such as recreation preferences, artistic tastes, and so forth. That is to say, most people naturally gravitate toward those with whom they share a great deal in common. Notice that this generally applies to any group of persons (anarchists, athletes, musicians, vegans, philosophers, etc.) who share mutual interests or concerns.

Even if we can imagine a society in which neighborhood or school segregation is not the problem that many of us think it is, there will continue to be reasons to support various forms of separation, even if it is only to provide important goods—such as belonging or membership—to the persons for whom such membership matters. Taken together, VS represents a response to particular circumstances enabling persons to resist the assimilating pressures of majority environments in favor of celebrating and consciously reproducing the culture, history, and experience of a group's members.

As I have tried to show, any robust account of VS must be built on the same framing principles used to defend integration. To that end, I have framed the prima facie case for VS on a particular reading of both equality and citizenship. Notwithstanding a number of qualifications, however, many readers will doubtless consider a defense of separation as defeatist. But here a number of points should be stressed. First, we should not forget that to one degree or another, de facto separation already is the prevailing norm within and across most societies. (Readers of this book are likely to fit that pattern as well.) Second, we must not forget the prima facie nature of the argument: separation per se is never a sufficient condition for its justification. Enabling conditions must exist if a justification for VS is to get off the ground. Third, as I have tried to show, separateness per se does not compromise equality or civic virtue. To the contrary, a number of resources made possible by spatial concentrations often strengthen them. Particular concentrations may be initiated by external forces, but voluntary responses often coincide. For example, both discriminatory housing policy and a desire to live among others like oneself commonly occur at the same time. Exceptions to the rule do not change the general pattern.

So while VS may begin with the fact of segregation, it need not be circumscribed by de facto realities. Instead, the aim will be to (re)define the experience of separateness on one's own terms. Accordingly, VS is not an argument against integration so much as one supporting constructive alternatives to the entrenched patterns of involuntary segregation. VS is therefore not cynical resignation; it accepts that many worthwhile and positive features attend segregation and that to deny their importance or seek to disrupt them is potentially to engage in harmful and unwelcome forms of social engineering—ones that wittingly or unwittingly undervalue the resources that spatial concentrations often provide.

There is no doubt that some conditions of segregation have been imposed; some remain structural obstacles to be overcome. Moreover, in some cases the negative features of segregation can outweigh the positive ones. But it is far from obvious that a direct cause-and-effect relationship exists between segregation and harm. In any case, the most effective response to involuntary segregation in many contexts is not to integrate neighborhoods or schools but to change the conditions under which segregated experiences occur. As I stated earlier, this is what distinguishes VS from involuntary segregation. VS thus represents an important response to what may be a less-than-ideal situation but that nevertheless can improve the conditions necessary for the cultivation of self-respect and civic virtue, whose benefits can have ripple effects beyond one's own community. Though it may be difficult, neither local attachments nor segregation need prevent us from having the skills and dispositions necessary to understand other points of view or to enter into deliberation with others to resolve disagreements when those occasions arise. Provided the right kinds of social supports and enabling conditions, VS can enable the cultivation of self-respect or civic virtue.

Given the various harms associated with segregation that I outlined in Chapter 2, for whom could VS possibly have an appeal? The motives and need for VS will vary from one context and group to another, and its duration also may fluctuate depending on external conditions. But VS certainly will have an appeal for those for whom equal treatment is lacking in mixed environments—that is, where stigma and discrimination are commonplace. There is in fact a long history regarding the road to separation, and its reasons will be familiar. When basic access to equal opportunities is denied, or assimilation is the cost for having access, minority groups have opted out of integration on terms set by others in favor of strengthening their own networks and institutions.

With respect to education, the same reasons apply; when there is an absence of quality education available in integrated settings, when education under terms of integration fails to supply the goods necessary for one to flourish, when those settings fail to supply the bases for self-respect, and when integrated education is not even an option, separation is the next logical step. In the United States alone, women, blacks, Jews, Roman Catholics, and the deaf all established voluntarily separate schools as early as the mid-nineteenth century. Many still exist today, and many receive state support, though of course for many the harm of stigma has arguably diminished. Meanwhile, in many Western countries there is rapid growth in educational experiments based on some articulation of VS; African-centered, Roma, Hindu, Tribal/First Nations, and Islamic schools, to take but a few examples, join their ranks.

Of course, simply being a member of a stigmatized group in itself is no argument for separation. Even with the benefits that culturally cohesive environments may provide, separation will not be an attractive option for everyone. Many will favor integration. Nothing in my argument speaks against this. Not only are stigmatized groups just as heterogeneous as non-stigmatized groups; members of stigmatized minority groups also will inevitably interact with mainstream society, at least some of the time, if for no other reason than that minority status makes this unavoidable. Whatever the case, separation will continue to be an appealing alternative for those whose equal status is not recognized, for those whose opportunities are impeded or denied, and where the possibilities for civic virtue may be diminished in integrated environments. Finally, VS offers an alternative for those for whom the possibility of seamlessly blending in with the mainstream remains a fantasy. Indeed, VS can really only make sense in environments in which segregation is already the norm.

Other readers will doubtless be thinking, *Even if I am willing to grant some provisional benefits to VS, for how long will separation really be necessary?* The answer to this question cannot be decided in the abstract. Too much will depend on the contextual circumstances, material conditions, and opportunities for those who stand to benefit from it. So long as involuntary segregation—or, for that matter, integration—fails to supply the conditions necessary for the cultivation and maintenance of self-respect and civic virtue, then perhaps for that long VS will be needed.[21] A longtime proponent of integration, later in his career Du Bois defended separation as an indispensable strategy for American blacks being denied equality under the terms of integration. To the question of how long separate schools would be needed, he wrote, "Just so far as it is necessary for the proper education" of vulnerable minorities who are consistently denied a quality education. Of course, integrated schools under conditions of equality may be preferred over segregated ones. In principle, Du Bois agreed. He wrote, "Other things being equal, the mixed school is the broader, more natural basis for the education of all youth. It gives wider contacts; it inspires greater self-confidence; and suppresses the inferiority complex."[22] The problem, as Du Bois knew all too well, is that other things are seldom equal. What was true in his day continues to be the case in ours—namely, segregation is a fact of life, and attempts to address inequality often must begin from a condition of separateness. Equality under terms of integration is comparatively an effortless affair for persons whose first language, religion, ethnicity, ability, or other identity markers correspond to the mainstream.[23] Obstacles, where they exist, include making new friends, mastering a new skill, navigating unfamiliar territory, and so on. But matters for stigmatized minorities under terms of involuntary segregation, but also integration on terms set by others, are not so simple.

Criticisms

In Chapter 2 I examined the case for integration, focusing chiefly on social cohesion and social inequality. There I offered a number of criticisms against standard integration arguments. However, now that a portrait of VS has been sketched, several integrationist criticisms come to the fore, in particular to argue that VS falters on several fronts. In the paragraphs that follow I will both articulate and respond to these challenges. The challenges are stratification, ethnocentrism, and deliberation. All three challenges in fact bear upon both equality and citizenship. Remember, too, that equality and citizenship intertwine, for civic virtue operates as a precursor to equality because equal recognition and treatment are equality's essential ingredients. However, stratification, with its emphasis on socioeconomic inequality, engages more directly with the notion of integration for equality. Meanwhile, both ethnocentrism and deliberation stress the importance of integration for citizenship. Each criticism in its own way holds that segregation of any sort is undesirable and that voluntary forms of separation in particular are wrong headed.

Stratification

The first criticism recalls the discussion in Chapters 2 and 3 underscoring the role of education in the distribution of equality. The criticism is that VS fails to reckon with what is most damaging about segregation—namely, stratification and poverty concentration. Stratification describes a differential relationship between members of particular groups and access to society's fundamental resources. Stratification suggests that a lack of access to critical resources effectively undermines the possibility of equality and citizenship if not also for opportunities tout court. Anderson writes, "Segregation ties children to a disadvantaged structure of social capital, thereby perpetuating the effects of historic discrimination in human capital development, even in the presence of effective antidiscrimination law, and even for children with innate potential equal to that of their more advantaged peers."[24] Remember, too, that the value of my education will partly be determined by the education others receive.

More than forty years of research on educational stratification seem to bear this out, suggesting that concentrations of school poverty make for a very difficult learning environment because students are likely to be surrounded by peers who are less academically engaged, have parents who are less active in school affairs, and have weaker teachers who have lower expectations. Disengagement with one's education in toxic school environments often leads to high dropout, unemployment, and incarceration rates. Taken together we not only see important liberties compromised by severe inequalities; we also see the seeds of civic virtue ruined before they even have a chance to germinate. Hence, to the extent that segregation coincides with poverty concentration, the issue is not the separateness but the absence of socioeconomic and political resources that dramatically curtail one's ability to mobilize and improve one's circumstances.

In light of these challenges, again, we hear that integration is the solution to educational inequality, dismissing the idea that equality of any sort can be achieved under conditions of segregation. As we saw in Chapter 2, by far the strongest proposal presently being championed is the integration of schools by social class.[25] The idea, the reader may remember, is that by mixing students from different socioeconomic backgrounds, one can raise the academic achievement of poorer students without harming middle-class children. The achievement of poor children will be raised, the argument runs, because poor (who incidentally are often minority) children will be exposed to the knowledge and social capital of their middle-class peers. This also has long-term effects, because "exposure" to middle-class children (and the social capital their parents and teachers bring to school) will provide access to social networks necessary for accessing career opportunities.

Integration enthusiasts have rallied behind this idea in part because they have been forced to contend with a variety of legal and moral challenges to standard race/ethnicity-based integration approaches, including that school selection on the basis of race/ethnicity obscures important social class differences and also leads to questionable assumptions about minority schools (i.e., that they are per definition inferior). Meanwhile, some governments have reversed course, stating that combating segregation is no longer a priority.[26] Further, parental resistance to bussing, redistricting, or inclusionary zoning policies are well known, and these often prevent most desegregation plans from having a substantial impact. So attempts to mix schools by social class, say, by limiting the number of students eligible for reduced-price meals per school, circumvents parental opposition and results in the mixing of schools by race and ethnicity indirectly.

While the argument for VS is not, strictly speaking, about educational opportunity but about equality for self-respect and civic virtue, if the presence of the latter is at least partly tied to former, then it is worth pausing to consider the argument and the evidence. Take the argument first. There is no point in denying that poverty, hunger, and poor health—all of which conspire to produce failure—work against academic achievement and correspondingly the possibility of equality and the cultivation of civic virtue. Second, it is arguably true that conditions for the underprivileged who live in segregated neighborhoods or attend segregated schools are worse off relative to those born into wealth and convenience. But while material advantage may afford one more access to power, it does not confer self-respect or more civic virtue. With privilege there is often a sense of entitlement, certainly not intuitively conducive to civic virtue. Conversely, being raised in less-than-favorable circumstances, while not ideal, ironically may be more conducive to the cultivation of virtue provided that other important conditions (e.g., acceptable levels of safety, nourishment, and health)—exist and that other vital resources (e.g., emotional support, employment opportunities) are also present. Each of these, and many others besides, effectively works in tandem to improve the opportunities of children born into relative disadvantage, and without them, schools—integrated or not—do very little indeed to foster equality.

Persons in positions of social disadvantage arguably are more perceptive about questions of justice; many routinely are expected to cross back and forth between cultural worlds and in so doing are likely to gain a much greater self-awareness, to know what opportunities they have (or don't have), and to understand how systems of privilege are structured to favor those in power. Even when the disadvantaged lack the immediate tools to redress the injustice, we should not forget—as leftist populist movements throughout Latin America, the Arab world, and Southeast Asia recently have shown—that even oppressed individuals can recognize and reflect on their subjugation as a means of surmounting it.[27]

What about the evidence? There is no doubt that gains in academic achievement have been observed in some integrated schools, and these have been attributed to the presence of positive peer effects, more middle-class parents, and qualified teachers.[28] These success stories have revived hope for those committed to seeing the dreams of integration realized. Wherever success occurs, it should certainly be celebrated. But two things can be said. First, similar to what I argued with respect to the knowledge and dispositions needed to function in a multicultural society, academic success also does not hinge upon a classroom being mixed. Instead, as we saw in Chapter 2, it hinges on the availability of vital resources—in particular, *effective instruction* and a *supportive school environment*. Both of these will include high expectations, caring staff, guidance and role-modeling, culturally relevant pedagogy, and an adequately challenging curriculum. Notwithstanding difficult obstacles to overcome, many schools comprised entirely of disadvantaged children nonetheless make very significant gains.

These gains can only partly be explained in terms of additional monetary resources allocated for the schools with higher poverty concentrations.[29]

Second, considering that segregation index levels across Europe and North America are either holding steady or worsening,[30] it is simply unrealistic to expect academic success to hinge on the elusive benefits that mixed settings ostensibly provide. Even if the probability of interacting with children of different backgrounds improves in mixed settings, both voluntary and involuntary clustering of students on the basis of shared background and interests virtually ensures that this is not occurring on a significant level. This is the case in every country where the phenomenon has been studied.

Ethnocentrism

Now we come to the second criticism. The civic virtue of VS lies in promoting the good of a community through the shared interests, concerns, and values of its members. Yet a pluralist conception of citizenship presents special challenges for VS. Indeed, while belonging to a particular community can make more expansive notions of cooperation both possible and meaningful, some worry that pluralism will allow for harmful forms of belonging. In Chapter 3 I referred to this as the threat of ethnocentrism. Partly in response to this threat, I examined the case for shared fate as a possible remedy for this concern, for it is shared dispositions and habits that will reduce prejudice and foster cooperation across difference. For these reasons, countless authors have insisted on the importance of a robust civic education.

The ethnocentric critique here has two parts: first, belonging too narrowly circumscribed may unduly restrict liberties of some group members—notably, children. Second, some worry that some group memberships will foment intolerance and hatred. These are not idle concerns. Research from Europe, for example, suggests that VS may serve to reinforce stereotypes of outsiders.[31] Ethnic and religious tensions in Northern Ireland, Nigeria, Kashmir, and the Balkans may also elicit disbelief in any good to come of VS.[32] Increasingly, for many, national or regional attachments are particularly strong in cases where supranational demands are being imposed.[33] And if we remain exclusively focused on the interests of our own community or group, the argument runs, any gains occasioned by group membership will be cancelled out by a failure to imaginatively engage with others whose lives are different from our own.

But it is important to recall, first, the relationship between bonding and bridging. One does not preclude the other. To the contrary, bonding that occurs by turning inward can help to reduce feelings of isolation and distrust, without which possibilities for bridging across cultural divides seem even more improbable. Second, it is important to remember that the justification of VS will depend on the strength and expression of its civic virtues. As I argued earlier, there are principled limits to what can be tolerated. The associational rights of gangs, cults, and militia groups (where they are permitted) are provisional precisely because they are highly prone to violating basic societal norms of decency and respect even when their freedoms of speech and association are begrudgingly protected. Left unchecked these may spawn violence. As such, memberships that promote hatred and intolerance may be forbidden when they violate the freedoms of others. Of course, even in the absence of hatred or violence, an inordinate focus on one's own cultural, religious, or political group (or sometimes all three rolled into one) will create an inability to listen to or understand experiences and perspectives one does not share. In any case, memberships that intentionally or unintentionally aim to undermine the possibility of cooperation across differences are undesirable given the threat they pose both to liberty in general and to other forms of belonging in particular.

But it is unwise to argue from worst cases. Pride in one's community is not tantamount to intolerance or hatred any more than liberalism is synonymous with colonial occupation or police brutality. Further, an expectation of abuse is not sufficient warrant for associational restrictions. Remember that VS as I defend it must adhere to basic moral principles, and these must be consistent with civic virtue. In order for VS to foster civic virtue, it cannot consist of core features that effectively discredit it (i.e., promoting idiosyncratic notions of communal good at the expense of others). Hence groups that subordinate its weaker members do not meet the requirement. Nor do groups that vilify, threaten, or condone violence toward others.

Nothing in what I have said will prevent majorities from questioning the loyalty of their minorities or exaggerating the threat of "otherness." Indeed, when loyalty becomes the standard, Melissa Williams writes, "there is a natural tendency to be suspicious of those whose outward forms and inward habits of mind are different from those of commonly recognized paragons of citizenship."[34] But critics who raise the specter of ethnocentrism are wont to downplay its common occurrence—and, frequently, its more virulent forms, xenophobia, and racism—among "silent majorities." Integration often entails an ethnically bound and politically restrictive understanding of civic virtue. There is a heavy price to be paid for the forced incorporation of stigmatized minorities into so-called mixed environments in which many are not made to feel welcome in the first place; where, in schools, children are labeled and sorted, adverse effects on self-image are widespread, and cultural histories are misshapen or left untold. And of course the cruel irony of integration is not lost on stigmatized minorities who are publicly chastised for remaining separate yet whose neighborhoods "turned" shortly after them moving in.

Certainly under the right conditions mixed environments can produce greater levels of tolerance and social trust. Be that as it may, without shared activities and institutions to facilitate them, spatial integration does not automatically lead to greater social interaction.[35] Further, very little evidence demonstrates that generalization of social trust in integrated environments occurs beyond the immediate setting.[36] Conversely, a fairly homogeneous environment that is appropriately structured, facilitating a sense of belonging associated with attachments to a particular group, is a powerful stimulant both for a sense of belonging and for the expression of social trust. In short, civic virtue does not turn on the environment being integrated. Indeed, it turns out that under conditions of VS, people often are freer to discuss, imagine, and pursue what civic virtue means when there are possibilities for parity of participation. Notice, too, how both equality and citizenship are appropriated in importantly different ways.

A related concern is that VS harms everyone by setting a dangerous precedent for intolerant groups who might use separation to indoctrinate and propagate hate. But the motivations for VS, in my argument, are nothing like those of intolerant groups such as racists or religious militants, and fears that radicals (e.g., fascists, religious extremists, ethnic secessionists) may seize upon or exploit the separation thesis are misplaced. First, VS of the sort I am describing is not driven by a sense of racial, cultural, or religious superiority;[37] that would indeed be a type of separation with disturbing moral significance. Rather, it is driven among other things by a desire for community membership and self-respect—not to mention a quality education.

Absent the opportunity to pursue VS, stigmatized minorities are far more likely to experience ambivalence toward a culture in which they commonly experience discrimination or exclusion.[38] Stigma can be greatly mitigated through affirming shared beliefs and practices not recognized in mainstream culture.[39] Attending to equality under conditions of VS can enable students to defend themselves, not only against the ignorance and prejudice of others, but also against their own fears and uncertainties, through the fostering of self-respect. Turning inward during the early stages of one's schooling can contribute to a child's capacity for self-respect, improved levels of well-being, higher academic achievement, and autonomous decision making. Hence what is different about VS in education is not the fact that the school population is segregated but the manner and terms on which the separation occurs.

Deliberation

A final worry regarding VS is an extension of the previous criticism—namely, that by focusing on equality as self-respect we downplay the importance of interacting with and learning to respect others unlike ourselves. As we saw in Chapter 3, the shared-fate argument emphasizes our interdependence with those with whom we have not chosen to be involved and stresses the importance of shared practices and institutions. Thick or thin, citizenship entails that persons from different backgrounds will act in various ways consistent with their rights and responsibilities and work together for a more equitable and better functioning society. Moreover, as we saw in Chapter 2, the social cohesion argument requires that persons who share a plural society come to understand one another through early and consistent exchanges. In contrast, VS appears to encourage focusing on the needs of one's own group and thereby to undermine a form of citizenship necessary for mutual engagement and cooperation.

Citizenship as shared fate, the reader will remember, entails a capacity for enlarged thought, the ability to see oneself bound up in relationships of interdependence with others, and the capacity to reshape the practices and institutions of one's environment. Taken together, citizenship requires the capacity for communicating with others under conditions of social equality and forging paths of social cooperation, even when there is limited contact. Notwithstanding the importance of legitimate partialities and local attachments, a citizenship of shared fate requires people to engage one another from time to time in order to address and find acceptable solutions for the challenges facing fellow citizens. Segregation, the argument runs, undermines this possibility to the extent that people remain isolated and disengaged from each other. Making matters worse, political elites remain distressingly unaware of their constituents' concerns. Accordingly, many theorists of citizenship stress the importance of integration so that deliberations necessary for promoting justice can occur.

A capacity for deliberation roughly describes the ability to engage with others on matters of social and political relevance in a respectful manner, exhibiting a give-and-take relationship that recognizes both the significance and the seriousness of other points of view. Deliberative democracy, its advocates insist, welcomes debate on matters of substantive disagreement. Where principled differences thwart consensus, a deliberative approach stresses the importance of finding a common ground. Indeed, it is the common ground of shared belief and practice in the public sphere that establishes both the rule of law and the legitimate exercise thereof.

Deliberation seems imperative precisely because many beliefs and practices are *not* shared, and without a consensus there is no shared basis of citizenship.

That is the ideal. But context also matters. Remember that VS is a response to very particular social and political conditions—ones in which members of stigmatized minority groups are "positioned by social structures that constrain and enable individual lives beyond their individual control."[40] Indeed, the context in which majority-minority relationships occur cannot be divorced from a specific history, as Daniel Weinstock explains:

> Beyond the assimilative pressures endemic to any majority/minority relation, minorities often find themselves in a cultural context that they perceive as at best indifferent, and at worst hostile, to their practices and beliefs . . . Muslims in France and Britain are not simply people who happen to practice a different faith from that of the majority. They are also erstwhile colonial subjects . . . Majorities and minorities are therefore rarely unrelated groups that happen to have been juxtaposed on the same territory. Minorities have often suffered at the hands of the majority, and what's more, culture and religion have often been invoked by the majority as justifying different forms of unjust treatment.[41]

Here we plainly see the involuntary context in which individual and group responses occur. We should not be surprised that many groups maintain a skeptical posture toward states whose rhetoric of liberty, equality, and citizenship has gone hand in hand with exclusion and violence. Too often we fail to understand how concepts like *integration* or *citizenship* look an awful lot like coercive pressure to conform.

Nancy Fraser has argued that deliberation as defined by majorities often serves as a mask for domination—that it in fact presumes a bourgeois conception of the public sphere that requires the bracketing of inequalities of social status.[42] The "public sphere" takes place on unlevel ground rather than in "counterpublics" where, she argues, members can control how they are represented. In these counterpublics, members are better positioned to actually reshape the practices and institutions of their environment. To the extent that there is voluntary separation, resisting, redefining, or reclaiming the terms of one's experience also improves the possibilities for self-determination.

Integrationists assume that integrated environments are the only ones capable of supplying the conditions under which authentic democratic deliberation among equals can occur. Only through pursuing the ideals of integration can we expect office holders to be knowledgeable, competent, and responsive to the needs and concerns of their constituents.[43] Insofar as these thoughts express important ideals, they should not be abrogated. Yet notwithstanding our habit of talking as if we were all equals, multiple counterpublics in separate spheres can contribute more to democracy so long as power is concentrated in the hands of the few and massive social inequality exists. With respect to deliberation, William Galston reminds us that it should avoid any comprehensive presumptions in favour of the exercise of public power. As we weigh the evidence in a liberal society, the burden of proof should rest on those advocating the use of that power in ways that significantly impede the ability of mature and competent citizens to live their lives in accordance with their own conceptions of what gives their lives purpose and value.[44] As the need arises, members of these counterpublics can formulate their own interpretations of their interests and needs and advance these for public hearing. But if fair channels of deliberation are not available and political elites do little or nothing by way of response to voiced concerns, we should not be surprised if counterpublics manifest themselves in the form of protest and dissent, a rejection of deliberation exclusively defined and delineated by others.

The idea of multiple counterpublics is consistent with civic virtues under conditions of segregation, particularly when the benefits positively impact marginalized communities. Accordingly, civic virtue does not hinge on integration. Under the right conditions integration may facilitate certain benefits, but it is not an irreducible good. Nor, as I have argued, must civic virtues reduce to political ones. A capacity for enlarged thought can be cultivated without it—say, through education—and the capacity to reshape one's environment begins, and often remains, within the local. I have no doubt that integrated environments can and do produce desirable effects where there is the possibility for parity of participation. But there is reason to doubt whether integrated environments that meet these conditions occur very often; indeed, achieving integration often entails toil and frustration disproportionate to the expected outcomes. As a political matter, citizenship as integration frequently overrides the interests of individuals as well as the communities to which they belong.

Integration may indeed be instrumentally valuable. It may supply access to goods and opportunities. But that applies equally to VS. As an expression of a counterpublic, VS does not mean that one has no understanding of other points of view or that its members lack the ability to cross borders. Rather, one of the strengths of VS lies precisely in its providing an alternative point of view—one very useful for agitating against social and economic injustice. In short, the flourishing of civic virtue under conditions of segregation not only is feasible but also may yield outcomes that rival the very benefits ideal integrated environments allegedly offer.

Conclusions

In this chapter I have provided a prima facie defense of VS. First, I defended a prima facie justification for VS for stigmatized minorities when conditions are more conducive to equality through the cultivation of self-respect. I have grounded my argument in a very specific notion of equality—one that accords high value to the role self-respect plays. It therefore holds that self-respect is fundamental to what it means to experience equality and that the equalization of resources or opportunities alone cannot compensate for persons for whom self-respect is compromised or absent. With respect to education, stigmatized minorities, like other groups, are not demanding integration so much as they are demanding a quality education.

Second, I argued that segregation need not undermine civic virtue and may even serve to enhance it. Segregation, particularly when there is a voluntary aspect present, often facilitates meaningful attachments that promote the good of the community and make other forms of social cooperation possible, even when other harms may be present. Provided that particular attachments produce and sustain civic virtues, these need not preclude moral concern for those belonging to other groups. Democratic and pluralist societies need individuals who are both strongly rooted in local communities and able to engage productively with those who are different from them. As I have argued, civic virtue may overlap with political virtue, but it need not reduce to politics.

Neither must spatial concentrations undermine the importance of shared fate. To the extent that VS is conducive to equality of self-respect and civic virtue, there is no reason to believe that its aims are at cross-purposes with shared fate. Even so, as I argued in Chapter 2, it must not be forgotten that there is much experience that is categorically *not* shared. Further, we must be careful not to conflate shared fate with the rhetoric of integration, which, more often than not, underestimates the significance of communal belonging and is vastly overrated when it comes to promoting a willingness to engage with others.

Undoubtedly some will continue to worry that VS will only magnify the stigma that some vulnerable groups already experience. As we saw in Chapter 2, many argue that only integrated environments can reduce stereotyping, prejudice, and mistrust. Yet as I argued earlier, even if prejudice reduction were to germinate from integrated environments, we have little reason to think that this effect is generalizable. Second, given both the nonshared experiences and nonideal conditions of contact, this outcome is in any case improbable in the absence of many other enabling conditions, which for stigmatized minorities are often absent in integrated settings.

In any case, stigmatized minorities cannot prevent themselves from being stereotyped and profiled by majority groups or excluded by the available opportunity structures. To the extent that social exclusion is institutionalized, one can only manage one's response to it. It is often imperative that minority communities preserve their right to remain separate by galvanizing their virtues in opposition to institutionalized oppression. But the manner of opposition will vary. Persons can make efforts to educate the public about institutionalized oppression, even in coalition with others whose lives are not directly affected by it. Civic virtue may also demand outright revolt. But civic virtue does not require this response, because civic and political virtues are not one and the same.

Critics may still worry that the civic virtues cultivated under VS will be restricted to one's own community, effectively sequestering institutional change without challenging or reforming the macrostructures that set the terms for accessing opportunities in the labor market or for leveraging power in the political sphere. But there is nothing in my defense of VS that precludes the development of autonomous and critical choices, the cultivation of political virtues, or even the mastering of the discourses of power. As I have argued in this chapter, it may be because of segregation that these can be more effectively pursued.

Yet whether articulated as necessary for the cultivation of self-respect or conducive to civic virtue, my prima facie defense of VS is not a defense of segregation per se. Nor do I take a position against reasonable[45] efforts to desegregate schools, provided that they actually foster equality. Integrationist ideals also need not lose any of their force as ideals, and under ideal circumstances, one would not be forced to choose between equality and integration. But equality should always be prioritized over analogous demands to integrate, especially when integration strategies for the most part continue to be designed in ways that are far less likely to supply the social bases of self-respect. Real integration at all levels of society does indeed imply that equality is not determined by something as arbitrary as the color of one's skin or the social class background of one's parents. But when segregation indices are not diminishing, it cannot simply be left to integrationist ideals to foster equality. We may lament segregation; indeed, there is a sense in which we *should* lament it. Yet however lamentable neighborhood or school segregation may be, it is unwise to conflate equality with integration. Pursuing equality through integration may work in many instances, but stigmatized minority groups need not wait for others to have a moral epiphany or for contrived occasions to arrive. Given that de facto segregation is the norm, they cannot afford to do so.

In the three chapters that follow I examine different case studies to either exemplify or test the claims of VS. All three chapters consider the circumstances of different stigmatized groups and the challenges they face—especially in the educational domain. I also confront a number of conceptual and empirical challenges confronting each case. As we will see, some fare better than others.

5

Religious Separation

Against the backdrop of a pervasive economic crisis—combined with a low autochthonous birth rate, unprecedented levels of non-Western immigration, high unemployment, a swelling elderly population, and ever-present xenophobic sentiments that infuse political debate at the highest levels[1]—a "politics of integration" in Europe has become commonplace. Though its meanings and uses are manifold, *integration* typically is taken to mean that a society's minority groups—be they immigrants, asylum seekers, or even natives—must accept the dominant political and cultural norms and values of the host society.[2] Naturally some groups are singled out more than others. Yet whether expressed as populist rhetoric or political mandate, *integration* continues to be an ideologically ambiguous concept with many implicit features whose meanings are not entirely evident to either the immigrant or the native population. Consequently, there is much debate concerning its indicators and requirements.[3]

The pluralist challenges European and other governments are facing are not new. Take schools, for example. Historically schools were, and arguably remain, the most effective means of enacting the political aims of integration. As we saw in Chapter 3, many political theorists espouse the rather benign view that the civic purpose of schools is mainly to inform citizens about how their government works and to encourage some type of participation in the political process. More robust versions may even insist that state schools cultivate both knowledge and virtue necessary for social cooperation or that civic education enable pupils to dispassionately evaluate different points of view and to respectfully regard perspectives with which one does not agree. That is to say, all persons (save, perhaps, those inimical to the idea of respectful engagement) should be worthy of equal recognition and treatment.

Whether these inspiring aims are achievable in schools will depend on the resources and characteristics defining the school environment. But as state institutions, schools indisputably have long served to assimilate the masses—that is, to promote social cohesion via conformity to social norms by championing the interests of its dominant groups. Language, culture, and religion have long served as the instruments for galvanizing a people around specific nationalist ideals.[4] Given the importance of fostering shared norms and values, it is unsurprising to find that citizenship education in many countries is compulsory. As we saw in Chapters 2 and 3, schools are at least partly envisioned as places where children of different backgrounds converge to learn together—and also to learn about, and from, one another.

But residential segregation as well as an educational system that often mirrors the local demography and facilitates segregation along other—denominational, pedagogical—lines presents serious challenges to integrationist aims. Of course not all schools with segregated pupil populations are alike; some are the legacy of de jure segregation and white flight (discussed further in Chapter 6), while others host relatively homogeneous minority pupil populations by choice. When spatial concentrations coincide with choice in such a way that segregation is turned into an advantage, we may say that they typify a form of voluntary separation (VS). As the first of three case studies, this chapter represents a brief exploration into two school types—Islamic and Hindu—that fit this mold. These schools consciously promote cultural and religious distinctiveness with the aim of facilitating, among other things, equality and citizenship by other means.

In what follows I explore the means by which Islamic and Hindu schools try to achieve these aims in a manner that is predicated on VS. Though in principle both types of schools are open to children outside the faith, their primary aim is to educate children of shared cultural and religious background. And like other schools whose instructional design is religiously specific, both Islamic and Hindu schools have faith building, identity formation, and emancipation among their central aims. I will explore the specific cultural and religious components that are used to form the identities of children and how these can be viewed as emancipatory practices. In particular I will examine how these schools concretely prepare pupils to negotiate their place in a society in which they are visible minorities.

To keep the analysis within feasible boundaries, I shall focus exclusively on the Netherlands. I circumscribe my focus to the Netherlands for several reasons. First, the Dutch school system is almost uniquely pluralist in character, allowing for the establishment, full state funding, and monitoring of various school types on principled constitutional grounds. Second, "emancipation" plays an important historical role in the Netherlands as this pertains to religious schools. A long struggle for equality of recognition and treatment by religious minorities has led to a variety of educational options that many see as evidence of integration and emancipation.[5] Third, the

Netherlands is the only Western country that hosts a significant number of fully funded Hindu and Islamic primary schools. Fourth, while Hindus and Muslims are not stigmatized to the same degree (or even stigmatized at all in other contexts—certainly not in Hindu or Muslim majority countries) in the Netherlands, both groups are frequently associated with "black"[6] schools—that is, schools that are themselves stigmatized due to a higher concentration of minority children. Finally, while the colonial and immigration histories are distinctive, the Dutch context (imperfectly) mirrors the situation of stigmatized ethnic and religious minorities elsewhere.

Background

The Netherlands presently has a population of 16.7 million inhabitants, of whom 1.6 million (9.3 percent) are Western immigrants and 1.9 million (11.6 percent) are non-Western immigrants. More than one-third of the Western immigrants come from the neighboring Germany, Belgium, and United Kingdom. Three categories of non-Western immigrants have come to the Netherlands since the 1960s: (1) immigrants from former Dutch colonies (Surinam and the Netherlands Antilles); (2) guest workers from the Mediterranean countries (e.g., Italy, Turkey, and Morocco) and subsequent waves of immigrants from these countries who come for purposes of family reunification and family formation; and, more recently, (3) asylum seekers and refugees from Eastern Europe, Africa and the Middle East. In 2012 the largest non-Western immigrant groups had the following origins: Turkey (393,000), Morocco (363,000), Surinam (347,000), and the Netherlands Antilles (144,000).[7] One characteristic shared by most non-Western immigrants is their comparatively low level of education. Another characteristic that sets most non-Western immigrants apart from both Western immigrants and native Dutch, especially since the 9/11 terrorist attacks and the murder of Theo van Gogh, is religion—specifically, Islam.[8]

Visible ethnic concentrations in Dutch cities certainly include Ghanaians, Chinese, Surinamese and Antilleans, but by far, the two largest groups are those of Turkish and Moroccan origin. Both groups, despite all sorts of internal divisions and widespread secularism, more often than not are summed up in one word: Muslim. Surinamese Dutch citizens of Indian descent face less discrimination today than their Muslim counterparts, but this was not always the case. Even with guaranteed Dutch citizenship, owing to their earlier colonial status, Surinamese immigrants in the 1970s and 1980s confronted racism and discrimination in Dutch society much as Indonesian immigrants had in the 1950s and 1960s. And both groups are still implicitly viewed as not belonging to Dutch society—they are routinely labeled *allochtonous* (*allochtoon*)—by the mainstream, owing to their relatively recent immigration history. That is to say, relative to other kinds of minorities, members of visible immigrant groups in countries like the Netherlands face a special kind of uncertainty—one that at least partly derives from their minority status.

Religious Schools and the Dutch State

Since the revision of its constitution in 1917, the Netherlands has guaranteed educational freedoms, together with full support for funding, to establish schools with religious or didactic aims and methods. Many of these schools (e.g., Jenaplan, Steiner, Dalton) have developed and expanded over the decades and remain very popular, especially among well-educated, middle-class white parents. Other schools that represent religious denominational differences also remain popular and in fact continue to educate a majority of Dutch children. Dutch constitutional freedom of education resulted from a struggle over equal treatment, specifically for equal financial support for both denominational and nondenominational or public schools. Article 23 of the Dutch Constitution was the result of an intensely fought-over school struggle (*schoolstrijd*) for equal and public recognition and funding between Protestants and Catholics on the one hand and secular liberals on the other. This struggle for equality can be seen as part of an emancipation process of the indigenous Dutch religious social groups.

However, the struggle was not restricted to education but was rather part of a general emancipatory process of social and religious groups in the Netherlands that penetrated all aspects of Dutch society. An important consequence of this has been the maintenance of a delicate balance between the autonomy of the different social and religious groups on the one hand and the integration of these groups within the encompassing framework of the nation-state on the other. Regardless of their specific denomination, most religious schools aim to promote, to one degree or another, shared beliefs, values, habits, and interactions among school and community members.

At the same time, there is a curious paradox in the Netherlands: while secularization has steadily progressed in all societal sectors since the 1960s, the number of religious schools largely has remained constant, with a market share of some two-thirds of all pupils.[9] At this moment, 33 percent of all primary schools are public schools, 30 percent are Catholic, 26 percent are Protestant, and the rest are of smaller denominations, including branches of Reformed Protestant, Islamic, Jewish, and Hindu faiths. Notwithstanding the fact that institutional religious membership and attendance has dropped off dramatically in the past forty years, it continues to be the case that religious schools are defended by many as an important avenue of emancipation. Proponents of Hindu and Islamic schools appeal to the role separate schools have played in the historical emancipation of, for example, Dutch Catholics and Jews.[10]

Both Hindu and Islamic schools represent a form of VS—one that appears to conflict with the demands of integration. Yet motives for establishing and choosing Hindu and Islamic schools vary, for they include the inculcation of faith, a desire to improve academic achievement, a belief that children ought to learn about and participate in the cultural background of their parents, and the hope that they will play a positive role in the integration of the next generation.[11] Because Hindu and Islamic schools follow the constitutional guarantees that permit schools to be founded on the basis of a worldview or philosophy, each is fully funded by the Dutch state. While they are permitted to favor teachers and principals of their respective faiths, all schools are expected to follow the attainment targets in terms of teaching matter set by the Ministry of Education. The vast majority of the pupils in these schools of course have either a Hindu or Muslim background, but in at least one Hindu school in Southeast Amsterdam, owing to its diverse neighborhood characteristics and strong academic reputation, more than 25 percent of the children are either Muslim or Christian. Perhaps also surprising is that this school has a number of Muslim teachers.[12]

The Dutch inspectorate of education visits all religious schools regularly[13] to see whether they are meeting the required instructional and environmental standards on a number of quality criteria. These criteria are elaborated in a framework that focuses on the structure of the learning process with the following elements: educational content, learning/teaching time, educational climate, school climate, teaching methods, response to individual needs, active and independent learning, results, and development of pupils. The following descriptions represent an idealized praxis of Hindu and Islamic education.

Hindu Education

The ethos of a Dutch Hindu school contains the following aspects: time for meditation is a part of daily school life; images of Hindu gods adorn classrooms and hallways; texts from scriptures such as the *Bhagavad Gita* and *Upanishads*, or epic poetic texts from the *Mahabharata* and the *Ramayana*, can be publicly seen; Indian dance and music may fill up as much as two hours of school time per week; and finally, though major Christian holidays are also celebrated, Hindu festivals such as Diwali and Phagwa (Holi) are celebrated as community-wide festivities and attract a lot of public attention and participation. Teachers aim to develop a Hindu worldview and identity by integrating cultural and religious beliefs into ordinary instruction. This is known as *dharma* education. Though the regular subjects are taught, the Hindu school also offers Hindi instruction for one to two hours per week (but in all subjects, instruction is given in Dutch). Hindu schools strive to foster unity among the staff and pupils through shared mantras, prayer (at the start and end of the school day), and a vegetarian diet (though not all Hindu families are vegetarian).

But far more than Hinduism, what children in a Dutch Hindu school mainly have in common is their Surinamese cultural background. Because most teachers have a Surinamese-Hindu background, staff and pupils share a common ancestral history and experience, which strengthens the relationship between teachers and pupils and overall internal school cohesion. This can also be seen in the school didactics—that is, the fact that more individual attention is given to the cultural needs of pupils.[14] In addition to their shared cultural background, the Dutch language provides additional cohesive support. Within the existing constitutional framework in the Netherlands, Hinduism—as a religious worldview—becomes the artifice for binding these items together. Even in the absence of constitutional provisions, religion frequently mediates cultural bonding among expatriates. As one researcher observes, "In immigrant contexts, religion becomes the means of creating ethnic communities and identities and so the attachment to religion and religious institutions is intensified."[15] While there is no doubt that Hindu schools aim to foster a shared Hindu ethos, through the propagation and repetition of basic beliefs and practices, the emphasis is importantly also culturally based, and thus the actual "Hinduness" of what Hindu schools do may not run very deep.

All children and school staff participate in the shared activities, tolerance toward other beliefs and traditions is strongly encouraged, and mutual respect toward one another in school is certainly expected. Active parental participation and involvement in the school life and at home is encouraged. However, this is not always accomplished. Reasons for this are that Surinamese children disproportionally (up to 60 percent) live in single-parent families, and if this is not the case, both parents work. Pupils at Hindu schools follow the same basic curriculum as pupils at other Dutch schools. This includes the obligatory subjects of intercultural education and religious and ideological movements (such as Christianity, Islam, and Judaism). While Hindu schools use the same textbooks as other schools, there is considerable flexibility in how the school meets its learning goals and attainment targets.

Islamic Education

Dutch Islamic schools aim to provide an environment infused with the teachings and ethos of Islam. In this basic aim, Islamic schools share a similar mission with their Hindu counterparts. Though there are different types of Islamic schools, including those with varying degrees of orthodoxy, strictness, and ethnic affiliation, many overlapping similarities unite them. To begin with, all Islamic schools aim to promote an awareness of Allah in all that children do and learn. Mindfulness of God is the central aim of an Islamic education, but maintaining equilibrium between the physical and spiritual realms follows from this, and there must be integration and balance in all forms of knowledge. Prayer times in Islamic schools are routine, and space is provided for pupils to carry out ablutions either in an adjoining mosque or in the school itself.

The language of instruction is Dutch, though the level of spoken and written Dutch even by some school staff is highly variable, and some instruction in Arabic is rudimentary, particularly in religious instruction classes and during study of the Qur'an. All prayers are typically recited in Arabic. All Islamic schools provide varying amounts of Qur'anic instruction (with recitation), including studies of the life of the Prophet and the period of the first four Caliphs. The example of the Prophet Muhammad, whose deeds are collected in the Sunnah and whose attributed sayings are collected in the hadīth, serves as the moral guide. All Islamic schools celebrate the two important feasts on the calendar, the Festival of Sacrifice and the Festival of the Breaking of the Fast.

Besides the usual subjects, art classes are sometimes available, but depictions of persons and animals are strictly forbidden because of Islamic sanctions against idolatry. Islamic songs are permitted, but music classes are available only in a few schools, and many instruments are forbidden. Because Islam compels modesty, dress codes are usually strict, not only for pupils, but also for staff, and Islamic manners are instilled.[16] Beyond a certain age (typically by nine or ten years old), it is characteristic for girls to wear a headscarf (*hijāb*) as a display of inward as well as outward modesty. Gender separation is a common practice in some Islamic schools, though separation is normally discouraged prior to the onset of puberty.

Islamic school staff understand their role as one that provides not only academic instruction but also counseling, role modeling, and spiritual support, for both the pupils and, occasionally, the parents. Though some changes have occurred in recent years, Dutch Islamic schools are more likely to attract parents who are recent immigrants than those who are second or third generation. The primary motivation for many parents in choosing an Islamic school for their children is simply to protect their children from secular influences in the public schools and in society and to cultivate a strong religious identity.[17] This seems especially to be the case for girls. Where boys are concerned, Islamic schools can mean more discipline, particularly for parents looking to correct delinquent behavior.[18]

Though a shortage of qualified Muslim teachers remains a problem, given the shared cultural background of many staff with their pupils and the parents, a sense of accountability to the community is higher than normal. Moreover, owing to the stronger formal relationships that usually exist between school board members and teaching and administrative staff, there is a strong stake in the performance and reputation of the school as well as the well-being of the pupils. Islamic school teachers, many of whom have considerable teaching experience in other public and private schools, often remark that Islamic school children are much better behaved than children in other schools. Staff attribute this to a school philosophy built on inner excellence and to a life guided by prayer, morality, and consciousness of God. Issues of faith are broached in the classroom and, theoretically, integrated into the teaching of different subjects.

Similarities and Differences

When asked what is distinctive about a Hindu or Islamic education, many teachers and principals report that the pupils feel at peace—that the school fosters better character and aligns the actions of pupils to a set of values that transcend cultural norms and other curricular aims. Others say that a feeling of unity and sense of belonging prevail among the student body. Whether it concerns sharing a dress code, praying together, eating *halāl* or sanctioned food, or celebrating religious holidays, pupils feel themselves in solidarity with their peers, and this may extend beyond the walls of the school. Further, being together in a Hindu or Islamic school means not having to face (at least not as often) bullying, peer pressure, gang culture, harassment, drugs, or, ultimately, a less friendly environment.[19] Other aspects contribute to student well-being, including a higher degree of adult supervision and concern (though as we shall see, this may have inhibiting effects for girls), fewer cliques, and more self-confidence among the student body.

Both Hindu and Islamic schools are predicated on many of the same principles invoked by other religious minority groups in the Netherlands. That is to say, its defenders argue that a religious education, one that takes account of the relevant cultural and religious values and backgrounds of the pupils, has the potential to enhance the self-respect of pupils, foster civic virtue in distinctive ways, and facilitate the learning process. Accordingly,

Dutch Hindu and Islamic schools recognize that instructional design, strong leadership, and school organization that builds on these shared features is the key difference between a school with a high concentration of minorities and one that has turned ethnic homogeneity to its advantage. In the opinions of many parents, the resources that Hindu or Islamic schools offer are in short supply in public schools with a comparable student population, which are generally the only option available to minority parents living in segregated neighborhoods.

Both Hindu and Islamic schools aim to prepare their pupils to live in a culturally diverse society by instilling self-discipline, tolerance, and mutual respect, especially toward adults. These are reinforced by explicit staff expectations and parental support of the school mission. Role modeling proper attitudes and dispositions reinforces a school ethos of peace and respect. Dutch Hindus and Muslims both believe they have a duty to themselves as well as to the community in which they find themselves. This dual obligation composes their educational and spiritual vision. The child is part of the school community and learns to function as part of this community. Both Hindu and Islamic schools also try to cultivate each child's development by attending to individual needs. Yet while both Hindu and Islamic schools claim to have a holistic orientation, they are generally more subject-matter oriented than process oriented and place a strong emphasis on discipline and cognitive achievement. In short, school is seen as preparation for membership and participation in society, and Hindu and Islamic schools endeavor to supply each child with the requisite dispositions, knowledge, and skills.

But there are important differences between Dutch Islamic and Hindu schools. For example, while the Dutch state has played a facilitative role in fostering educational pluralism, not all religious schools have been welcomed with open arms. While other minority groups (e.g., Protestant evangelicals) have struggled for the right to open their own schools, in their 25-year history, Islamic schools have struggled under an image problem; during periods of political crisis (e.g., following 9/11 or the murder of Theo van Gogh in 2004), public sentiment briefly turned against the Muslim minority, and a number of Islamic schools were vandalized.[20] Recent scandals involving fiscal mismanagement by the schools' boards only worsened their reputation, and a few schools were later closed for reasons having to do with low enrollment and poor academic achievement.[21]

Most worryingly, it had become clear to many that in terms of their pupils' achievements, the 43 Islamic primary schools in existence had not, until very recently, succeeded in living up to their expectations. Then, in 2012 following three years of intensive internal reforms, evidence emerged showing significant academic improvements at a number of Islamic primary schools. By early 2013 two Islamic primary schools had been awarded the title "Excellent School 2012" by the Ministry of Education.[22] The news was hardly noticed by the public, but to those who were monitoring their progress, the revelation was nothing less than astounding. Meanwhile, those who had worked hard at improving the quality of these fledgling schools were less surprised.

Other differences between the two groups should be noted. Within schools, faith and adherence to revelation play a much stronger role in Islamic schools. With respect to school practice, unlike in most Islamic schools, girls and boys in Hindu schools take not only academic classes but also physical exercise and swim classes together. Stigma, too, for Dutch Hindus has lessened over time. While the vast majority of children who attend Dutch Hindu schools have a Surinamese background as well as parents with lower socioeconomic status (SES), Dutch Hindus appear not only to perform, on average, better than other minority groups in schools[23] but also to "integrate" at a faster rate than other non-Western immigrant groups. Certainly there is a linguistic factor here, as the Surinamese already speak a Dutch dialect, but also significant is that social aspirations among Dutch Hindus are consistently high and that, in general, their orientation is toward the mainstream culture. Many Dutch Hindus report that one has to adapt to the country where one lives, actively participate in its social and political life, and abide by the laws of the country.[24]

Assessment

In Chapter 2 we saw that a central point of equality is to secure liberty for all on terms of equal recognition and treatment. We also saw how equality entails a fundamental regard for self-respect. To the extent that specific Hindu and Islamic schools succeed in this area, in this regard they satisfy basic equality demands. We also saw how pluralist accounts of citizenship allow for a variety of civic expressions that need not be overtly political in nature and that permit prioritizing and pursuing those things that matter to the persons in question. Typically this entails priority to group memberships and local concerns. So beyond the basics of a shared membership within a political space, with mutual rights and responsibilities applied equally to all, wide latitude is given to citizens for acting out or expressing their citizen-like roles. So how well do Hindu and Islamic schools in the Netherlands measure up to the framing principles?

Equality

Within the Dutch context, religious schools have long been seen to fulfill an egalitarian purpose. That is to say, the constitutional freedom to establish religious schools is seen as an expression of fair and equal treatment. For non-Protestant groups, religious schools may even represent a type of emancipation. They are emancipatory for reasons both external and internal to the educative process. Some of the external reasons have to do with colonial and postcolonial practices and identities: stigmatization owing to their visible minority status; experiences with prejudice and racism; the rhetoric of integration that permeates government discourse; and, finally, the tremendous pressures imposed on certain visible minority groups to somehow demonstrate that their cultural loyalties are directed first and foremost toward the Netherlands. Additional pressures arguably apply to the Hindu community, whose characteristics match those of the model-minority stereotype—namely, expectations to outperform other, less favorably evaluated minorities and to show oneself as more "integrated."

Yet reasons internal to the educative process may also be cited, including the aim of promoting personal well-being and improved academic performance that derive from culturally responsive learning strategies. School environments that aim to be culturally responsive potentially yield both epistemologically and instrumentally important benefits. Epistemologically, learners can be expected to benefit from a pedagogy that places them at the center of instruction. Children who routinely encounter stories, characters, and achievements of those with whom they share important traits in common can be expected to identify more with what is being taught and to be more intrinsically motivated to succeed. Instrumentally, culturally responsive pedagogy can help to mitigate psychological and cultural dislocation, assisting young people in cultivating more self-respect and preparing them to enter society more confident of who they are and where they come from.[25] (I address the worry about cultural essentialism in Chapter 6.)

Both Hindu and Islamic schools cater mostly to a cultural and religious minority, but more important, they also cater to a higher-than-average percentage of socioeconomically disadvantaged children.[26] With respect to improved academic performance, Hindu schools have managed to improve themselves from being what were some of the lowest-performing schools in the country twenty years ago to being among the better-performing schools.[27] They also are fewer in number and have not been subject to scandal, and recent school openings have been welcomed by the Ministry of Education. Meanwhile, Islamic school performance until very recently was an ongoing topic of concern. However, as we have just seen, there is new evidence to be cautiously optimistic about academic improvement in Dutch Islamic primary education. What was not very long ago a rather tenuous situation facing Islamic schools in the Netherlands now looks more promising.[28] Yet in both communities, a strong correlation will continue to exist between the socioeconomic status of pupils and their academic achievement, particularly if and when there is low proficiency in the Dutch language.

Finally, Hindu and Islamic schools are sites not only where faith and culture can be incorporated into the instructional design but also where shared values and expectations frame much of what members of the community care about and pursue. Like other community-based schools, Hindu and Islamic schools aim to provide a number of vital resources, including a caring ethos, high expectations, a culturally relevant curriculum, and a core set of shared concerns. More than the curriculum itself, its daily rituals, routines and practices, role modeling and leadership, relational bonds and trust, and strong community support all aim to contribute to a unique learning experience in which, at the heart of its pedagogy, each child is given equal recognition and treatment.

Notwithstanding these positive features, for Islamic schools there continues to be concern in at least one area: gender equality. While there are many notable exceptions, anyone who has visited a variety of mosques and Islamic schools cannot help but notice that women and girls take a backseat—quite literally—to men in terms of authority and equal freedoms to move about. Notwithstanding references to equal treatment,[29] Muslim girls are usually more restricted than boys in the freedoms that they enjoy, both inside and outside of school, and in the expectations that some feel imposed on them to become mothers or to forgo a career.[30] Limited opportunities are more acute for girls who have parents with little education or who follow the customs of another culture that constrain what girls can do; the pressure to marry young and to begin conceiving children is not uncommon, though it is far less common than it once was.[31]

Careers, for example, often must take a subordinate position to family duties (including, for many, the obligation to care for the husband's family as well), and leadership roles, especially in Islamic affairs, are normally assumed to be the exclusive domain of men. Limitations on what Muslim girls are permitted to say or do have important implications not only for the breadth of experiences and aspirations that female pupils are permitted to have both inside and outside of school but also for the range of democratic freedoms Islamic schools are purported to uphold. Even if these concerns are less evident in Dutch Islamic primary schools, to the extent that even Islamic primary schools engage in questionable forms of differentiated treatment, these are legitimate worries.

At the same time, I am under no delusions concerning equality of the sexes in Western culture or even in the Netherlands, where women continue to be sorely underrepresented in top management positions as well as prominent leadership roles in both higher education and business.[32] Notwithstanding the tremendous gains feminists have made over the past one hundred years, legislation to actively promote equal rights for women in Western countries is indeed a fairly recent phenomenon, and the "glass ceiling" remains implacably in place in many domains. Muslims are correct to point both to this historical record (including the right of women to vote, which came later in Western countries than in some Islamic ones) and to the questionable beliefs that sexual freedom or equal representation in the highest positions of management is tantamount to equality with men.[33]

Of course, the failure of liberal democracies to consistently live up to the democratic ideal of equality of opportunity for women does not let Islamic schools off the hook; nor is it an argument in favor of perpetuating the practice of gender inequality under the guise of religiously circumscribed gender roles. For while Muslims believe that Islam breaks down many national and ethnic differences, differentiated expectations for girls continues to be a troublesome issue in many Islamic schools, notably for many of the female pupils in high schools (in the West, mainly in England and North America), where equal treatment between girls and boys remains a sensitive issue. Yet a critique of gendered practices need not originate outside of the Islamic school; there is considerable anecdotal evidence to support the claim that feminist challenges are emanating from within the Western *ummāh*.[34]

Citizenship

When we come to the matter of citizenship, the charges are familiar: religious schools aggravate segregation within the education system, facilitate some not-very-healthy forms of ethnocentrism, and possibly contribute to permanent societal isolation. Ethnic separation within the education system will coincide with ethnic separation within other societal institutions that will produce more ethnic enclaves or even ghettos.[35] I examined several of these objections vis-à-vis VS in Chapter 4 and will not repeat them here. However, it is possible that religious schools raise a new set of concerns to the extent that they may promote comprehensive and exclusive truth claims.

As I detailed in Chapter 3, among the demands of citizenship are the capacities necessary for both engaging with others on principled grounds and reasonably disagreeing when necessary. Citizenship also asks that we be able to imaginatively engage with others whose perspectives and experiences are different from one's own and to work together to sustain or reform the political institutions to bring about positive change. As these items bear upon Hindu and Islamic schools in the Netherlands, three responses immediately come to mind. First, religious school segregation is not unique to minority faiths. Indeed, as we have seen in earlier chapters, while minority groups certainly exhibit preferences for living close to one another, the same can be said of majority groups for reasons having to do with social class affinity or shared background and interests. A large percentage of schools in the Netherlands are all white and either Protestant or Catholic—and certainly not by accident.[36] Moreover, segregation is of course also determined by involuntary forces outside the control of specific persons or groups, including the cost of rent and middle-class flight. Second, as I argued in Chapter 4, it is difficult to see how, on the face of it, religious schools are less equipped to promote civic virtues than other schools. Indeed, presented with the task of addressing the specific needs and challenges of ethnic and religious minorities, they may in fact be better equipped to do so, given the resources they have at their disposal.

Third, as I also argued in Chapter 4, spatial concentrations frequently open up possibilities for cultivating civic virtue. Certainly for proponents of Hindu and Islamic schools, like proponents of any form of VS, what they do is not "segregationist." Rather their aims represent a particular response to segregation. Moreover, as I argued earlier, many Hindu and Islamic schools serve to reinforce the potentially fragile self-image of children from immigrant families who are more likely to experience bullying, harassment, discrimination, exclusion, and also ambivalence toward a culture with which they may not (yet) identify.[37] Attending to these concerns in a protective environment improves the chances of escaping imposed stereotypes offered up by the media and a school system that otherwise does not address cultural or religious difference except in the most superficial way.[38] Proponents of Hindu and Islamic schools in the Netherlands see that one of the best ways to do this is to explicitly address the minority position of these children relative to the broader Dutch context.

In what remains of this section, I shall limit most of my remarks to Islamic schools. I do this for two reasons. First, notwithstanding their visible minority status and many challenges and setbacks, immigrants with a Hindu background have managed to "integrate" reasonably well in the Netherlands.[39] Integration here should not be taken to mean that Hindus are more widely dispersed than other groups. However, owing to a shared

Surinamese background, their command of the Dutch language, high rates of intermarriage with native Dutch, and a historical relationship with the Netherlands[40] have eased their transition relative to other groups. Other evidence suggests that the hierarchal, cohesive, and community-oriented Indian community, combined with an entrepreneurial work ethic and high social aspirations, all combine to explain the rapid advancement of Dutch Hindus. In addition to support from the Surinamese community, Hindus also enjoy government-sponsored weekly television and radio programming, organized and run by Hindus, that focuses on issues affecting the Hindu community in the Netherlands and abroad. Today Dutch Hindus are seen by many as model minorities—certainly when compared to Muslim minorities.[41]

Meanwhile, though a highly differentiated group itself, Muslims continue to be seen as problematic both in the Netherlands and throughout Europe. First, putting isolated instances of extremist violence aside, Muslim male youth in particular are considered a problem population in the Netherlands. Irrespective of whether or not families are particularly religious, in terms of ethnicity, Muslim boys of both Turkish and Moroccan descent rank very low in the mainstream. School performance is low, and dropout rates are very high—incarceration rates are high, too. From time to time, Moroccan boys also have been found to harass gay men as well as members of the small Orthodox Jewish community in certain neighborhoods.[42] And second, as we have seen, Islamic schools have continuously been in the spotlight for a number of years, most of the time receiving exclusively negative attention. Questions pertaining to the treatment of women, attitudes toward homosexuality or Darwinism, anti-integrationist attitudes, and sympathy for religious laws (e.g., ritual slaughter) that for some appear to conflict with liberal democratic institutions all contribute to a negative image—hence the focus on the Islamic case.

For the moment, it remains unclear just how much interaction pupils in Islamic schools have with "otherness." This is the case for at least four reasons: (1) some Muslim parents who select Islamic schools are often reluctant to allow their children to form close friendships with non-Muslims or even with Muslims from different cultural, ethnic, or theological backgrounds; (2) analogously, "protection" from different points of view, or, if one prefers, cultural coherence, is partly the raison d'être of Islamic schools, and indeed, Islamic schools at least partly exist in order to counter the prevailing (materialist) cultural attitudes in liberal democratic societies; (3) the enrollment of non-Muslims in Islamic schools remains very low, and indeed, the overwhelming majority of Islamic schools contain no non-Muslim pupils; and finally, (4) most Muslim minorities already live in segregated neighborhoods. All of this suggests far less contact with difference for a majority of pupils in Islamic schools, especially in the early years when paternalistic control over what children do is more stringent, and limited contact portends worrying trends for inclusive and democratic education.

These are not trivial concerns. Even so, it is important to bear the following items in mind. In a country as densely populated as the Netherlands, very few segregated neighborhoods are isolated. Mainstream culture is pervasive. As anyone living in cities like Amsterdam, London, or Paris can observe, observant Muslims come in all stripes, but a significant percentage are thoroughly Westernized. In countries like the Netherlands, even a majority of Muslim girls who wear the headscarf also use cell phones and wear designer jeans and makeup. Of course, it is true that materialist possessions don't tell us very much about attitudes or orientations, and there can be no doubt that extremism is alive and well among a small but seriously alienated minority of young men. The point here is simply that the isolation hypothesis is quite exaggerated.[43]

Similar observations can be made about many Islamic schools. Important to note, Muslim pupils raised in Western societies, particularly by the time they reach adolescence, expect that reasons or justifications ought to be given and that blanket authority is insufficient and even unacceptable. Islamic secondary education in the Netherlands is hardly an option, but as Mazen Istanbouli found in his study of an American Islamic high school, many pupils are not afraid to question the principles of Islam or the authority of their teachers. He quotes a school administrator:

> If you question certain principles of Islam in certain communities, they call you a heretic and they will attack you sharply. I like the fact that [our] kids are a lot freer and they question everything. A lot of that is found in the early Islam but not in the Muslim communities now spread all over the world ... [our kids feel] that "so what if you are the teacher, unless you earn [our] respect, I am going to question you." And "so what if you are the principal." I feel that this is the right approach. When you deal with those kinds of kids, you respect them and you earn their respect. You produce leaders and not sheep.[44]

As the quotation from the principal of an Islamic high school suggests, many pupils of Islamic high schools, precisely *because* they are raised in a Western context, are generally freer to question and challenge traditional thinking when no reasons are given and to rethink how to be a Muslim from a different cultural or political point of view. In many respects, pupils in Islamic schools—again, in the higher grades—can be expected to reflect on their beliefs to a higher degree than children who accept mainstream values, for some of their commitments will evidently be at odds with much of what the larger society values, and this will require greater attention to the reasons for maintaining those differences. In a small number of Islamic schools, Muslim pupils are even given the freedom to openly question the dictates of faith. The more the foregoing types of exchanges occur, the more one can expect Islamic schools to enhance, rather than inhibit, the kinds of civic virtue that liberal Democrats value. However, it must be borne in mind that Islamic education in the Netherlands is largely limited to the primary school. As such, the amount of critical thinking taking place is on a level similar to that of other primary schools—which is to say a rather low level.

To the belief that a diverse student body is essential for promoting civic virtue, much has already been said. First, as I demonstrated in Chapter 2, even if diversity remains an attractive ideal, levels of segregation often remove this option from the realm of possibility. Second, as I argued in Chapter 4, spatial concentrations can in fact foster both "bonding" and "bridging" capital. Third, in principle there is reason to think that, over time, both Hindu and Islamic schools may come to serve more diverse student populations—just as most Protestant and Catholic schools now do—provided their reputation for academic excellence prevails. Indeed, as we saw earlier in this chapter, that possibility is already coming to fruition.

Criticism

There are two criticisms routinely brought against religious schools. The first, which typically alleges something specifically about Islamic schools, is that they promote violent and extremist views. The second criticism maintains that religious schools are inherently indoctrinatory and thus inhibitive to the development of autonomy. That is to say, religious schools somehow interfere with a child's future interest in self-governance.[45] I will not pursue either of these criticisms in detail for two reasons. Related to the first allegation, inspections by the Dutch Ministry of Education have repeatedly shown these fears to be largely unfounded. Indeed, Islamic schools are more likely to *minimize* feelings of stigma and exclusion, thus dampening whatever extremist tendencies a handful of isolated and militant individuals may have.

As for the second allegation, it is important to remember that VS expressed as religious separation must conform to rather substantive conceptions of equality and citizenship. Schools that do not conform to the requirements of the framing principles are not included under the prima facie defense. But more to the point, critics of religious schools often construct untenably demanding notions of autonomy that not only are naive about the degree to which imposed values and socialization shape our choices and how we think about and pursue them; these empirically implausible notions of autonomy also have the effect of censuring virtually all parents who "nonautonomously" pass along their (religious or nonreligious) beliefs and values to their children. While some content and methods of religious instruction undoubtedly impede rational and critical thought, one should not assume that the mere presence of dogma occludes rational thinking or that fidelity to religious tenets precludes the thoughtful consideration of dissenting views. Religious persons can espouse their views in a perfectly reasonable way, capable of engaging with others whose views differ manifestly from their own.[46]

Demanding notions of autonomy also fail to appreciate that autonomy is a matter of degree and too seldom take into account the appropriateness of *heteronomy* for many types of reflection, judgment, and decision making. In any case, all children are raised heteronomously long before they are capable of carefully considering the reasons for continuing to hold, revise, or jettison their beliefs. In short, not only is it dubious in most cases to speak of autonomy in younger children, but demanding notions of autonomy have the effect of censuring most parenting practices around the world, whether the practices are religious or not. Others and I have addressed a number of these concerns elsewhere,[47] so I will not pursue them further here. However, as I hope will become clear, a basic conception of autonomy is strongly implied in my discussion in the following section.

Well-Being

One criticism, however, that I will pursue and that certainly deserves serious consideration, is this: VS may very well make sense for adults, whose choices may or may not be impaired by structural obstacles but who nevertheless are able to makes decisions for themselves, but what right does that give parents to impose these choices on their children? After all, children have very little say in the matter. In addressing this criticism, I leave aside the obvious justification invoked by defenders of religious schools—one that we saw clearly in Chapter 3. Here I speak of the nonfacilitative principle of liberty and the constitutional guarantees that support it. Instead, I take up the concern that in selecting Hindu and Islamic schools for their children, parents potentially disregard what is in their children's best interest.

Though variable in its expression, well-being involves essential enabling conditions and outcomes. For instance, in order to speak of well-being there must be basic protections from harm. Well-being also will require that one's general material and emotional needs are being met. But well-being also entails the promotion of certain capacities; it will, for instance, equally entail the capacity to think and speak for oneself and the capacity to take up pursuits (e.g., vocations, relationships) that contribute to a flourishing life. Here we can see how autonomy and well-being might be mutually reinforcing.[48]

With respect to well-being, the claim against religious schools goes something like this: parents who place their children in religious schools extend their influence and control over their children's ideas and beliefs to such an extent that it severely inhibits the development of critical thinking and closes down the range of opportunities available to them, owing to the degree to which they have come to uncritically embrace their own parents' views. When legitimate expressions of parental partiality are combined with constitutional liberties to select religious schools—and children are therefore segregated according to, say, the religious preferences of the parents (and religious preference and ethnic homogeneity in the Netherlands frequently overlap here)—the implications for integration are not good, at least as defined by integrationists. If and when religious teaching approximates indoctrination or thwarts one's capacity to cooperate with others whose views one does not share, the threat of ethnocentrism looms, and the possibilities for deliberation with others fade from view.

Good intentions and healthy motives from parents (e.g., to improve academic performance) can be mixed with ones that are less so. With respect to religious school choice, this may include less toleration of views with which one does not agree. In particular it may be the case that some parents with strong conservative views will select a school whose aim is to nourish commitments that seem to militate against both a child's well-being and the public good. Taken to an extreme, religious commitment can erode the civic minimum needed to support and sustain democratic institutions. Irrespective of whether most children develop antisocial tendencies or not, many feel that it cannot possibly be in a child's interest to be raised or schooled separately.

And the fact is that some religious schools simply do *not* do well by their pupils. Some *do* aim to indoctrinate children and fill them with fear of the judgment to come as well as an intolerant disposition toward those who do not share their point of view. Moreover, virtually all Islamic schools condemn homosexuality, at a minimum creating difficulties for children whose sexual orientation deviates from heterosexual norms.[49] Further, as we saw earlier, some Islamic schools restrict what girls can do. All of these are legitimate concerns bearing upon a child's well-being. In short, whatever it is that religious schools may provide, surely these alone are not enough so as to allow us to remain optimistic about what, say, parents' motives are—or for that matter, how more conservative-leaning schools may impair a child's ability to flourish.

When it comes to education, both the parents and the state make claims on what is best for children. Given the potentially indoctrinatory tendencies of a separate religious education, the state should ensure that what is a positive alternative for some is not used by others as a vehicle to control children's minds or promote intolerance toward others. Its paternalist function accordingly serves to protect its citizens, and no less its children, and to ensure that their basic interests are looked after. The challenge lies in determining just which sorts of environments or personal attention meet the threshold prerequisites, not least of which because the scope of any child's needs is naturally a complex affair and at least partly will be determined by personal characteristics as well as contextual constraints. Hence when we examine the well-being of children vis-à-vis education, a one-size-fits-all approach is not only impractical and unpopular but also likely unjust.[50] Of course, avoiding a one-size-fits-all approach does not remove the concerns about a child's well-being, but a number of things need to be stressed here.

First, recall the discussion from Chapter 3 about the importance of liberty and its relationship with parental partiality. There we saw how liberty functions as a nonfacilitative principle: rather than facilitating integration, its exercise perpetuates segregation. Moreover, in that same chapter, I argued that on the basis of the Dutch Constitution, the European Convention on Human Rights, and the Universal Declaration of Human Rights, in choosing Hindu or Islamic schools, Hindu and Muslim parents act as do other parents who want what is best for their own children. In the Dutch context, this means that parents who select Hindu or Islamic schools are doing more or less the same thing as the majority of parents, whose children attend Protestant and Catholic schools.

However, parental liberty in shaping children's preferences through schooling or any other pursuit is not unrestricted, and states possess the right to intervene to protect the interests of children. Their rights and freedoms are contingent on their ability to fulfill their responsibilities as parents, at least at a basic threshold. Failing that, their right can be revoked. But while parents do not have limitless liberty in how they express partiality toward their own children, they nevertheless are well within their legal and moral rights in giving priority to their own children by selecting religious schools. Importantly, as we have seen, these rights and guarantees are enshrined within both national and international law. Though it is true that not all religious schools will serve the interests of children well, the same can be said of many nonreligious schools.

Second, as we have seen, part of what it means to enjoy a flourishing life is largely defined by the associational memberships we have, and these frequently are facilitated through expressions of partiality. Legitimate partiality will describe a justifiably special regard for another, normally on the basis of a unique sort of relationship. By virtue of the right kinds of partiality, parents not only pass along something of value to their children; in doing so, in most cases, they also demonstrate their love and concern. Further, as an expression of legitimate partiality, meaningful memberships within particular communities are cultivated on the basis of shared values, habits, and preferences.

Third, while religion and our framing principles do occasionally come into conflict, especially as it concerns exclusive and absolute truth claims, religiously inspired ideals per se do not operate at cross-purposes with concerns for a child's well-being. Indeed, it often is the case that by taking one's cultural and religious background seriously, one is able to yield outcomes conducive to equality of recognition, treatment, and self-respect. Nor need religious ideals conflict with the demands of citizenship, whether that be respect for the rule of law, basic human freedoms, or the capacity to engage in discussion with others whose views one does not share.[51] Not only the basics of citizenship can be reconciled with what it means to be religious; as we have seen, citizenship allows for many different articulations of civic virtue.

Fourth, the reasons for choosing religious schools are varied and complex. For instance, many parents choose a Hindu or Islamic education for their own children to pass along their faith or to solidify cultural attachments. Others want a more demanding curriculum or more discipline. Still others are looking for shared values or smaller class sizes.[52] Parents of every background wish to see their children educated in a safe environment where they will not be bullied, labeled, or neglected. Considering the hostile political climate toward non-Western immigrants in Europe in general and Muslims in particular, these are very reasonable concerns for many parents. Moreover, and perhaps most important, all parents hope that the school their children attend will improve their children's academic performance. So long as the teaching methods used are not purposefully indoctrinatory (read: aiming to promote blind obedience) and the ideas are not patently false (e.g., teaching that evolutionary biology is a conspiracy), claims that religious schools harm children—that they promote irrationality, ethnocentrism, or hatred—amount to little more than sweeping and indiscriminate allegations.

If we examine Hindu and Islamic schools contextually, it should not be forgotten that the religious school monopoly in the Netherlands has not waned since the 1960s. Nearly 70 percent of all Dutch pupils continue to attend a denominational school of one kind or another. The fact that the religious profile of most Protestant and Catholic schools has considerably diminished over time does not mean that conservative Christianity has disappeared.[53] Nor, incidentally, does the decline in Church membership across Europe mean that the influence of religious beliefs has been muted, as large, religiously motivated protests in April 2013 in France against gay marriage plainly demonstrate. Irrational beliefs, too, are widespread; across the Netherlands and "secular" Europe, New Age ideas are commonplace.[54] Therefore, to single out Hindu, Muslim, or other religious minorities over concerns about children's well-being seems rather arbitrary. Hindu and Islamic schools represent but two types of denominational schools within the Dutch school system, in which each institution is subject to state-mandated standards and inspections. Should any Hindu or Islamic school not satisfy the Dutch inspectorate, they are subject to closure. Moreover, should any Hindu or Islamic school clearly fail to promote the well-being of children or foster outcomes consistent with equality and citizenship as I have defended, then the prima facie case for their existence collapses.

Conclusions

In this chapter I examined the case for VS with respect to stigmatized minorities in religious schools. Notwithstanding the strong legal and philosophical reasons I have provided in their defense, none of what has been argued is at loggerheads with efforts to integrate. Under the right kinds of conditions, many benefits can accrue to pupils from different backgrounds that rival or exceed what can be offered under the conditions I have defended for VS. This does not diminish worries routinely expressed about segregated schools in the Netherlands. But more thinking needs to be done beyond simply mixing schools. Most of the benefits for social outcomes that are predicated on the integrated school argument continue to be hypothesized rather than demonstrated.[55] While a mixed pupil body is certainly one variable worth taking into consideration, other important features consistently have been found to promote strong outcomes, which, as we have seen, include a caring ethos, cultural recognition, and positive role modeling.

In the Dutch context, Hindu and Islamic schools can be seen as an avenue of integration by other means. That is to say, they function in a manner that is historically consistent with the idea of emancipation. However, unlike mainstream Protestant and Catholic schools in the early portion of the twenty-first century, the aims and praxes of these schools contribute to emancipation by attending to the specific needs of stigmatized minorities. Attending to those needs often increases equal recognition and treatment as well as enhanced self-respect. Further, there is no reason to think that either Hindu or Islamic schools are unable to demonstrate robust forms of civic virtue. This is nothing to sniff at for many children who normally face higher risks of school failure. To the extent that Hindu and Islamic schools can contribute to the self-respect of their pupils, we may speak of psychic integration. To the extent that Hindu and Islamic schools contribute to the good of their respective communities, we make speak of communal integration. Finally, to the extent that schools can contribute to the academic and language skills of disadvantaged youth, we may speak of potential cultural and economic integration. Important to note, all of these have implications for equality and citizenship in the sense that they can facilitate—rather than obstruct—integration into the mainstream. But in many cases, integration first entails cultural, economic, and political separation, which is to say *integration within one's own community*. Without this, integration into the broader society, to the extent that it occurs, more closely approximates assimilation.

To be sure, as a group, Dutch Hindus continue to be a rather successful minority when compared with Dutch Muslims. The Dutch Hindu community, while not without its fractures, is less ethnically and ideologically divided than the Dutch Muslim community. Hindu schools, too, reflect this tight community structure—but also greater fluency in the Dutch language, high social aspirations, and a greater concentration and retention of qualified Hindu teachers. This is far less true of the Islamic schools, which have their success stories but continue to struggle with ethnic and ideological differences between schools, fewer qualified Muslim teachers, a lower retention rate of teachers in some schools, and much higher concentrations of children with poorly educated parents. Whether Islamic schools in the Netherlands will ever match the successes of many of their counterparts in the United Kingdom or North America remains to be seen, but the "achievement gap" between Islamic schools on opposite sides of the Atlantic has much to do with social class differences between immigrant groups.

Despite my generally positive assessment of both school types in the Netherlands, challenges remain. Earlier I focused my attention on Islamic schools given the inordinate amount of attention they have received compared to Hindu schools but also given the influence of Islam in the West as compared with Hinduism. But Hindu schools also are not without potential weaknesses. In my view, Hindu schools must take their belief and practice of mutual respect seriously not simply by fostering a live-and-let-live attitude but also by critically examining Hinduism's historical role in establishing fixed castes of people, with some persons destined to permanently lower positions and others relegated outside the caste system altogether—namely, the Dalits. Other topics in need of critical attention include various patriarchal customs (e.g., control of temples) and the limited freedom to exit one's Hindu culture.[56] To be sure, these topics may not be appropriate for elementary school–aged children and therefore may have to wait until the Dutch Hindu community establishes its first secondary school. Even so, Hindu schools have the ability to use religion as a critical resource—one directed against cultural practices that fail to exhibit either equality or civic virtue.

Both Hindu and Islamic schools represent an institutionalized form of VS. To the extent that they make good on their aims and purposes, they buttress the prima facie case. But whether Hindu or Islamic schools will be necessary in the future or serve the same purposes they now serve remains to be seen. Though unlikely, changes in constitutional freedoms to establish and receive full subsidies for religious schools may not last forever. Religious schools in the Netherlands, too, are closed down when they fail to meet basic requirements, like adequate enrollment numbers and acceptable academic performance. More likely, however, is that over time Hindu schools will become rather like mainstream Catholic and Protestant schools that cater mainly to nonreligious children and offer more in the way of academic excellence and less in the way of religious difference. Given the upward mobility of the Hindu community in the Netherlands, this outcome is conceivable. Meanwhile, whether a significant number of non-Muslims ever will be drawn to well-performing Islamic schools remains to be seen.

6

Cultural Separation

In this chapter I focus my attention on the North American context and examine voluntary separation (VS) with a cultural base for stigmatized and poor blacks in the inner city. As we saw in Chapter 2, it has long been an orthodoxy that the answer to urban segregation is to integrate schools. Yet for some time now, many African Americans have questioned the aims of integration—"diversity" and "multiculturalism," in twenty-first-century vernacular—claiming them to be little more than attempts to assuage liberal guilt and maintain white cultural and economic dominance. Indeed, given the grim realities of black community life in a number of American cities, many African Americans believe most educational reforms to be either woefully inadequate or misguided. In various urban neighborhoods, teenage pregnancy and crime rates among black youth remain at worrisome levels, unemployment remains scandalously high, many children grow up in schools and neighborhoods overrun by gangs and drug trafficking, and more African American fathers are incarcerated than graduate from high school.[1]

Notwithstanding often dauntless efforts by ministers, parents, and community leaders to resist hopelessness, the sense of crisis—characterized by some as a slide toward nihilism[2]—is palpable, a downward spiral continues for many youth, and despair abounds. One institutional concomitant of the general malaise of urban and poor black communities, particularly in northern states, is highly segregated schools characterized by poor achievement, dilapidated infrastructure, ineffective leadership and teaching, high levels of violence, and low high school graduation rates, particularly for males.

While people on both sides of color-based and economic lines—lines as tangible as street names in many cities—point the finger and pass the buck, a group of African-centrist scholars, educators, and community leaders have attempted to turn de facto segregation to their advantage by putting the educational process back in the hands of African Americans. Their efforts have spurred the creation of a small but rapidly growing number of African-centered schools across the United States.³ The creation of these schools has been facilitated—somewhat paradoxically, considering their "radical" agenda—by the success of charter school and school voucher movements, which are often identified with the most conservative elements of American society.

African-centrist scholars consider blame, no matter where it is placed, to be a losing strategy that erodes the sense of nationhood required to develop black consciousness; in its place are the inspiration and energy required to cultivate a positive and productive culturally based identity for "New World Africans."⁴ African-centered schools endeavor to supply that cultural base, placing the history, culture,⁵ and life experiences of individuals of African descent at the center of everything they do. Those involved in the African-centered education movement believe that even institutionalized racism and unfavorable economic circumstances cannot determine one's purpose and direction if there is a strong cultural base informing one's community and family. As such, African-centered education (ACE) shares much in common with other identifiable groups (e.g., religious minorities and women) that defend VS as a means of building group efficacy. Indeed, ACE represents a powerful and inspiring response to despair as well as a form of resistance from below.

Just as I did in Chapter 5 with Hindu and Islamic schools, I will describe the background context out of which ACE arose, its central aims and purposes, and then assess the case for VS using the framing principles of equality and citizenship. I then respond to worries about cultural essentialism. As I proceed, I am aware of two things in particular. First, a variety of interpretations of ACE exist, and these are incorporated in schools in different ways.⁶ Nevertheless, I attempt to supply a fairly conventional, or normative, reading of ACE in describing the curricular choices, learning goals, teaching strategies, and performance assessment of practitioners in African-centered schools. Second, African-centered schools have many critics, both white and black. Few schooling experiments have elicited such vociferous debate. I aim to be responsive to ACE's critics but also true to ACE's core mission, which is to educate African American children well.

Background

The story of black people in the United States has a long and intricate history. However, for the purposes of examining the interface of African-centered education with VS, it will suffice to begin with the landmark 1954 Supreme Court decision (*Brown v. Board of Education* 347 US 483)

I touched on in Chapter 1. Remember that *Brown* famously outlawed de jure school segregation, repudiating the dastardly logic of "separate but equal" codified in the *Plessy* decision (*Homer A. Plessy v. Ferguson* 163 US 537) some sixty years earlier. In the American context, *Brown* has become the benchmark text on which many integrationist assumptions are based. Indeed, many hoped that *Brown* (and subsequent rulings in the 1960s and 1970s) would correct the inherent inequalities in schools, but for a large number of African Americans, *Brown* effectively marked the dismantling of thriving segregated institutions and communities. To be sure, in fits and starts, mandatory desegregation did bring modest success. Proponents of integration, including many African Americans, have pointed to the fact that many schools, particularly in the South, became far more integrated than they had ever previously been. Yet the lived reality of desegregation in public schools would not have the salutary effects that integrationists had envisioned. Indeed, the painful and often violent outcome of the integrationist agenda was that tens of thousands of black children would leave their relatively safe—albeit manifestly "unequal"—learning environments for integrated schools where they would be rejected by many of their white teachers and peers.[7]

The effects of school integration on the African American community were both immediate and devastating: literally scores of mostly black schools were closed; tens of thousands of black school personnel were displaced from 1954 to 1965; and by 1966, fewer than 2 percent of black teachers worked in desegregated schools.[8] Further, the 1970s witnessed ruined experiments with bussing and rezoning that resulted in fragmented black communities and a greatly diminished role for black parents. Time and again, black children moved from an educational context in which their identities were centered on black culture and communal life to one in which their endeavors inevitably would be compared with their white counterparts and found wanting. Some authors continue to argue that in most urban and suburban public schools, minority pupils are expected to exist in an environment that "negates their language, denies their historical existence, and demeans their culture."[9]

The education of a larger number of black pupils in predominately white schools has contributed to "white flight" (involving either residential relocation or migration to private schools), as many whites continue to see schools with a critical mass of black or Latino pupils as a marker of poorer school quality and, where enrolment increases do not result from bussing, as a guarantee of deflated property values.[10] White teachers and administrators, from liberal to conservative, often have been inclined to view black children as slower and as intellectually inferior in some fundamental way as compared with white children. Even as middle-class blacks seek out greater social and economic opportunity, African American pupils frequently suffer from any or all the following: "stereotype threat" in integrated settings, ambivalence and conflict in suburban schools, the pressure to "represent" for their group, pressures to form a raceless identity in order to assimilate, and the expectation that they express group loyalty as a form of "fictive kinship" in resisting institutional norms.[11]

Today many American schools are, in fact, well integrated; many have effective black leadership, and racial tension is relatively minimal. But as we saw in Chapter 2, when black pupils attend more integrated high schools (including magnet schools), racial stratification often occurs inside the building—through referrals for special education, a lack of mentoring, tracking mechanisms, and disciplinary procedures.[12] Indeed, blacks are far more likely to be grouped or tracked low, to be cited as having behavioral and learning disorders, to be suspended or expelled, and to drop out. By disproportionately using disciplinary action and tracking black pupils into lower academic tracks, "school systems [have been] able to limit interracial contact and thereby reduce White flight. In the process, most Blacks have received lower-quality educational opportunities. Consequently, [efforts] to desegregate defy the intent of *Brown,* as this nation witnesses the persistence of practices that result in inherently unequal schools."[13]

Further, schools that have a majority of black pupils are also far more likely to be located in urban districts with an eroding tax base, induced by the flight of businesses and social institutions that once sustained them, high unemployment rates, high mobility rates, high dropout rates, fewer teachers with terminal degrees in the subject they teach, and inadequate facilities and learning materials. These all generally contribute to a substandard education.[14] While the black middle and professional classes have expanded greatly since the *Brown* ruling, and while many African Americans have moved to the suburbs and exurbs, social and economic conditions for the disproportionately large black lower classes have steadily deteriorated over the past 25 years, and school segregation, along with seemingly intractable lines of residential segregation, has increased.

It is therefore perhaps the cruelest irony that African-centered schools are accused of rejecting integration in favor of segregated schooling. Critics who charge that African-centered schools foster segregation fail to reckon with the fact that a significant number of urban schools are already segregated; it is virtually impossible for African-centered schools to segregate their pupils any more than they already are. What is different about African-centered schools is the manner and purpose for which they are segregated. They are but one of several choices African American parents have vis-à-vis de facto segregation; many also select religious schools, for example. But in the absence of a repaired public school system or, at any rate, one in which black community interests are both represented and integrated into public school institutional cultures, most black parents prefer to have choices such as African-centered schools rather than to be assigned a school that could possibly fail to educate their children.

African-Centered Schools

Though both involuntary and voluntary forms of separate black education in the United States dates back centuries, the first African-centered independent schools opened in the late 1960s. African-centered schools were organized as a response to the demand from the black community for equity, high educational standards, and cultural expectations to which public schools, owing to the ways in which they were bureaucratically structured to maintain the status quo, had failed to adequately respond.[15] In a few cases, entire school districts (e.g., Atlanta and Detroit) have managed to infuse the curriculum with African-centered content with the support of teachers, parents, and school board officials,[16] while in the private sector, the Council of Independent Black Institutions (CIBI) aids parents in locating schools with African-centered character. Today there are more than four hundred African-centered public schools, while in the private sector, African-centered schools serve more African American youth than all schools except Catholic schools.[17]

The proliferation of African-centered schools in the 1990s coincided with a series of Supreme Court decisions related to the termination of court-decreed desegregation orders, the outcome of which was the lifting, at least in part, of most of these orders. The main message of the court was that only school segregation that was related to past or present intentional discrimination or that produced the social and personal stigma that the *Brown* court identified as the main damage of de jure segregation could be judged unconstitutional under *Brown*. School segregation related to residential segregation or other causes was not proscribed.[18] In this context, several legal scholars discussed the constitutionality of African-centered schools, some arguing for their permissibility and even necessity[19] and others recommending caution in sanctioning any kind of ethnically segregated schooling.[20]

Together with churches, mosques, neighborhood organizations, and families, African-centered schools present themselves as an important vehicle for transmitting an alternative historical perspective that putatively embodies the core cultural values of the African/black community. These values include self-respect, cultural pride, and communal responsibility. According to proponents of ACE, a school that does not live by these values cannot foster the ethos of institutional caring that is requisite for constructing a positive self-concept, working well with others, and succeeding in academic endeavors.[21]

The founders and proponents of ACE have maintained that the quality of committed staff is critical to the success of African-centered schools; from the principal to the teachers and the custodial and kitchen staff, each must desire to work in the school precisely because it is an African-centered school—because they are committed to the core aims of ACE and to the character development and academic success of black children. Each staff person is expected to be a role model for the children, fostering trust-based relationships and a positive self-image. Teachers are expected by school leaders and parents to have high expectations for pupil learning and success, even as the teachers provide a strong basic skill foundation for greater continuity and stability. Teachers sometimes loop for three years with the same pupils in order to maintain trust and cohesion, while in some African-centered schools, teachers also are also expected to make numerous home visits each year so that they might establish strong connections to the children's homes and maintain rapport with the parents or guardians. To allow for further contact with families and the community, activities are organized after school and occasionally on weekends. Children are also provided mentoring from other adults in the community who can support and advise pupils.[22]

While African-centered schools aim to have strong parental support,[23] they also strive to have strong leadership and a teaching staff committed to its core values. Of course, these desired outcomes are also supported by a number of ameliorating conditions, including small classroom size, family-like bonds between the staff and the pupils, minimal regulatory features (often facilitated by charters), and the affirmation of African-centered practices in everything that occurs within the school. Each of these must come together to produce a school culture that is stronger than the home culture the children may bring with them, a culture compromised by the myriad problems associated with urban poverty and cultural disintegration. Indeed, African-centered educators maintain that absent resources such as strong community bonds, compelling role modeling, and effective cultural foundational development, teaching efforts aimed at bringing about the schooling success of black children are a doomed project. Whether they are public by charter or other district arrangement, voucher dependent, or private, African-centered schools have important affinities with other successful community-based schools.

There is already much that African-centered schools do well. These strong points include building character, pride, and self-respect; facilitating meaningful and purposeful activities; and fostering personal and collective responsibility and solidarity. Many African-centered schools appear to be building coalitions with community leaders, church groups, and businesses, though certainly more work is needed to bring the aims of ACE into the community and families of some children. It is worth noting that most of these innovations, such as small class sizes, strong teacher-pupil relationships, and active parental support, have well-documented positive effects on pupil learning, most of which are extremely lacking in the "integrated" public schools that most black children attend. Perhaps most important in an era of greater state accountability, there is some evidence to suggest that a number of African-centered schools are raising not only black self-awareness and determination but also black academic achievement to impressive levels.[24] This is highly relevant given the decreasing number of African Americans generally entering the teaching profession and the chronic dearth of adequate preservice training that equips teachers with the pedagogical skills to effectively educate black youth.[25]

African-Centered Education

Nearly all mainstream multicultural narratives assume that African American history and identity begin in slavery and move toward emancipation. In the traditional American story, emancipation has been a long, arduous struggle fought for by African Americans, but it is also one that has been given by whites. ACE acknowledges that important changes have occurred, at least partly, as a result of efforts to redress past wrongs. Still, the liberal doctrine is seen as falsely reassuring insofar as it operates on the assumption that educational opportunity for blacks is largely dependent on white altruism and magnanimity. African-centered pedagogy rejects this narrative—from degradation to freedom—as inaccurate and devastating in its psychological effects. Ronald Takaki maintains that there can be nothing so dispiriting as to read the history of one's nation and find oneself and one's family missing or misrepresented.[26] Schooling in many mainstream schools, saturated with the symbolic capital of whiteness—institutionalized in both the formal and the hidden curriculum, inconsistent cultural messages, expectations, and communication styles between home and school—produces in black pupils a kind of psychic dissonance that interferes with learning and psychological well-being.[27] Psychic dissonance may be exacerbated by a weak or absent self-concept or identity. The combination is, for ACE, legitimate cause not for zero tolerance but rather for a different kind of schooling that promotes the healthy development of black youth.

With respect to its curricular and pedagogical aims, ACE entails the investigation, interpretation, and explication of all reality through an African-centered lens or from a perspective grounded in African-centered values. African-centered pedagogy assumes a cosmic order to the universe—an ontology in harmony with both nature and one's ancestors and forbearers. Persons of African descent are not individualized. Rather, black people are incorporated into the collective; personal development is subsumed to community goals and purposes,[28] and responsibility to—and solidarity with—others of African descent is paramount. In pursuit of these goals, Peter Murrell posits that black children need a "figured world of African American culture and intellectual life that invites the participation, development, and achievement of African American children."[29] Of what does this figured world consist? Although a number of interpretations are in circulation,[30] complete consensus remains somewhat elusive, and individual schools approach the sources differently. However, some shared elements exist.

There is, of course, a historical dimension whose inception is Africa, the cultural locus of all African-centered instruction. Therefore, ACE requires that children engage in a critical study of ancient and modern African history. Children also study, inter alia, the ancient civilizations of Kemet, Nubia, Axum, Meroe, and Kush; these are linked to other African cultures, including the Zulu, Yoruba, and Ife. The periods of enslavement and resistance in the American Diaspora are also examined but not in isolation from African and Asian slave trades; nor does the period of enslavement overshadow American history. Similarly, the roles of the Black Freedom Movement and the Black Power Movement on the African continent, in the United States, and elsewhere are also studied in light of important contextual realities. Critical study of modern African nation-states requires that pupils be attuned to the colonial influences that subordinated previously existing cultural and ancestral norms. Consequently, knowing that African achievements continue to be evaluated in relation to European standards, caution is urged in appraising educational models in modern African states whose authorship derives from a colonialist perspective.

Although ACE does not fixate on the narrative that puts white racism at the center of black history and ontology, this is not because white racism is not real. Indeed, institutional racism is assumed, and teachers are only too aware of what children will likely face in mainstream society. African centrists are invested in rescripting educational opportunity in a different way—one that is not mired in a victim-focused curriculum. Defenders of ACE accept as fact that most public schools facilitate the educative process in ways that further alienate black children from their cultural heritage. Simply put, far too many black children have been "deculturated." *Deculturation* has been defined as "a process by which the individual is deprived of his or her culture and then conditioned to other cultural values."[31]

Deculturation does not require the complete absence of group or cultural identity but rather involves the practice of denying access to, or refusing to acknowledge, an individual's culture or the role that it may play in an individual's well-being.

Operating on the assumption that most African American children have lost touch with their authentic selves, ACE places black children at the center of instruction by reenculturating pupils into the "majesty" of African/black consciousness and identity. It aims to reenculturate black children into a set of habits, dispositions, and behaviors—in short, an identity—that centers them on a firm understanding of who they are. In order to accomplish this, the black child must occupy the space at the center of instruction so that he or she may be viewed as the subject, and not an object, of that instruction. In doing so, the learner comes to interpret the world through a cultural understanding that has been constructed within, about, and for his or her own community. What follows, according to African centrists, is greater self-esteem and higher academic achievement.

By providing African American pupils with a safe cultural space within which they are able to express their racial/cultural identity—a separate space where they can unlearn internalized stereotypes and feel culturally anchored—ACE aims not only to facilitate an important coping strategy in a racist society but also to improve the academic performance and social relationships of pupils. When children, but perhaps especially cultural or ethnic minority pupils, begin to explore questions of identity in early adolescence, the pedagogical framework will require that they are provided with identity-affirming experiences, positive expressions of racial identity, and information about their cultural group, which is precisely one of the core aims of African-centered schools. At such schools, one typically finds a caring community deeply committed to the nurturing, development, and academic success of black children. Indeed, far from being a merely intellectual exercise, African-centered symbols, rituals, role modeling, and instruction have the explicit intention of centering the black self both psychologically and spiritually.[32]

The developmental purposes of ACE accord with Phinney's notions of healthy ethnic identity development. Phinney suggests that a person cannot hope to participate fully in an American society in which identity and self—particularly those of minority citizens—are under constant scrutiny (if not the subject of active discrimination) without having integrated a positive cultural/ethnic identity with a coherent sense of belonging in the broader world with "others."[33] Kal Alston conceptualizes this stage of racial identity development—a goal of ACE—in terms of achieving increased visibility, but visibility that counters the historical visibility of black abjection: "To remain visible, in the face of erasure, is to act against the juridical comforts of color blindness or the aesthetic comfort of assimilated familiarity [both of which Phinney identifies as eventually unsatisfying identities]. Visibility on this account is not simply a matter of allowing oneself to be an object of perception for others, but of shaping a visible subject ... The responsibility for visibility rests with those who can work from the visible subject position, turning racial knowing and being into value and valuing anew Blackness—known, experienced, undergone, transcended, released and celebrated."[34] The ability to "work from the visible subject position" is one of the primary aims of ACE, and this generally gives hope for fuller participation by blacks in American society.

Assessment

As much of the foregoing depiction suggests, ACE plays a crucially important therapeutic role that serves to inoculate children from the invidious effects of stigma and racism. Indeed, one of the core purposes of African-centered schools is the protection of a stigmatized minority from violence of all sorts during essential stages of identity development in which pupils have few resources with which to combat this violence on their own. Positive identity construction works in tandem with character development and fosters a deep respect for oneself, the society, and the broader world as well as a sense of service and communal responsibility first and foremost to the African American community.[35] ACE then serves not merely to construct a culturally coherent, historically grounded self-concept[36] but also to foster equality of self-respect. But how well does ACE measure up to both framing principles? How well, indeed, if citizenship demands more of us than simply being in solidarity with others of African descent? Let's start with equality.

Equality

Notwithstanding whatever benefits African-centered schools may supply, we should not suppose that equality of self-respect is an adequate substitute for equality in more material terms. As we saw in Chapter 2, equality is open to different interpretations, and equality of self-respect cannot brush over debilitating forms of socioeconomic inequality. Indeed, as we saw in Chapters 2 and 4, when there are refractory concentrations of poverty, we have legitimate reasons to be concerned. In those chapters I examined ways in which many segregated schools can be harmful to pupils, owing to the absence of resources, such as broader course offerings, a fairer distribution of better teachers, and more motivated peers. In that same discussion I also considered how integration might provide access to social networks that are crucial for economic opportunities down the line. Those whose own socialization is bereft of meaningful interactions with minorities are even less likely, when the time comes, to select them for positions at hiring time. These social networks, the argument goes, are simply unavailable under conditions of segregation. So if voluntarily separate schools are impoverished in terms of resources, then they cannot possibly make good on their promise of advancing equality beyond the most rudimentary level.

Given the relationship between a quality education and its intrinsic and instrumental benefits, it is absolutely right to worry about these things. But, again, this is to take a very narrow view of resources. Take the standard argument for the equitable distribution of high-quality teachers. Many studies show not only that better-qualified teachers on average prefer to work in schools that have more privileged children but also that when schools are integrated, principals retain their best teachers by matching them to classes with more female pupils, fewer pupils with learning disabilities, and fewer pupils who are eligible for subsidized lunch.[37] Schools serving the poor conversely have teachers with fewer qualifications, less experience, and fewer skills for dealing with the challenges poor children bring with them to school. If that is the general trend, then equality—of, say, instructional challenge and high expectations—is denied to pupils who have less access to the resources better teachers supply. One way to redress this problem is to offer financial incentives to attract and retain better teachers in high-poverty schools.

But here it important to remember that incentives used to attract and retain more experienced teachers to high-need schools have not been effective, and this is not difficult to understand. When the organizational structure, leadership, and working climate are not favorable, work becomes unsatisfying. Combine these factors with schools serving high concentrations of poor and minority pupils, and the retention of high-quality school administrators and teachers becomes a losing battle.[38] One researcher astutely observes, "Teachers have little financial incentive to teach at undesirable schools. Since observably better teachers will be hired over weaker teachers and all teachers are likely to apply for the most desirable jobs, schools with undesirable working environments will have teachers of lower average quality."[39] There are certainly exceptions to the rule, and black teachers—owing partly to proximity to work but also to cultural similarities—are far more likely to remain in schools serving black children,[40] but the general pattern holds. While it certainly is preferable to have both high salaries and positive working conditions, if there must be a trade-off, *working conditions* seem to matter far more. This means that if there is a meaningful choice to be had, few personnel want to deal with inflexible bureaucratic structures, high mobility rates, truancy, antiacademic peer pressure, limited parental involvement, and regular bouts of low morale. But notice that these conditions routinely describe many integrated as well as involuntarily segregated schools.

VS such as we find in many African-centered schools offers a real alternative. High-quality teachers are far more likely to be attracted to schools that may have fewer material resources[41] but nevertheless have a core set of shared values and institutional norms reinforced by parental and administrative support.[42] Policies that aim to undo some of the effects of involuntary segregation—for instance, transfer programs or magnet schools[43]—certainly represent one way to address inequality. But given the relatively small number of pupils such programs serve (and the even smaller number of pupils who succeed in those programs), these cannot possibly be the only option.

There will undoubtedly be those who say that ACE simply represents a type of resignation. Faced with limited options, unattractive alternatives, and perhaps even desperate circumstances, proponents of ACE merely have adapted their preferences to their less-than-ideal state of affairs. Rather than choose what would actually benefit them, the integrationist avows, urban blacks acquiesce to the inequalities that involuntary segregation produces, and ACE is the inevitable result. Rather than expand the number of alternatives, policymakers should implement assignment policies that balance the mix of pupils across a particular school district so that no one school is left tackling more than its fair share of poor children.

There are two components to this criticism: the first is about the ability of the poor to know what is best for themselves, and the second is a paternalist policy response aimed at an integrationist outcome. First, if the poor and disadvantaged are not good choosers where the well-being of their children is concerned, much certainly can be done to restructure the environment to improve informed decision making. Eradicating poverty is a favorite theme invoked by egalitarian philosophers, but its realization remains notoriously difficult given the epigrammatic truism that those with power concede nothing. Nations may adopt more progressive taxation policies in order to *reduce* poverty, but its eradication in a world of scarce resources is the stuff of fiction, and in any case the more privileged always will benefit from various other genetic, environmental, and interpersonal advantages.

Be that as it may, serious efforts to mitigate inequities are both feasible and afoot: guaranteed equitable access to affordable health care, more transparent school registration processes, and extra resources for schools serving more poor children—these are all consistent with VS. But if concerns for equality govern how we think about things like self-respect, then the best way to proceed will not be to restrict parental liberty—which will affect minority liberty as well (recognized freedoms of association and movement make this improbable from the outset)—but to expand the quality of choices available to the poor and to make sure that the social bases of self-respect inform the choices they make. This would certainly include having access to reliable information but also means supplying real alternatives in seeking educational equality when segregation defines much of their experience to begin with. Second, to the suggestion that integrationist policies should be adopted rather than ones that may harden patterns of segregation, I have responded to many of these concerns in Chapters 1, 2, and 4. There I examined both voluntary and involuntary factors that make spatial concentrations inevitable. In any case, as I have argued, mixing and dispersal policies unavoidably involve asymmetrical power relations inasmuch as the minority group they are intended to "help" is too often adversely affected, in part because the attitudes and assumptions underwriting those policies assume schools with minority—and perhaps especially black—concentrations to be inferior.

There can be no question whether certain risks attend VS where the matter of educational equality is concerned. The provocative claim that black disadvantage is caused not only by fewer material resources but also by a "lack of social and cultural capital, which can only be acquired through interracial interaction"[44] is an unwittingly racist assumption that takes a deficit view of education controlled by minorities as well as a curiously narrow view of which resources for self-respect really matter.[45]

Citizenship

ACE promotes critical thinking skills that enable black children to question, explore, and understand causes and their effects. This begins by situating children within a meaningful and relevant cultural framework so that learning can proceed from a coherent center. Only after children are properly centered, its apologists argue, are they prepared to confront alternative understandings. In other words, they will not possess the tools for questioning their cultural bearings without first being led to a world view that focuses on individuals of African descent across the span of human history. Here we recognize a similar epistemological benefit to the one we encountered in the previous case study.

Dei suggests that ACE entails a political education that equips teachers and pupils with the cultural capital necessary to eradicate "the structural conditions that marginalize the existence of certain segments of the school population."[46] But because ACE is principally concerned with the emancipation and empowerment of black people, its core beliefs are inspired by, and connected to, the struggles of African peoples around the world: "[ACE] seeks the truthful reconstitution of Afrikan [sic] history and culture and transformation of the Afrikan man and woman and their world ... It is informed by the struggles of fellow Afrikans and by similar struggles of other people. It aspires ultimately to inform concretely and positively the human condition."[47] This orientation toward demarginalization on the one hand and orientation toward a pan-African consciousness on the other is, then, a precondition for "freedom" in learning. The aim of ACE, like those of many other community-based schooling practices, is to counter the depersonalizing environments of bureaucratic public schools by providing more meaningful curricula and instruction; stronger relations between teachers, staff, and pupils; more intimate surroundings; opportunities for exploration; and generally a more caring milieu. Taken together these form the bonding capital that serves as the basis for civic virtue.

Again, the critic might say, that is all fine. But how well could ACE possibly prepare African American children for building bridges with others who do not share their world view? How will an education centered on one's own cultural group prepare one for a shared fate with others? As I argued in Chapter 4, focusing on the needs of one's group does not necessarily lead to troubling forms of ethnocentrism. Rather, ACE can simply provide the original context from which others are seen, understood, and appreciated. "Before a group can enter the open society," Stokely Carmichael (Kwame Ture) and Charles Hamilton observe, "it must first close ranks. By this we mean that group solidarity is necessary before a group can operate effectively from a bargaining position of strength in a pluralistic society."[48] Closing ranks coincides with the notion of cultural coherence. On this view, the road to citizenship must first be paved with its psychological precursors. Provided that ACE entails the essential democratic features—namely, nonrepression of reason (including the freedom to dissent), nondiscrimination, and reasonable engagement with different views in a pluralist society[49]—children in African-centered schools will have been prepared for life in a democratic society, even if that life outside of the workplace remains rather segregated.[50] But nor does a learning environment infused with ACE preclude or inhibit critical thinking. Higher-order thinking skills stand central in its pedagogy and certainly to a degree beyond what many African American children currently experience in mainstream schools.

Even though African-centered schools are, in practice, staffed almost entirely by black people and undeniably preoccupied with "blackness," there is nothing in the curriculum or the underlying philosophy to suggest that separatism per se, or segregation outside the school, is its aim. Proponents of ACE do not reject all knowledge offered from non-African-centered perspectives. Rather, the purview of ACE is inclusive; it accepts the best of what mainstream culture has to offer.[51] Although evidence for the time being is anecdotal (these are certainly the answers that I heard myself time and again), African-centered teachers routinely report that they are far more inclusive of diverse cultural, historical, and literary traditions than their public or private school counterparts. Such an expansive approach suggests that ACP is entirely compatible with an education that prepares one for flourishing in a democratic society—but also one, if we are honest, that will remain largely segregated. So while ACE recognizes the need to equip black pupils with the skills and dispositions necessary for thriving in a democratic society, its more immediate aims are to "eliminate those bureaucratic and classroom practices that prevent African-American children from competing on an equal footing with their non-minority counterparts."[52] African-centered schools accomplish this, like other community-based schools, by supplying pupils with strong role models and mentors, a more culturally intimate and caring school ethos, more culturally relevant curricula, and high expectations.

The purpose of ACE is therefore not to encourage pupils to separate themselves from the multicultural American world in which they live or to disparage members of other cultural groups. Indeed, defenders of ACE repudiate the suggestion that African-centered schools represent just another kind of ethnocentrism that valorizes its own accomplishments at the expense of others. Rather, African-centered schools simply provide essential learning opportunities to pupils that are missing from mainstream public schools—ones where it is possible to cultivate both the cognitive and noncognitive dispositions necessary for constructing, maintaining, participating in, and critiquing mainstream institutions. The relevant noncognitive dispositions would include things like assertiveness, self-control. and perseverance, while the cognitive dispositions certainly would include a capacity for understanding, respecting, and evaluating differing views in a pluralist environment in which there are multiple, often conflicting, conceptions of the good, described in cultural, philosophical, or political terms.

Criticism

Because of the psychological and physical violence endemic to the experience of black children in public schools and the historic persistence of systematically misrecognizing black people in American society achieved partly through the erasure of African American cultural history in schools, a strong case can indeed be made for both responsive and voluntarily separate schooling. Moreover, I have shown that ACE is compatible with our framing principles. Even so, this does not absolve ACE from other difficulties. ACE is an instance of VS on cultural grounds, but does this idealized culture not possibly conceal elements that potentially compromise its mission and success?

Cultural Essentialism

Earlier I noted that ACP aims to impress on black children a firm understanding of "who they are." Language like this induces many critics to argue that ACP (and black nationalism generally) essentializes "blackness"/"Africanness"; romanticizes African and African American history; and elevates heterosexist, patriarchal norms to privileged heights at the expense of women, sexual minorities, and persons of mixed race.[53] Further, ACE also stands accused of glossing over important social class distinctions among persons of African descent, lending itself to the construction and maintenance of "African tradition" as the property of the ruling classes and as something that may not necessarily function to protect and recover an authentic ethnic identity.[54] In other words, ACE stands accused of failing to recognize or respect the diversity of black American experience or identity and of seeking to impose a system of "foreign" values on children, some of which (e.g., patriarchal sexism euphemistically dressed up as gender "complementarity") might be just as damaging as white racism. This tendency is addressed with characteristic incision by bell hooks: "Many African-centred critiques trash Eurocentrism for its unitary representations of culture, the universalizing of white experience, its erasure of African ways of knowing, while constructing within these same narratives a unitary utopian representation of Africa as paradise, a motherland where all was perfect before white imperialism brought evil and corruption. Utopian Afrocentric [sic] evocations of an ancient high culture of black kings and queens erase the experiences of servants and slaves in the interest of presenting contemporary black folks with super heroic models of black subjectivity."[55]

Undoubtedly, among some of its defenders, one finds unsettling aspects in certain interpretations of ACE, including a carefully circumscribed role for women, a denigration of homosexuality and gay people, and a propensity to sponsor a very limited and noninclusive canon of "black heroes" that does not necessarily contribute to, and may even undermine, its attempt at cultural coherence. Given the historical record of that mode of thinking generally, and for blacks specifically, it is indeed odd that many African centrists appeal to an underlying philosophy grounded in racial and sexual essentialism. Indeed, the reenculturation process opens up a plethora of questions concerning what it means to be black when the sanctioned definitions and ascriptions are predetermined.

Some contend that patriarchal orientations are not dictated by the underlying canon of ACE, within which a prominent place is given to historical figures like Queen Hatshepsut and to the central place of the woman—as the symbol of good character—in Yoruba cosmology. Molefi Asante writes that "the liberation of women is not an act of charity but a fundamental part of Afrocentric project . . . It is impossible for a scholar to deal effectively with either the cultural/aesthetic or the social/behavioural concentrations without attention to the historic impact and achievement of women within the African community."[56] Yet high principles are no guarantee against sexism, overt and covert, and some practitioners of ACE, like some practitioners of liberal arts education, are guilty of denigrating women even as they idealize all things feminine.

The very real result of an essentialized past may be the denigration of "real" black culture. That is to say, the peril of championing a fictional black culture is that only those who conform to the prescribed roles and typologies of blackness can pass muster with those who police the boundaries of authenticity. Critics of ACE in this regard are fueled by statements such as that by one of its leading lights, Molefi Asante, who declares, "When I say that [Supreme Court Justice] Clarence Thomas is not black I am not saying anything about his complexion or his ancestry; I am rather speaking about virtue."[57] Yet if the logic of the African-centered story is essentially "racial" or "ethnic/cultural," it risks being interpreted as no more than the opposite of whiteness, for its guiding principles will have been "formed largely within the domain assumptions of a science it opposes."[58] That is to say, gate keeping the boundaries of authentic blackness is susceptible to the same structural domination to which ACE is unconditionally opposed. One result is an inversion of the binaries of discourses that legitimize domination; also, those who affirm black identities that do not conform to the figured world of ACE risk being condemned as "selling out" or aping white norms. Guided by cultural notions reconstructed from ancient and misty origins, ACE may be a parochial instance of "structural nostalgia," which creates a mythical past to avoid constructive dialogue with the real past, present, and future.[59]

As the foregoing discussion suggests, there is much in ACE, including some of its questionable historical revisionism, that is vulnerable to criticism. Even so, I do not join those who rush to caricature ACE, dismissing it as "gallant but misguided"[60] while misperceiving the important aims of African-centered theory and practice. I concur with Patricia Hill Collins, who observes, "The deep-seated belief in the promise of Afrocentrism [*sic*] by many everyday African Americans cannot be analyzed away as false consciousness. This would only aggravate existing divisions both between Black academics and African Americans outside the academy and among Black intellectuals within higher education. Much more is at stake than questions of the logical consistency or empirical merit of Afrocentrism."[61] On Collins's view, ACE is a completely understandable response to "epistemic imperialist violence" and may be desirable so long as racism—and, I would add, segregation tout court—continues to inform many of the schooling practices available to black children.[62] Therefore, in the final analysis, even essentialism in ACE may be an unavoidable but also needed—albeit provisional—pedagogical tactic. It is unavoidable because all identities, including white ones, possess essentialist trappings. No identities are unimagined or absent of biased historical interpretation. Indeed, whether from a socioethnic or developmental psychological perspective, the very idea of identity is essentialist by nature. Historical accuracy is important, to be sure, but equally important is the quality of the imagination in delineating a personal and collective identity worth embracing.

Given the smorgasbord of ephemeral identities served up by popular culture, including many associated with street corner narcotics, unemployment, and gang violence, those offered by ACE are an inspiring and desirable alternative. Further, to the aforementioned concerns about "structural nostalgia," ACE advocates can simply point out that integrationism is also based on various historical myths—such as equal opportunity—that do harm to black children. Essentialism may also be a needed pedagogical tactic, because its idealized cultural construction provides (in ways that integrated environments cannot) the cultural coherence that has proven effective for emotional healing and the sociopolitical empowerment of black youth. In her visit to an African-centered school on the American east coast, noted critical race theorist Gloria Ladson-Billings observed, "I was amazed at the sheer number of pupils in attendance who had previously been identified by traditional public schools as mentally, emotionally, or learning disabled. Of course, in this setting it was virtually impossible to distinguish the formerly 'labelled' children because they were performing on par with the other pupils."[63] A healthy black identity development[64] requires that one come to terms with one's own identity status before attempting integration with a broader social identity.[65] African-centered pedagogy provides an institutional structure in which this development can take place.

But the essentialism of ACE must be provisional, and this is for two reasons. First, the cultural coherence that ACE provides is not able (nor is it meant) to shelter black children from other cultural expressions or identities, including the many ways of being black in America and in the world.

Indeed, all persons possess culturally hybrid identities, and the blending of those (hybrid) cultures leads to continual adaptation and change. Important to note, the overwhelming majority of children who graduate from African-centered primary schools move on to non-African-centered school environments, and many if not most also do not have parents who sustain African-centered practices at home. Indeed, one of the biggest challenges that teachers in African-centered schools face, particularly in poor neighborhoods, is the general lack of correspondence between the culture of the home/neighborhood and that of the school. In other words, cultural coherence may only exist within the walls of the school and not beyond. Consequently, teachers and staff struggle to maintain a notion of black identity and culture that may not closely correspond with the notions of identity and culture that children and their parents confront daily.

As I stated earlier, the development of the psychological resources important to healthy identity can be liberating, but these resources might also turn out to be ineffective for facing unforeseen challenges. The worth of an African-centered education, then, will be measured in terms of how well it prepares its pupils to leave the sheltered environment in which they have been educated. This necessarily includes a cultural anchoring not only for vigorous and healthy identity development but also for critical thinking skills that should be at the heart of any citizenship education worth its name. These skills are vital for developing in children the capacities to examine the ways that mass media depict the plight of the dispossessed in Somalia or Niger as well as in North Philadelphia and Brussels. But these skills must also be able to tackle problems of greed, corruption, and ethnic strife on the African continent as well as the machinations of the global economy that threaten to destabilize African cultures more than colonialism ever did. Finally, these critical thinking capacities must also enable pupils to question the core beliefs and habits inculcated in African-centered schools. In other words, if ACE is true to its own objectives in fostering higher- and lower-order thinking skills, there will be no indoctrination.

The second reason essentialism must be provisional is that the black identities ACE fosters may minimize the fact that many black youth have sufficient agency to create their own viable and valuable identities and communities. Ironically, then, African-centered schools provide a haven within which black youth can create themselves, though perhaps not in the image imagined in ACE (which, after all, may not be culturally relevant to the experiences of black youth). Rather than seeking in every instance to replace the cultural contributions that black youth have to offer, proponents of ACE would do well to consider the alternate cultural experiences that black youth express and have reason to value.[66] Doing so will help proponents of ACE avoid the trappings of identity politics—namely, collective agendas swallowing up individual expression and also the habit of downplaying important social class and sexual differences that agitate against uniform cultural identities.

There is no point in denying that certain personalities and trends within African American culture risk reproducing the kind of misrecognition upon which relations of dominance rest—that is, through an essentialized and exclusionary black identity. Yet given the strength of institutional racism and the way that it perniciously structures residential patterns, hiring decisions, and educational opportunity, I must again stress that an essentialized—albeit provisional—discourse that valorizes black culture and identity as a means of providing empowerment and hope for the future may not be as ill advised as many think. Again, Collins notes, "Despite its problematic treatment of gender, economic class, and sexuality, Afrocentrism [sic] remains important to both Black men and women. In a climate of institutionalized racism that valorises Whiteness, Afrocentrism offers an affirmation of Blackness, a love ethic directed toward Black people. In this sense, it reaches out to everyday African American women and men in ways lost to even the best academic antiracist, feminist, Marxist, or postmodern social theories. While sociology provides knowledge and postmodernism stresses tools of critique, Afrocentrism offers hope."[67]

Critics who charge that ACE is merely another foolhardy attempt to unite a disparate people may have a short-term view of things. The hope that ACE offers is as much a political project as an intellectual one. But as African-centered schools continue to grow, they will have little choice but to engage with alternate readings of the past and present. Doing so will not only determine their contemporary viability but also chart their future.

Conclusion

In this chapter I examined a case of VS on cultural grounds. I also interrogated its cultural essentialism. In particular, unitary tropes that underlie some conceptions of ACE, particularly those that "reinscribe patterns of domination rather than disrupt or alter them,"[68] need to be interrogated. So must undifferentiated notions of culture. While ACE offers a particularly strong indictment of bureaucratic public education, its racially constructed, essentialized notions of black culture and the "authentic self" are at best a provisional necessity. Essentialism depends in part on a historical reconstruction at odds with mainstream versions of black history. Yet while some psychological resources instrumental to healthy identity development can be liberating, many are not, and therefore they may aggravate, rather than remove, the psychic dissonance that many blacks already experience.

But continually reexamining how best to conceptualize ACE need not threaten its core principles; many of these will remain, though they will be interpreted anew. (So, for example, sexism within certain conceptions of ACE will likely fall away as more and more women play important leadership roles in revising African-centered pedagogy and in directing African-centered schools.) As a result, ACE may evolve into a more expansive understanding of African and African American culture, one that is inclusive of many ways of cultivating and experiencing blackness. Such expansiveness is consistent with the core aims of ACE but also with a more comprehensive embrace of humanity. That is to say, ACE and the practices that flow from this story are not destined to employ the same essentialist racial logic that guarantees the existing relations of domination. Yet the meaning of blackness—including, as hip-hop artists come under greater scrutiny, what black people themselves are permitted to say—continues to be hotly contested terrain.

As with the example of VS on religious grounds, the African-centered example is compatible with the facilitative principles of equality and citizenship and therefore is prima facie defensible. Provided that there are crucial resources in place, such as strong leadership, high expectations, and a nurturing staff, ACE can prove vital to the psychological health and academic success of African American children as well as in preparing them to enter a democratic society not only in which there are competing cultural, religious, and political notions of what is good and right but also in which most black children will lead segregated lives and encounter racism in one form or another.

As a clear statement against integrationism, African-centered proponents flatly reject the suggestion that blacks need whites in order to obtain a quality education.[69] Rather, African centrists champion a different vision—one of cultural congruity and holistic learning, where schools promote processes of self-rediscovery and reintegration into a community from whence the understanding of that self derives. The goal that drives ACE is not only a more integrated, centered self but also more successful academic outcomes—and thus more life chances and opportunities—for black children. Consequently, while African-centered schools are not the only means of combating psychic dissonance in the black community, they are rightly perceived by many to be a radical departure from the conventional approaches used to address black underachievement—and in more ways than by simply denying as necessary the presence of (middle-class) white pupils or personnel.

Some will worry that African-centered schools will only serve to amplify the visibility of poor urban African Americans, potentially increasing stigma or prejudice. But here it is important to remember, first, that, owing to residential patterns of segregation, integrated schools are not even an option to most children who attend African-centered schools. The alternatives to VS are almost always schools that are already involuntarily segregated, and these too often fail to provide the bases of self-respect. Second, neither VS in general nor ACE in particular prevent imaginative solutions to underachievement that takes other forms. Many magnet, religious, Montessori, and also well-run public schools with no particular cultural identity or core values other than high achievement also can and do serve many black children well.[70] But then again, so do most African-centered schools.

Concerning its many triumphs, a critic might say that African-centered schools that become successful owe less to their being African centered or voluntarily separate or even to their particular organizational features and more to a special x factor (e.g., a charismatic leader) that is notoriously difficult to replicate elsewhere. There is something to this criticism, but notice that this will be true not only of successful African-centered schools but also of all other kinds of schools. It goes without saying that schools with strong leadership will do better than schools without it. To the related worry that I idealize what voluntarily separate schools can accomplish, I can say two things. First, I no more idealize African-centered schools than proponents of integration idealize the typical public school as the site of equal opportunity and civic engagement. At present, far too few involuntarily segregated schools serving the urban poor supply the social bases for self-respect and civic virtue that members of stigmatized minority groups deserve. The result is, predictably, that involuntarily segregated schools are undesirable places to be much of the time.

My second response is that there will always be some cleavage between principles and their implementation. It also is important to remember that establishing an educational climate that can provide the relevant goods takes time, and it would be unfair to blame schools prematurely for failing to supply them when they must begin from a position of relative disadvantage. I therefore categorically reject the idea that ACE represents a pitiful surrender to inequality. African-centered schools on my argument need not be left to fend for themselves. As I suggested in Chapter 5, under the right regulatory scheme, schools may still be eligible for extra resources and also be expected to meet certain standards. States certainly ought to play an important supervisory role in seeing that children receive a quality education irrespective of the type of school they attend. But when the state fails to play this role, or when options available to parents are clearly unsatisfactory, alternatives must be available—and preferably ones that do more to promote both meaningful and realistic forms of equality and citizenship.

7

Social Class Separation

In Chapters 5 and 6 I examined specific instances of voluntary separation (VS) within an educational context. Both case studies focused on specific visible minority groups whose position in the societies they inhabit can be fairly described as disadvantaged or stigmatized, albeit to varying degrees depending on other factors, like social class, gender, sexuality, and immigrant status. Moreover, both case studies illustrate and exemplify VS in the form of concrete educational experiments whose aims are both to reduce the effects of stigma and to produce positive outcomes in terms of creatively reproducing cultural and/or religious identities as well as in terms of enhancing equality and citizenship. As I indicated in Chapter 1, education is certainly not the only area of life in which these goods can be pursued. For instance, as we saw in Chapter 4, communities often facilitate a variety of opportunities for and expressions of civic virtue. This means that fostering greater self-respect also may be pursued in countless ways within minority communities where spatial concentration is the norm. But owing to its central role in the lives of most people, education represents a uniquely institutionalized response to the problems of inequality and stigma.

But what happens when stigma and disadvantage are less visible, owing to other traits like skin color, national citizenship, and first language? How, for example, should we respond to groups whose stigma coincides with whiteness and even historical privilege? Tackling this hard case is the focus of this chapter. Specifically, the challenge is to see whether the arguments for VS could plausibly apply to a group whose shared characteristics and social class position for decades has very much been marked by poverty, stigma, and social exclusion. Though examples can be drawn from several national contexts, to give this chapter a sharper historical focus, I home in on the white working class and working poor of postindustrial England.[1] To abridge matters, I refer simply to the white working class.[2]

This demographic category, spread over a wide region but arguably more concentrated in the Midlands and northern middle-sized and large cities,[3] is a particularly vexing one for several reasons. First, the white working class does not constitute a minority, even if many have become a numerical minority within their own communities. Second, whites are a historically privileged group, even though this privilege is context dependent, is not evenly shared, and when combined with other traits may actually produce stigma. In any case, relative to the middle and affluent classes but also upwardly mobile immigrant groups, privilege for the white working class has been significantly eroded over the past forty years, inducing, in many, profound feelings of despair and bitterness.

Third, the very idea of white separation is inevitably viewed with suspicion, and it is not difficult to understand why. White institutionalized separation by the English and Afrikaners in Rhodesia and South Africa, for example, instantiated the most abhorrent forms of racial hatred—forms established to subjugate and humiliate indigenous black Africans. Also in the Americas, institutionalized white separation aimed to systematically deny important resources to the enslaved and colonized; it served to reinforce white supremacy. In some cases, the efforts to promote white supremacy entailed cultural genocide, as was the case with reservation/boarding schools across Canada and the United States and with "stolen generations" of aboriginals taken from their families in Australia. These and other examples have led David Gillborn to say, "Historically, white identity has only ever been destructive and violent."[4]

Yet when your social class position is one of severe disadvantage, or when pride in your working-class identity has been all but erased, is the option for VS available to you? And if it is, are the essential resources necessary for promoting self-respect and civic virtue available? Unlike the previous two case studies, where institutions—and schools in particular—have been erected to address a situation of disadvantage and marginality, except for morally reprehensible forms of white nationalism, most institutions around which white working-class identities were based (e.g., trade unions, churches) have faded inexorably into the background. So the white working-class problem poses a dilemma. While not entirely unique (other white minority communities can be examined as separate cases), it nevertheless raises important questions and challenges for any theory of VS, specifically for equality and citizenship. However, as I will argue, provided that analogous enabling conditions similar to those in Chapters 5 and 6 can be located, the possibilities for VS can be explored, albeit tentatively.

Background

The reach of the British Empire, once so vast and seemingly unassailable, is now difficult to fathom. Yet for more than two centuries, the British garnered untold wealth and political dominance for commerce and the Crown while subjugating and exploiting nations and tribes as far afield as Barbados, Jamaica, and Guyana in the Americas; Egypt, the Sudan, Kenya, and Rhodesia in Africa; India and Burma in South Asia; and Papua New Guinea and Fiji in the Pacific. Its colonial rule was not exclusively imposed on nonwhites, as the history of North America, Australia, and Ireland makes abundantly clear. Yet particularly following the independence of India (and subsequent partition with Pakistan) and, later, with successive African and Caribbean independences, large numbers of former Commonwealth citizens began to immigrate to the United Kingdom, a substantial percentage of whom settled in industrial cities and towns in England to take up factory work and other manual forms of labor. Though legally entitled to immigrate, such a massive influx of unskilled immigrants was rightly or wrongly perceived as a direct threat to the jobs working-class whites occupied and very much took to be their special domain. By the mid-1960s, the cities were, in the opinions of many whites, being overrun with "darker" peoples (foreigners)—those whose language, culture, and racial and ethnic differences were viewed as steadily undermining the very notion of what it meant to be English.

Backlash

In 1968 an eloquent and fiercely independent-minded conservative by the name of Enoch Powell delivered an incendiary address that was to trigger both a groundswell of support and a countermovement. Powell prophesized that "rivers of blood" would pour through the streets of English cities were the tides of immigration not immediately reduced to a trickle. His entire speech, which heralded the imminent decline of English culture and values owing to the unprecedented demographic changes in cities where the ethnic composition seemed to be changing overnight, was a match set to a tinderbox. Skillfully tapping into the rage and resentment spreading among the white working class, he wrote, "But while, to the immigrant, entry to this country was admission to privileges and opportunities eagerly sought, the impact upon the existing population was very different. For reasons which they could not comprehend, and in pursuance of a decision by default, on which they were never consulted, they found themselves made strangers in their own country . . . The sense of being a persecuted minority which is growing among ordinary English people in the areas of the country which are affected is something that those without direct experience can hardly imagine."[5] Alarmed by what he had witnessed in India between Muslim and Hindu factions as well as race riots that had occurred the previous year in American cities like Newark and Detroit, Powell compared the immigration policy of the United Kingdom to "watching a nation busily engaged in heaping up its own funeral pyre." He could not imagine that a multicultural society—much less an integrated one—was possible or even desirable. "As I look ahead," he wrote, "I am filled with foreboding, like the Roman, I seem to see the River Tiber foaming with much blood." The "ordinary English people" whom, it must be said, the rather aristocratic Powell sought to defend, were of course the white working class. By narrating the tale of a frightened and widowed elderly white woman whose neighborhood had been "taken over" by nonwhite immigrants, Powell touched the very nerve of fear and uncertainty experienced by dozens of white communities across Britain.

Powell's provocation was calculated in its intent to upstage his political rival Prime Minister Edward Heath and to preempt the Race Relations Bill, whose intent was to eliminate racial discrimination in the housing and labor market. Yet his speech, seen by members of his own party as an indiscretion and viewed by thousands more as the worst sort of racist fear mongering (at one point a reference was made to "wide-grinning piccaninnies"), led to his swift dismissal from public office. The fact that he was a member of the Tory Party was ostensibly of little consequence, for his speech resonated profoundly with the voting core of the Labor Party, still at that time a much more working-class party than it is today.

While barroom prejudice and backstreet racism were nothing new (there had been race riots in Notting Hill as early as 1958), a respectable conservative in the chambers of government had now given credibility—however fleetingly—to a widespread sense of resentment and rage against immigration policies that facilitated the rapid changes to their neighborhoods, schools, and workplaces. Powell believed that an antidiscrimination bill toward nonwhites would only create a sort of reverse discrimination against "ordinary and decent" white English people. Indeed, tens of thousands were to come out in public support of Powell, many of whom had already come to the conclusion that immigrants—Indian Sikhs and Hindus, Jamaican Christians, and Pakistani Muslims—were being given special privileges and opportunities that were steadily being withdrawn from white native Britons. The Race Relations Act was of course ratified shortly thereafter, a nascent but expanding antiracist movement gathered pace, and official multicultural policies by the government ensued. Consequently, Powell and the brazen rhetoric with which he had come to be associated were to be increasingly marginalized in British politics and public life. Even so, his words would have a profound impact on British society—in ways even he could not have foreseen.

The hullabaloo surrounding Powell's speech and the subsequent fallout eventually were to coincide with the inexorable decline of heavy manufacturing, mining, and industry across Britain and elsewhere. Steady deindustrialization, global commerce, and neoliberal economic policies ruthlessly pursued by successive Conservative and Labor governments (particularly under Margaret Thatcher) facilitated the weakening of trade unions, a marginalized position for the working-class male in the technology-driven economy, and a sense of social malaise in many communities. Entire industries across northern Britain—mills, foundries, engineering workshops, and storage depots—were decimated by aggressive deregulation and free-trade policies, profoundly affecting entire communities whose livelihood depended on such labor. Council estates increasingly gave way to squalor, and unemployment and criminality too often replaced gainful employment that already was in scarce supply.

In the years to follow there would be events that for many would inescapably evoke the foreboding words of Powell about the violence to follow from multicultural policies that many believed had eroded a much-needed sense of "Britishness": the 1981 and 1985 race riots in Brixton; the 1988 Rushdie political conflagration; the 2001 riots in Oldham, Burnley, and Bradford; the terrorist attacks of 2005 in London (and subsequent attempts in Glasgow); and most recently, the explosive riots that spread across Britain in the summer of 2011. As political pundits cast about for explanations and causes, many would point to the failures of multiculturalism and growing concerns about segregation, inequality, and social exclusion. As Prime Minister Cameron had noted earlier in 2011, segregation had encouraged people to live separate lives without learning to interact with others.[6]

Against this backdrop, the arrival and subsequent growth of immigrant communities was never welcomed by many within the white working classes. The perception that foreigners were simply taking jobs and services that did not belong to them gathered steam. Indeed, any gains made by minorities were perceived to be losses to the white working class, particularly to union-member males. Equally relevant is that, from the perspective of many working-class whites, immigration from South Asia and the Caribbean has resulted in a demographic transformation of British cities that has massively transformed the way "their" neighborhoods once looked as well as what it means to be British.

These frustrations, of course, have boiled over many times. Many find it enormously frustrating that it is no longer socially acceptable—as it briefly appeared to be in Powell's day—to publicly criticize ethnic minority groups in any way, even if there may be legitimate reasons to do so. Nowadays, to express frustration about one's lack of decent schools, employment prospects, or housing conditions is sometimes couched in terms of what others are receiving, and it is this framing of the problem that is widely seen as evidence of incorrigible backwardness and racism.[7] For a minority, these frustrations find cruel expression in gangs and street violence. Elsewhere, organized political movements step into the void—in particular, the British National Party (BNP) and the English Defence League (EDL).[8] Replacing once proud and distinctive working-class modes of belonging, new group identities involve reconstructing what it means to be British (i.e., white, Christian, and native English) in contrast to others (e.g., immigrant, Muslim). English nationalism has in fact become a logical, if tragic, attempt to regain self-respect where so much self-respect has been lost to irrevocable changes in the economy as well as in the wider British culture.

Stigma and Disadvantage

As the foregoing paragraphs show, a large percentage of the white working class and working poor in Britain continues to feel left behind if not altogether written off. Even if we can bracket the overtly racist manifestations of white rage, there is little disagreement about whether the position of relative strength white working-class Britons once enjoyed has been profoundly eroded. It certainly is the case that the white working class in the twenty-first century is very much affected by involuntary—chiefly economic—forces beyond their control, which both restricts the options available to them and eats away at self-respect. Indeed, many of the reasons for once being proud of one's regional, working-class, or even religious identities have virtually disappeared. In fact, some would say that many formerly working-class whites have imperceptibly slipped into an underclass.[9] Chris Haylett explains why it would be a mistake to underestimate this:

> During the early 1990s the idea of a British "underclass" emerged through a dominant motif of degeneration. Characterised by a stamp of difference and division from the rest of us—middle class and respectable working class—this group was cast as a national aberration but also a warning sign of national decline. "Underclass" works as a discourse of a familial disorder and dysfunction; of dangerous masculinities and dependent femininities; of antisocial behaviour; of moral and ecological decay. The production of "underclass" discourse has not been limited to the predictable sites of right-wing journalism, although its flourishes are found there. Significantly, it has engaged commentators across fields of journalism, politics, and academia,

and across political divides. From the early 1990s its themes of economic impoverishment, social disorder, and cultural decline became the subject of mainstream musings on the state of society.[10]

Haylett writes that most media and academic depictions of this disparate group unsurprisingly are marked by "positions of disparagement or retreat from people who are seen to embody an unsettling mix of whiteness, 'working-classness,' and poverty. Frequently these [descriptions] are marked by silences which speak of disappointment, embarrassment, and abandonment."[11] Perhaps more than anything else, it is contempt for the white poor—concerning their habits, modes of dress, speech patterns, types of work, and places of residence—that serves to reinforce a sense of entitlement as well as an insurmountable cultural and social class divide between the haves and have-nots. When combined with unprecedented unemployment, alarming school dropout rates, and disaffection with "the system," a stigma is firmly established.

When silence *is* interrupted by public commentary, derision of the white poor (sometimes adopting the derogatory "white trash" or, for boys, "chavs") continues to have widespread currency.[12] Though it has taken on a more insistent tone in the past twenty years, ridicule and dismissal of a demographic category for class-related markers is not something new. Indeed, as any reader of Dickens will know, the history of white lower-class stigma runs much deeper than that which coincides with an unfortunate downturn in the economy. Indeed it can be argued that this social class history provides the longstanding foundation upon which current middle-class disdain of poor whites rests.[13]

This is not to say that appeals to justice can no longer be heard. Left-leaning members of the middle-class media and academia periodically express dismay and concern about the position of the poor. But as I demonstrated in earlier chapters, none of this does much to alter general patterns of segregation. Further, even structural changes with the aim of reducing inequality appear to do little to alter the choices and behaviors of the privileged. Stephen Lawler astutely observes, "The point is not whether or not the middle-classes are well-meaning, but whether they enjoy privileges that mean they can claim valuable characteristics such as progressiveness as part of their selves. Clearly there are conflicts and ambivalences going on within the middle-class, as within all classes. But this should not blind us to the ways in which it is middle-class people who are able to claim a monopoly on the normal and are in a position to make judgments and to make them stick."[14] Moral judgment heaped upon a socioeconomically disadvantaged though indigenous demographic category, combined with a battered sense of communal identity and eroded self-respect, unsurprisingly yields defensiveness, anger, and hostility toward not only the middle classes but also anyone believed to occupy a more advantaged position.

And the problems associated with stigma and disadvantage come into even sharper focus once we consider the educational predicament of white working-class children. For years, the situation in British schools for this demographic category has been rather bleak. Like disadvantaged children elsewhere, white working-class children are more likely to have teachers with less experience and lower expectations, fewer role models, and to experience curricular silence with respect to their own community and history. Taken together, working-class children are more likely to have leveled aspirations, and a significant percentage drop out of school without five GCSEs (the English equivalent of a high school diploma).[15]

Meanwhile, in many places and irrespective of gender, a number of reports suggest that white working-class children are more likely to fail at school than any other demographic category. During the past few years, considerable media attention has argued that poor and working-class whites (and boys in particular) were the lowest-achieving demographic category in Britain.[16] Whether or not that is in fact consistently true—both black and Bangladeshi children also continue to do rather badly—no one seriously disputes the fact that white working-class children *as a category* continue to underperform relative to many other groups, white and nonwhite. Many attend what some refer to as "sink schools"—a label that further stigmatizes them. While a number of initiatives have been implemented to address the underachievement and exclusion of other minority groups, only comparatively recent attention has been raised about the alarming failure of white working-class children.

Compounding these problems, there continues to be disapproval of the communities from whence many of these children come. Explanations for school failure move in different directions, but they frequently circle back to the environments in which young people are growing up: "sink estates" with high unemployment, addiction, gang culture, low aspirations, and general aimlessness. In short, both the community and home culture are held culpable for the failure of white working-class children.[17] Moreover, consistent with a conservative ideology that extols individual responsibility for success and failure, many poor white youth who do badly at school internalize the view that they have only themselves to blame. Hence their failure merely confirms what many others already think of them—namely, that they are expendable.[18]

Integration Revisited

In the wake of the July 7, 2005, terrorist attacks in London, Tony Blair argued the following in a speech called "The Duty to Integrate": "Integration, in [the British] context, is not about culture or lifestyle. It is about values. It is about integrating at the point of shared, common unifying British values. It isn't about what defines us as people, but as citizens, the rights and duties that go with being a member of our society."[19] With the tenor of his speech accenting "British values" in general and the importance of tolerance in particular, Blair's comments were chiefly directed at pockets of Islamic extremism and therefore seem to have little explicit application to the white working class.

Indeed, in the context of immigration and the "multicultural society," integrationist efforts that aim to promote "Britishness" are particularly ill suited to the position of the white working class. White working-class history and attachment to Britain cannot be compared to other stigmatized and disadvantaged groups—say, Pakistani Muslims or the Roma. In any case, the white working class is "integrated" in all sorts of ways: with respect to first language, cultural norms specific to their surroundings, and even the emotional attachment many undoubtedly feel toward Britain.

Other articulations of integration—notably multiculturalism—broadly aim at inclusion, antidiscrimination, and a general celebration of diversity. But "multiculturalism" rewards the middle classes for their own professed values and choices while inadvertently classifying as "backward" and "retrograde" the experiences and concerns of the marginalized white poor. Multiculturalism in any case disallows the relevance of social class and offers poor whites nothing in the way of a cultural background they can celebrate without apology. At any rate, multiculturalism in Britain has become a term of derision, discredited by extremists and dismissed by Prime Minister Cameron and many others.

Meanwhile, efforts to address white privilege and entitlement have been taken up in various forms of antiracist education. But in practice, antiracist education too often assumes that it is principally the white working class (and not the so-called cosmopolitan middle class) that is the object of its critique. Moreover, the celebration of cultural difference showers recognition on groups that the white working class often perceives as posing a direct threat to its way of life. Teacher of the Year Phillip Beadle writes,

> It's all too easy for those living outside such communities to dismiss such views. But I too have sat through whole rafts of assemblies about Nelson Mandela, Rosa Parks and Jessie Owens. The only white person mentioned all term is Adolf Hitler. And I've watched the white kids squirm with guilt,

embarrassment and shame as they are force fed a daily diet of the doctrine of their own obsolescence... The white working-class never really feel part of the education system simply because they are not represented in it. When a teacher arrives in school who looks, behaves and sounds like them, in my experience, they react positively.[20]

And the fact is, with the exception of right-wing nationalist rhetoric, very few public discourses are available that speak to the interests of the white working class. With respect to equality, the rhetoric of neoliberalism, labor market participation, and welfare reform generally downplays the significance of wealth disparities and distributive justice. Further, by ignoring endemic class structure and its inequalities in British society, this rhetoric does not address the effects of poverty that both define and afflict a large number of citizens generally and poor and working-class whites specifically. With respect to citizenship, the uptake of integration in political pronouncements concerning Britishness, social cohesion, and shared norms and values has invariably undercut class interests. Expressing his worries about the corrosive effects of national interests, Harry Brighouse observes, "National loyalties lead to unacceptable disregard for the universal obligations owed to all persons... national loyalties and ties disrupt class loyalties which socialists have seen (not without reason) as the primary motor of moves toward justice. Nor is the fear that workers will fail to unite across the world, but that ties to the members of their own domestic bourgeoisie will inhibit their ability to unite with other members of their domestic working class."[21]

In different ways, both of the previous comments point to this: while a disproportionate amount of attention has focused on raising awareness about and redressing past and present injustices for which whites as a group are responsible, very little has been tried in postindustrial Britain to take up constructive modes of resistance in school among the white working class. This is disconcerting to say the least, and if correctives to this imbalance are not available, antiracist education may simply chip away at what may be all that is left of a once vibrant and proud working-class culture and, in its place, simply foster more isolation and resentment.

Assessment

So where does the foregoing discussion get us in terms of VS? Is separation even remotely a viable—not to mention desirable—strategy for the white working class? Would it have anything to offer them? Perhaps more to the point, can such a group be delineated without being tainted by notions of cultural membership or nationalism that violate the framing principles delineated in Chapters 3 and 4 and applied in Chapters 5 and 6 to ethnic/religious and racial/cultural minorities? Remember that a prima facie case requires that certain conditions be met and hence that the argument only holds to the extent that it satisfies those conditions. Accordingly, each application of VS to a particular group must be tentative.

I suspect that many readers perhaps willing to entertain a case for VS as it applies to specific minority groups will be extremely reluctant if not adamantly opposed to doing so here. But are there grounds for applying the arguments presented in earlier chapters to the evidence we have about a group whose position with respect to equality and citizenship might be improved?

Consider the following facts bearing upon this case:

1. I have circumscribed a specific group of whites—hence not whites generally—within a specific national context whose experience in many respects is already segregated by social class but also profoundly disadvantaged for reasons not exclusively having to do with their socioeconomic position. Further, I have underscored their failure in the most important institution serving them—that is, schools—and the stigma that others have imposed on them, which quite plausibly is being internalized by many members of the group and undermining self-respect. In short, here is a specific demographic category whose experience is already both segregated and stigmatized.
2. Nothing in what VS may have to offer the white working class opens the floodgates to justifying white separation tout court. VS does not entail moving white communities away from where they live in order to sequester them from others. Rather, VS is a conscious and pragmatic response to a set of conditions that already exist with the aim of resisting, redefining, and reclaiming the terms of their segregated and marginalized experience. The directions that this may take are not limited to one expression or institution. Indeed, constructive modes of resistance can be pursued through organized labor, community organizations, or religious institutions. Yet given the drastically weakened associational links with these in recent decades, a strong case can be made for focusing on schools.
3. Finally, a prima facie case for VS with respect to the white working class in England must conform to the framing principles that I have outlined and defended. Its aims must be framed by equality and citizenship. With respect to equality, VS that does nothing to improve equal recognition, status, and treatment will fail to meet this criteria.

With respect to citizenship, VS motivated by odious forms of ethnocentrism or nationalism is untenable. Further, VS whose bonding capital fails to produce bridging capital—that is, that inhibits group members from interacting with nongroup members—fails to meet the conditions of my defense, owing to an exclusive focus on one's own group at the expense of others.

In short, the position of the white working class in England in many ways is at least in important ways analogous to the stigmatized and disadvantageous position of other groups. Like the case studies in Chapters 5 and 6, VS for this demographic category would need to attend to the constructive ways in which they can respond to and change the conditions under which their segregated and stigmatized experience occurs. Accordingly, VS represents a pragmatic and only partially institutionalized response to existing segregated conditions—ones where integration either is not an option to begin with or is defined and imposed by others.

Of course, important questions remain. First, does a working class identity—whatever that entails—still survive, or have the effects of deindustrialization been so overwhelming that only its vapors remain? Second, do the relevant institutions still survive to supply the enabling conditions essential to working-class separation? More specifically, can a school that hosts spatial concentrations of white working-class children in fact adopt organizational features that could be responsive to the needs of this demographic category generally and aim to foster more equality and citizenship specifically? Are there cultural resources available to this demographic category that are analogous to those that the groups from my other case studies have at their disposal?

There might be. Efforts can be deployed to recapture or reclaim a suppressed working-class history, and attention can be devoted to the local struggles as well as more regional and national struggles of labor solidarity. But reconfiguring what these resources are for white children of working-class backgrounds in the twenty-first century certainly will require more imagination than either of the case studies in the previous two chapters. Indeed, with the steady weakening of community organizations (e.g., trade unions, media, political parties, churches, neighborhood associations) that arguably once provided a cohesive center for the white working class, reestablishing—or reinventing—any of these will encounter formidable obstacles. So if a tentative case for VS is to be made, there must be enabling conditions present, combined with the right kinds of cultural resources. But before proceeding further, a number of concerns must first be addressed.

Equality

The first concern is that VS for poor whites cannot begin to accomplish what it sets out to do, because even if equality as self respect can be accomplished, this will do very little to change the actual socioeconomic conditions of which poverty is the overriding factor. To correct for segregation by socioeconomic status, integration is imperative. We saw this argument in earlier chapters. Recall from Chapter 2 that the integrationist narrative posits that mixing communities and schools by social class not only will reduce social isolation and exclusion but also will improve the prospects of those who are worse off through a transfer of social capital that the middle class possesses. According to that narrative, one of the worst things society can do is turn its back on the poor and disadvantaged by doing nothing about segregation.

Rather than abandon stigmatized groups to their stigma or the disadvantaged to their disadvantage, policies must be designed and implemented that aim to integrate children—especially poor children—with a view to breaking down prejudicial attitudes and expanding opportunities in terms of the quality of education they receive, the career options that open up as a direct consequence, and the resulting chance for them to join the political elite. Further, as we saw in Chapter 4, socioeconomic integration in particular will improve the overall quality of the school, because more middle-class parents will invest in the quality of the school, and this ineluctably will produce magnet effects with respect to other parents, teachers, and peers. That is to say, a critical mass of middle-class children bring the social capital of their parents with them and contribute to the retention of more qualified and experienced teachers and peers whose contributions redound to those who are less advantaged.

The rhetorical strength of this appeal is not difficult to ascertain. But the consistent failures of integration should surprise no one given the way the nonfacilitative principle of liberty works. In Chapter 6 we also saw that even the distribution of teachers cannot be neatly disentangled from this principle. Particularly when cashed out in terms of parental partiality, liberties of conscience, movement, and association, the exercise of liberty generally facilitates patterns of segregation. Recall, too, how in Chapter 2 we encountered difficulties with the conceptual vagueness of an adequate education: When is an education "inadequate," and how much is one's "fair share"? Notwithstanding the grip egalitarian claims may have on the liberal imagination,[22] there is little reason to believe that a majority of middle-class parents will content themselves with what is merely "adequate" for their own child; nor is it reasonable to expect that most will feel compelled to do more than their fair share. The most recent and reliable studies in the United Kingdom confirm this repeatedly,[23] and what can be said of the United Kingdom in this regard can certainly be said of many other countries.

Second, the integrationist narrative is unwittingly both condescending and naive. It is condescending because it is taken as gospel that schools serving higher concentrations of poor and/or minority children are ipso facto inferior. As we have seen, the integrationist narrative implicitly assumes that the empowerment of the poor is something to which the middle class give access. Accordingly, integration is an imperative, because access to social capital crucial for upward mobility is dependent on cultural and intellectual benefits that only the middle class can provide. Working-class children essentially are viewed as victims not only of an unjust society and its inequitable distribution of wealth and opportunity but also owing to their own poverty and ignorance. Integrationism assumes that by failing to vigorously pursue integration as a strategy for the working class and poor, society effectively abandons them to sink schools and capitulates to the status quo.

But I have also argued that integrationism is naive about what it can accomplish given its repeated failure to translate into practice. Various initiatives have been adopted to engender more integrated communities, yet even when modest integrated patterns emerge, these typically do not yield the expected outcomes. Mixed-income housing policy, for example, certainly produces more spatial integration and better access to certain public services. But spatial integration only rarely translates into substantive interaction that would facilitate the sharing of common interests or transfer of social capital, as integrationists commonly assume.

That goes for schools as well, where we find very little evidence that the way *actual* integrated schools are organized will produce impressive gains for the less advantaged. As we have seen, it is usually the structural mechanisms integrated schools rely on that create and maintain segregation by "ability," and this frequently translates as segregation by ethnicity and social class.[24] A leading authority on middle-class behaviors in England, Diane Reay in her research again and again has shown that even in mixed secondary schools that have jettisoned grouping practices, "social class looms" and a "potent sense of unfairness and unequal treatment infuses [working class pupils'] attitudes to both seating and levels of teacher attention."[25] She has repeatedly argued that England still has "an educational system in which working-class education is made to serve middle-class interests."[26] Added to this, pupils create and join peer groups where they feel they can belong, which is to say with others with whom they share things in common. Sometimes this means crossing ethnic or social class boundaries, but much of the time it involves reinforcing oppositional behaviors toward doing well in school.[27] Finally, as I argued in Chapter 2, even if we can imagine schools perfectly balanced by social class, or even a society in which the quality of all schools was exactly the same, the educational advantages transferred outside of school simply become more important.

So the strength of the integrationist argument will depend importantly on the enabling conditions and organizational features that integrated communities and schools manifest. Certainly there are important steps one might take. As we have seen, some of these may include the refusal to use ability grouping, the availability of transfer programs to better schools, means-tested vouchers, teacher incentives, court orders that require demographic "balance," and priority in selecting schools based on income. Integrationists are right to be inspired by successes if and when they occur on terms fair to the disadvantaged. The problem, of course, is that integrationist strategies—particularly those entailing dispersal and 'balance'—are too seldom effectively implemented and generally fail to effectuate and sustain institutional change.

Citizenship

So far I have demonstrated that the position of the white working class is one of stigma and disadvantage. But just because there is segregation, stigma, or disadvantage, or because there are analogous circumstances and challenges to our other case studies, it nevertheless may not be expedient to pursue a course of action applicable to other groups. Something may be morally permissible but still not advisable given its potential for abuse. Here the worry is that VS applied to this case will only sanction white racism. A consciously race-focused separation with respect to whites in the British context would conflate class disadvantage with racial disadvantage and accordingly miss what is crucially relevant to their experience. Notwithstanding dramatic levels of social exclusion, people in this demographic category are not stigmatized for being white.

In part because of the opprobrium associated with Powell's rhetoric on the one hand and overt xenophobia from the EDL and BNP on the other, the very idea that stigma could attach to white persons for being white seems so improbable that if there is stigma at all, it must be attributed to something else—for example, sexual orientation, social class, or disability. David Gillborn, for example, writes, "White people do not all behave in identical ways and they do not all draw similar benefits—but they *do* all benefit to some degree, whether they like it or not."[28] Gillborn is reacting to the suggestion that any kind of class bias directed against whites is somehow also a race bias. He writes, "In the eyes of the [white working-class] pupils themselves, these disadvantages are re-imagined as the workings of a system biased against them as *white* young people. In this way the inequalities born of class structures, institutionalized via funding and selection procedures, are racialized so as to fuel racist sentiments that project minority pupils and their communities as the problem, and white working-class youth as race victims."[29] To accept the idea that the white working class suffers from race bias not only denies the various ways in which whiteness mitigates other kinds of disadvantage but also provides fodder for manifestly racist groups for whom whiteness and class position are melded into a toxic nativist breed of Britishness.

While critical race theorists like Gillborn are sympathetic to the loss of a collective consciousness poor whites once could rely on by virtue of a strong working class solidarity, they remain deeply skeptical that poor whites can legitimately express real grievances with respect to their change in status without simply bemoaning a loss of white privilege that merely serves to thinly veil a racism toward minority groups whose advances are perceived as taking something that is by birthright theirs. One need not try very hard to find evidence for this. Demands for equality issued by the BNP invert the usual association with ethnic, religious, or sexual minorities whose position historically has been marginalized. It is of course a clever ruse—one that conveniently wraps itself in the flag of British patriotism while seeking to privilege one group, indigenous whites, over others.

I am broadly in agreement with Gillborn and others who argue that "white solidarity" is but a thinly veiled racism—that is, a morally illicit type of ethnocentrism corrosive to the core values of liberal democracy generally and likely to pollute and contravene the framing principles of equality and citizenship specifically.[30] Indeed, in a country where whiteness is unavoidably associated with what it means to be English, and where whites are not stigmatized simply for *being* white, VS that plays the proverbial "race card" simply will not be viable. Therefore, race cannot serve as the basis on which to hang the argument. To the extent that a prima facie case for VS *can* be made, the right basis, it seems to me, is to start with working-class identity and with what I will call its concomitant cultural features without essentializing what it means to be a member of the working class.

But two points must be stressed here. First, as I argued in Chapter 4, when guarding against virulent forms of ethnocentrism, it is a mistake to argue from worst cases. It simply will not do to talk about the "backwardness" or intolerance of poor whites as if racism is the principal characteristic that defines their lives or motivates their genuine concerns. Just as essentialist or unjustly ethnocentric readings of other groups should be avoided, the same holds true in this case. The stigmatized and marginalized position of poor whites and the genuine frustrations they feel must be validated, even if some of that frustration is unjustly misplaced onto other groups.

Second, while it is correct to disaggregate class and race where this concerns the disadvantage of the white poor, it is not clear to me how ignoring race would be expedient. Chris Haylett asks, "Once traditional forms of welfare and work have been removed from the white working class, what happens to their whiteness?"[31] In the British context, while being white symbolically indicates privileged status relative to nonwhites, privilege is of course relative—particularly in a class-based society like the United Kingdom. Privilege of any type depends on favorable conditions, and when those conditions dramatically change or are removed, privilege is destabilized. After all, many members of the white working class are at least partly stigmatized, not only for being unemployed and poor or "uncivilized" and lazy, but also for dishonoring what it means to be respectably white.

Moreover, derision directed at the white working class is given carte blanche in the British press in a way that would never be tolerated against other identifiable groups.[32] It is therefore not entirely correct to say that whiteness is irrelevant to the shared experiences of the white working class and poor. To the contrary, as labels like *chav* evocatively suggest, whiteness can in fact embody shame. Any articulation of VS that would take up the concerns of the white working class would also need to incorporate positive constructions of whiteness. In reconstructing positive white identities, it also will be crucially important to discuss, examine, and critique the ways in which "whiteness" is used and mobilized to pernicious ends. If this task is neglected, one should expect illegitimate racial articulations to fill the gap—articulations that will capitalize on the resentment, anger, and isolation felt by those who already believe that others are receiving special treatment and protection while their own needs and interests are ignored.

A Tentative Case for Voluntary Separation

To the degree that educational VS might apply to the segregated experience of members of the white working class, it must entail opportunities for pupils to examine who they are, where they come from, and what they care about. The historical study of class loyalties in England may bring to life a number of issues that for too long have been neglected. Young people with working-class backgrounds can come to the understanding that commonalities of class are "more motivationally efficacious than the ties of nationality"[33] and that class loyalties often have played a much more important role than integration in distributive justice. Marx argued this a long time ago. "It is altogether self-evident," he wrote, "that, to be able to fight at all, the working class must organise itself at home *as a class* and that its own country is the immediate arena of its struggle."[34] The fact that class loyalties as expressed, say, in trade unions have been considerably weakened does not mean that other channels of class loyalty cannot, or should not, be pursued. Whichever directions this may take, one task should be to resist, redefine, and reclaim the shamed and stigmatized class identities with the aim of constructing more positive meanings and associations than those either imposed by a condescending mainstream or inherited by a defeated generation that preceded it.

And this is precisely the central aim of VS—namely, to redefine what it means to be a member of a stigmatized group and to reclaim and transform the terms of one's own segregated experience. Michael Bonnett argues that rather than blaming poor whites for racism, antiracists "should be engaged in the task of identifying and enabling this emancipator dynamic, of harnessing it in the service of the transcendence of white identity, and its supersession with a politically defined identity."[35] Transcending white identity would mean coming to see one's position in society as the fundamental thing and not the incidental feature of whiteness. Accordingly, and provided that the right kinds of enabling conditions are in place, schools that host segregated concentrations of children with white working-class backgrounds might set about turning de facto segregation to their advantage. Paradoxically, then, it might be the existence of schools segregated by social class that may actually foster important forms of equality and a more engaged citizenship.

With respect to equality, recall that this entails an important recognition aspect. It begins with equal status and treatment, and from these the possibilities for self-respect can flourish. For equal status and treatment to be realized, strong leadership and role modeling are essential, expectations must be high, and school ethos and classroom instruction should take the experiences of the pupils and their families into account. But, of course, equality also has material aspects. As we saw in Chapter 3, it requires distributive arrangements to be in place that can assist in leveling the playing field of opportunity. Education cannot be separated from good health, safety, and decent housing. But where schools are concerned, it means that there are decent facilities and qualified teachers and also that knowledge and skills are promoted that have immediate and long-term relevance and impact.

With respect to citizenship, as we saw in Chapter 4, civic virtue will entail cultivating the relevant dispositions and actions that promote the good of the community and makes their lives go better. But this first entails an inward-turning move, and bonding capital serves to mitigate feelings of isolation and distrust, without which possibilities for bridging capital across cultural and social class divides are far less likely. Similarly, in Chapter 3 I argued that robust accounts will include the capacity to challenge authority, to reasonably disagree with other points of view, and to dissent on principled grounds from positions sanctioned by the majority. As a specific response to social class segregation, VS can facilitate a more engaged citizenship by fostering critical reflection on one's position in society and the power structures—political, educational, social, and economic—that benefit some and hinder others.

Targeting middle- and upper-class ignorance and snobbery, Diane Reay has argued that a "revalorizing of vocational and working-class knowledges and a broadening out of what constitutes educational success beyond the narrowly academic is long overdue."[36] Her critique is echoed by Nicola Ingram: "The conceptualisation of working-class identity as a hurdle that needs to be overcome relies on the assumption that it is an identity that is invalid within the educational field, thus denying the attribution of any value to being working class."[37] In addition to these changes in attitude, more also will need to be done from working-class actors themselves. Here is where VS might borrow something from resistance theory. Partly inspired by the work of Paulo Freire, who argued that "freedom is acquired by conquest, not by gift,"[38] resistance theory has rejected the totalizing implications of its theoretical predecessors (e.g., cultural deficit, social reproduction) and instead focused on the critical perception and response of those positioned unfavorably in relation to power. Resistance must not be seen merely as opposition. Opposition is more akin to an orientation that effectively may undermine one's own education and future prospects. Rather, resistance theory insists on the possibility of identity reconstruction, community solidarity, and constructive political action. Its proponents maintain that oppressed individuals can come to recognize and reflect on their subjugation as a means to surmount it.[39] As a form of resistance "from below," resistance theory has much in common with the aims of VS inasmuch as it categorically rejects victimology and seeks to develop alternative modes of empowerment. It recognizes that marginalized or stigmatized groups are not dependent on the goodwill of others to formulate their own responses and to cultivate forms of equality and civic virtue necessary for their own self-determination. Accordingly, the white working class in England must be capable of responding to and resisting hegemonic forces on their own terms—which is to say, even in the absence of integration.

To the extent that culturally responsive and dialogic pedagogies can be mobilized and combined with other enabling conditions, we can begin to speak of communities and schools with high spatial concentrations of the white working class as potential counter publics. As I argued in Chapter 4, such counter publics for members of stigmatized groups can serve not only to cultivate civic virtues but also to reshape the practices and institutions of one's environment. And recall that inward-looking virtue need not exclude outward-looking virtue. Civic virtue also includes uniting with others against injustice. With time, VS will entail one imaginatively engaging with others whose perspectives and experiences are different from one's own and working together to sustain or reform the political institutions to bring about positive change. Schools with such a mission can use various strategies to raise pupil awareness about societal inequalities and build solidarity with each other, and in doing so they help to remove both physical and psychological barriers that impede revolutionary thinking and action. Such solidarity inevitably begins with members of one's own group in the local context but eventually can be expanded to include solidarity with others whose circumstances are equally disadvantaged if not worse. This expansion should include joining forces with others in combating intolerance and racism.

Formidable Difficulties

Nothing I tentatively argue for in the previous section will be easy to accomplish. There are two major obstacles. First, the social milieu in which young people with working-class backgrounds are growing up is often a toxic environment—one of chronic failure and hopelessness in which unemployment, poverty, domestic violence, gang activity, and alcohol and drug abuse are prevalent. Exacerbated by stereotypes, alienating school experiences, and a scarcity of positive role models, the environment in which white working-class children grow up will undoubtedly dispose many to acquiesce to their own failure. As Jay Macleod puts it, structural factors can lead to the "internalization of objective probabilities."[40] In concrete terms, this means higher rates of truancy, discipline referrals, dropout rates, and, for a disproportionate number, unemployment and prison.

The point is that the enabling conditions of neighborhoods and schools will be difficult to create and sustain. School environments that are to rise to the challenge of providing the conditions necessary for academic success, not to mention equality and citizenship, will have to be that much stronger than the home and neighborhood environments in which a substantial percentage of children from working-class backgrounds are growing up. Of course, neither voluntary nor involuntary forces—agency nor structure—can adequately capture both the complexity of constraints and the range of feasible responses to them. Other intermediate factors—positive family interventions and role models, high expectations, and real (not rhetorical) opportunities—can produce surprisingly positive outcomes, and the obstacles are no excuse not to try.

A second and perhaps more redoubtable obstacle is the English institutional context itself. While Scotland and Wales each have their own education system and have been more successful in fostering and restoring strong cultural, linguistic (in the Welsh case), and national identities, mitigating some of the class distinctions, England is particularly poorly suited to the task of doing the same. With separate legislatures, Scotland and Wales have intentionally engaged in far less testing and streaming in their schools than has England. Further, neither country has quite the extreme public and private school distinction that one finds in England. Religious schools, too, are far less selective with their intake in Scotland and Wales. In fact, class action, to the extent that one may speak of such things in twenty-first-century England, seems to be taking place much more among the middle and upper classes.[41] In order to regain some of the strength that class loyalties once provided, different kinds of alliances once commonplace among the working class in England need to be restored. Succeeding in this endeavor, however, remains an uphill battle.

I do not wish to understate any of these criticisms or obstacles. Particularly the two obstacles I mentioned make the tentative case for VS sound rather improbable. Even so, it turns out that a responsive pedagogy for the working class is not entirely farfetched. At least two schools—the Robert Clack school in Dagenham and the Marine Academy in Plymouth[42]—have garnered some attention for what they aim to accomplish with white working-class children, focusing on the historical background, shared struggles, and particular needs of the working class but also offering them an awareness of the wider world and the knowledge and skills to access it. Innovative approaches like these, it seems to me, are precisely the work that a well-thought-out form of VS can deliver—namely, an institutional response whose aims are to improve the recognition and status of its members and to cultivate important forms of civic virtue capable of transforming that community and thereby mitigating—if not removing—both its disadvantage and its stigma. For the moment, both schools serve as an incipient indication of what is possible on a broader scale, albeit in severely modest proportion to the need.

But two words of caution are in order. First, isolated success stories will not suffice. The same criticism I have brought against integrationist responses also must apply to the prima facie argument for VS, perhaps especially in this case. That criticism is this: a prima facie case cannot simply depend on a few inspiring success stories. The difficulties of replicating success in integrated schools holds true here as well. The second caution is that it is essential that one avoid essentializing or romanticizing what it means to be a member of the working class. Depending on one's particular history, including the absence thereof, some creative reconstruction (as we saw in the African-centered example in the previous chapter) may be necessary, but such reconstructions come with a price. A person's identity cannot be reduced to a single marker. It is a truism that identities are fluid, complex, and evolving; any one person may identify more as a father, a worker, an Englishman, a sibling, a homosexual, a patriot, a footballer, a walker, a Catholic, and so forth depending on the context or moment in time. All self-definitions will be highly situational and contextual.[43] Accordingly, what those precise cultural features are or should be will depend on a variety of other factors: location, religion, industry, dialect, and region.

Conclusions

In this chapter I considered a particularly difficult case for VS. In pondering whether VS might apply in this case, I argued that we should consider the position of stigma and disadvantage attending the experience of many white working-class and poor communities in Britain. Whether VS could in fact work in a manner analogous to the case studies involving African Americans and Dutch Hindus and Muslims is an empirical question that awaits a definitive answer. But if the relevant features of their segregation and isolation are true, as indeed they appear to be, then at least at the level of theory it strikes me as entirely plausible that VS might be applicable in this case, even if it is more cautiously circumscribed. Where VS suffers a less optimistic outlook is with respect not to the whiteness of the group but rather to the devastating effects of decades of neoliberal policies and deindustrialization. Working-class identities have been worn down to but a semblance of what they once were.

Consistent with my other case studies, I have not repudiated integration as an option for pursuing equality and citizenship. Integration in one form or another may indeed be an option for some. But consistent with how I have argued throughout this book, the alleged benefits that may accrue to working-class children simply by virtue of living in more integrated neighborhoods or attending more integrated schools strikes me as wishful thinking given the way that associational freedoms, generally, and social class affinities, more specifically, tend to work. For integration to begin to have the impact that integrationists say it should, the organizational features of integrated schools themselves would need to be thoroughly overhauled. In the United Kingdom, this would require the abolition not only of elite private schools but also of virtually everything about the way most comprehensives function—not to mention how middle- and upper-class parents behave. Middle-class attitudes and behaviors, including of those who choose integrated schools for "exposure" to others, would need to be drastically different than they are. Yet given the way that anxiety, competition, and even commodification of cultural difference govern middle-class behaviors, the options for the white working class remain rather dim.

Finally, at the macro level, opportunity structures—including monies needed to pay for higher education—need to be much fairer than they currently are, creating new paths for labor market participation and upward mobility. At the micro level, different ideas about education and its intrinsic and instrumental value need to be cultivated and pursued within working-class communities. Without a reason to get excited about education and what it can offer, all the rhetoric in the world about equality of opportunity will not make a dint. Until either or both of these occur, it simply fails to inspire confidence to argue that integration represents a satisfactory answer to the challenges afflicting the working class and the poor. When segregation patterns continue to hold as firmly as they do, integration cannot be a proxy for justice. Indeed, other routes for fostering more equality and citizenship must be available. However, if the critical enabling resources are absent, then VS will not work either.

Afterword

The central aim of this book has been to challenge some of our most familiar notions about segregation and integration. In particular, I have defended the idea that persons belonging to stigmatized minority groups have reason to consider and pursue voluntary separation (VS) when integration either cannot deliver on its promise or simply is not an option to begin with. I have not argued that one should be complacent about segregation but rather that "integration" set on terms that favor the majority risks ignoring the relevant interests of the marginalized. Indeed, alacrity to combat segregation may do more harm than good when well-intentioned persons take a deficit view of those they presumably mean to help.

To that end, throughout this book I have persistently criticized *integrationism*—that is, the belief that integration will serve as a proxy for justice. In order to show why this belief is either inattentive to the facts or simply naive, I have interrogated a number of integrationist assumptions on both philosophical and empirical grounds. Equality and citizenship have served as core principles in mapping the integrationist argument as well as in framing the prima facie case for VS. Moreover, I have argued that both self-respect and civic virtue serve as crucial thresholds for what both principles entail. Liberty, too, compliments and reinforces both equality and citizenship. But with respect to the themes in this book, liberty has not served as a framing principle, for even when restricted in important ways, both our personal choices and associative memberships tend to foster varieties of separation. "Picking one's company," George Kateb writes, "is part of living as one likes; living as one likes (provided one does not injure the vital claims of others) is what being free means."[1]

Though the "voluntary" inevitably will be exercised against seen and unseen involuntary forces, VS represents a pragmatic response to the daily experience of stigma and social exclusion—one very much informed by concerns about equality and citizenship. As I have argued throughout, VS is meant to capture actions that resist, rearrange, and reclaim the terms of one's segregation. Insofar as VS is instantiated in communities and schools, I have maintained that it is driven, among other things, by a desire for equal recognition and status as well as community membership and self-respect.

Under the right conditions and with the right purposes in mind, VS is a justifiable response to social inequality where parity of participation in integrated environments does not exist. As such, VS exemplifies a vital counter public.

With respect to segregation, I have argued that we should be more attentive to the features attending spatial concentrations: its voluntary and involuntary elements; the presence or absence of enabling conditions; and even, where poverty is present, whether the requisites necessary "to create a shared consciousness of oppression that can generate concerted resistance"[2] are available. I have further argued that it often is segregation, when redefined and reclaimed, that can make the fostering of many types of civic virtue possible. In other words, spatial concentrations may create possibilities for promoting the good of the community, and these benefits often redound to those beyond the community in which they are generated. In short, I have defended prima facie arguments for VS for the purposes of promoting both equality of self-respect and civic virtue, particularly among stigmatized minority groups.

Does my account offer anything to those who find themselves in segregated environments bereft of the relevant enabling conditions? Well, no. As we saw in Chapter 7, when segregated environments are characterized chiefly by corrosive and antisocial forces, then VS very well may be an unattainable, if not simply inexpedient, option. However, whether integration is the answer to these corrosive forces also is a matter that cannot be settled *in abstracto*. Too much hangs on the position of group members in society, the structural conditions of the environment, the cultural and economic resources available to the group, the opportunity structures inside and outside the community, the concerns of particular parents, the needs of particular children, and so on. In short, judgments about the appropriateness of VS must be suspended until more is known about the presence and strength of relevant enabling conditions. As for the sociopolitical contexts in which VS may be applicable, what may work in one place may not work in another for reasons that may not be obvious to anyone.

However, to the extent that integrationist ideals take the long-term view of how things ought to be, they continue to serve an important purpose; they embody goals that aim to facilitate a pursuit of justice, even if its actualized expressions continue to elude us. Further, to the extent that integrationist ideals express valid concerns about the many harmful effects of involuntary segregation on members of disadvantaged groups in the general population, they are of inestimable importance. Further still, to the extent that integrationist ideals, to a considerable degree, have called attention to egregious forms of inequality and not only improved how majority populations view minorities but also, to an important degree, equalized certain opportunity structures, much good has come of them. Many neighborhoods and workplaces are more mixed than they used to be, interethnic/racial/religious relationships in industrialized societies are increasingly common, and growing representation of various minority groups can be observed across the economic spectrum, all of which point to important moral and social progress. Finally, in cases where integrated neighborhoods and schools create the conditions of equality that produce self-respect, equal recognition, and treatment as well as parity of participation and substantive opportunities, we may speak of an advance in the cause of justice. Even the absence of ideal conditions for ensuring the success of integration does not dilute any of its force as an ideal.

Yet the dogged pursuit of ideals under nonideal conditions may be ill advised if not futile. When integration ignores what vulnerable communities and their members prefer, or when conditions that facilitate the realization of integrationist ideals simply do not exist, it may be time to reassess. A staunch advocate of integration, Lawrence Blum concedes, "Under less than ideal conditions—including those currently obtaining in many classes, schools and districts—it may be reasonable to favour policies that do not press toward racially mixed schools, or even that facilitate certain kinds of single-race (or single-race-dominated) schools."[3]

There still will be some readers for whom even a carefully circumscribed pragmatic argument for separation effectively signals defeat. Even if one is willing to accept the empirical facts concerning the plight of stigmatized minorities in mainstream schools (facts that incidentally recur in the academic literature year after year), and even if, as a matter of principle, most are willing to concede that stigmatized minority groups have the same associational liberties to pursue their own interests on their own terms, many will continue to view VS as subversive. After all, they argue, stigmatized minorities are not the only casualties of segregation. As we saw in Chapter 2, segregation also produces moral costs for persons of privilege, for whom an absence of interaction with stigmatized minorities (or perhaps more generally, anyone who is significantly disadvantaged) amounts to missed opportunities to learn from other points of view or to expand one's moral horizons through the cultivation of virtues such as empathy.

But why do stigmatized minorities have an obligation to see to the moral uplift of the privileged? Why, indeed, when it is the privileged who so frequently keep away? Why do stigmatized minorities have an obligation to "integrate" environments when those very environments too often serve not to eliminate stereotypes and prejudice but to reinforce them? As Roy Brooks observes, "dignity harms in restaurants, shopping malls, and other places of public accommodation, as well as discriminatory episodes within the workplace are the unfortunate byproducts of mixing."[4] Further, what incentive do parents have to "integrate" their stigmatized children into a school where too few teachers possess the skills needed to bridge cultural and social class difference—not to mention ability levels—in the classroom; or where stigmatized minorities are routinely described as "difficult" or "problem pupils"; or when they also are far more likely to be labeled as having learning disabilities, sentenced to low-level instruction, or simply excluded by school policies whose orientations are punitive rather than supportive?

My critic may concede these points but still insist that the best VS can offer is a temporary and piecemeal solution. Even well-organized efforts to resist, redefine, and reclaim the terms of one's segregated experience simply cannot suffice to combat the institutional injustices of residential or school segregation. Nor, they may argue, is VS likely to address larger economic injustices. At any rate, a failure to have brought about more substantive change in the past is no reason to relinquish current efforts. Perseverance, coupled with better implementation, will eventually pay off. In short, for some critics VS represents a sad capitulation to the status quo rather than a determination to "fight the good fight."

That sunny optimism, however, is difficult to reconcile with at least two things. First, as we have seen, the repeated attempts to implement comprehensive integrationist measures often are inattentive to the actual circumstances on the ground—in particular, how integration is just as capable of facilitating persistent forms of inequality for various stigmatized minority groups. Second is the widespread and resolute belief in integration and its incongruence with many of our actual decisions and behaviors, particularly with regard to where we choose to live and send our children to school. Advocating for integration while continuing to select homes and schools on the basis of shared background and interests or what benefits our children often is to give the lie to our integrationist ideals.

It is important here to recall my remarks in Chapter 2 about social desirability bias and implicit bias. To illustrate the phenomenon in familiar terms, it is particularly commonplace for left-leaning middle-class parents publicly championing diversity and fair play to promptly move to a more homogeneous neighborhood or go shopping for a "better" school shortly before their first child reaches the age of attending school. Those who remain in urban districts as a matter of principle will almost certainly make sure that their own children get into the choicest public schools on offer (even if that means having to jump on a waiting list or playing the odds in a magnet school lottery); other parents, as we saw in Chapter 2, will offer themselves clever excuses for going private.

Travelling in academic circles as I do, I observe this as a matter of routine among the highly educated middle class in both Europe and North

America.⁵ That is to say, many of us publicly register our dismay over segregation and affirm our commitment to integrated neighborhoods and schools, but our private choices all too often pull in opposite directions. Naturally we are careful to justify these choices. We say, for instance, that we want our child to receive a good education. But of course that is what every parent wants. Or we blame the system for failing us or blame others for not doing their fair share. Further, citing concerns about teacher quality, school safety, or a more demanding curriculum, we avoid having to talk about the racial, ethnic, or socioeconomic composition of a school so that if asked, we can explain why we feel it necessary to select a better one.⁶ Iris Marion Young describes this behavior thusly: "Well-intentioned whites persist in exclusionary acts that they rationalize in bad faith."⁷

And it is for these reasons that it is almost superfluous to point out the role that liberty, as both a crucial moral principle and a constitutional right, plays in maintaining current levels of segregation. We may have completely valid reasons for favoring or disfavoring neighborhoods and schools that reinforce segregation, but at the end of the day, *we* decide whether or not a neighborhood or school is good enough for us and our children, and it requires very little imagination to justify our choices, even when "good enough" often translates as *better than* the options available to others.

My aim here is not simply to be flippant about middle-class behavior or to expose the hypocrisies of the earnest. As we saw in Chapter 3, middle-class parents, like all parents, enjoy very wide latitude in the decisions they make regarding the education of their own children. The middle classes, too, are confronted with nonideal circumstances and conflicting priorities not straightforwardly amenable to whatever an integrated ideal might require. Indeed, most of us choose as best we can given the options available. Moreover, we may or may not be consciously aware of our implicit biases. Yet none of these things effectively alters the fact that many of us who decry segregation and its harms are at the same time at least partly responsible for its maintenance.

We still may have good reasons to lament this state of affairs. Many of us can still vividly recall the momentous occasion of Martin Luther King's 1963 "I Have a Dream" speech symbolically delivered in front of tens of thousands on the steps of the Lincoln Memorial in Washington, DC. Those who have studied the speech may pause on these poignant words: "One hundred years later, the life of the Negro is still sadly crippled by the manacles of segregation and the chains of discrimination; one hundred years later, the Negro lives on a lonely island of poverty in the midst of a vast ocean of material prosperity; one hundred years later, the Negro is still languished in the corners of American society and finds himself in exile in his own land."

In that same year, in his *Letter from a Birmingham Jail*, King penned this indictment: "All segregation statutes are unjust because segregation distorts the soul and damages the personality. It gives the segregator a false sense of superiority and the segregated a false sense of inferiority."[8]

The target of King's moral outrage was an institutionalized racist segregation already centuries in the making and deplorably successful in its oppression and dehumanization of blacks. Within a few short years, massive institutional and social changes would sweep the American landscape, giving many the impression that racism had been trounced once and for all. In the age of Obama, there are many who would like to believe we are now living in a postracial society. To my mind, that impression is decidedly false. Notwithstanding tremendous moral progress, inequalities are still very real.[9] Indeed, the stirring cadence of King's words continues to resonate, so much so that any positive assessment of segregation—however tentative—will strike many as absurd given the historical opprobrium of de jure segregation as well as subtler forms of imposed segregation and its corollaries, chief among them concentrated and persistent urban poverty.

Accordingly, some critics will say that my argument cannot possibly make sense for some groups, owing to their uniquely inauspicious history. In Chapter 2 we encountered a number of arguments to that effect. Particularly in the United States, integrationists who adamantly believe that blacks and whites must be integrated in schools draw not only on King's speech but also on an equally familiar and compelling narrative—specifically, the 1954 *Brown* decision, which I briefly touched on in Chapters 1 and 6.

Remember that *Brown's* intent was to rescind the de jure basis of segregation as set down in *Plessy*, a racist notion of "separate yet equal" entailing the inferior status of blacks. Brown was truly a heroic decision, but it was not without its flaws. First, in declaring segregation in the educational sphere to be "intrinsically unequal," *Brown* inadvertently invoked a racist logic of its own—namely, the idea that "black space" was inherently inferior. Second, while noteworthy for unequivocally repudiating the despicable legal justification of racial segregation, the Supreme Court failed to address the broader social conditions in which poor black children were being brought up. Third, as I have argued in earlier chapters, there are other variables that account for (black) spatial concentrations that cannot simply be explained by (white) racism. And finally, and contrary to widespread liberal opinion in the United States about *Brown*, a very large percentage of blacks themselves were not so enthralled with the prospect of their children being integrated into schools with white children, as they were to finally have leverage for demanding both equal treatment and equal resources.[10]

A speech delivered by Stokely Carmichael in 1967 made this abundantly clear, and his was by no means a minority view: "This country has been feeding us a 'thalidomide drug of integration,' [and] some Negroes have been walking down a dream street talking about sitting next to white people [and] people ought to understand that; that we were never fighting for the right to integrate, we were fighting against white supremacy."[11] Although expressed in less acerbic tones, James Baldwin had offered similar thoughts a few years earlier:

> White Americans find it as difficult as white people elsewhere do to divest themselves of the notion that they are in possession of some intrinsic value that black people need, or want. And this assumption—which for example, makes the solution to the Negro problem depend upon the speed with which Negroes accept and adopt white standards—is revealed in all kinds of striking ways [including] the unfortunate tone of warm congratulation with which so many liberals address their Negro equals. It is the Negro, of course, who is presumed to have become equal—an achievement that not only proves the comforting fact that perseverance has no color but also overwhelmingly corroborates the white man's sense of his own value.[12]

These ideas can still be heard in the black community today. In 2012, Cheryl Davis, a PTA president in Brooklyn, New York, offered related sentiments. "'I don't know that segregation is this horrible thing,' [Davis] said. 'The problem with segregation is the assumption that black is bad and white is good. Black can be great. That's what I instill my kids with.' Would she prefer an integrated school? 'I can't say that I would.'"[13]

As we saw in Chapter 6, there will be those who merely see this as evidence of distorted preferences or sad resignation to less-than-ideal circumstances. The idea here, one we encountered in previous chapters, appears to be that some groups are composed essentially of victims who just can't (effectively or intelligently) help themselves. But this condescending paternalism must be categorically rejected—and not only because it profoundly undervalues the importance both of voluntary association and group solidarity. More importantly, it exhibits a failure to demonstrate equal respect toward stigmatized minorities. The failure to respect is instantiated through the inscription of victimhood as an essential characteristic of the stigmatized group rather than being inscribed in the behavior and disposition of those who stigmatize.

Carmichael, Baldwin, and Davis were not naive about institutional racism. They simply were aware that racism could not possibly be the only relevant variable needed to explain the presence and importance of black communities. They also were aware that meaningful forms of equality and citizenship can be achieved by resisting, reclaiming, and rearranging the conditions of one's segregated experience on one's own terms. Failing to recognize this means that integrationists, preferring their imposed varieties of integration, will continue not to be cognizant of the complex set of variables facilitating segregation. Failing to recognize this also means that integrationist imperatives will continue to ignore what many minority communities themselves want, as the first two cases studies in Chapters 5 and 6 clearly demonstrate.

Even if we could imagine a utopian world extirpated of its racism, prejudice, and discrimination, we should still expect to find black neighborhoods—of all varieties—just as we would expect to find Cuban, Turkish, Jewish, Korean, and Serbian ones. Even in a world devoid of social exclusion, we would still expect to find Roma, Cree, Acadian, and Sami communities. And it seems to me that this fact—the existence of separate enclaves—takes absolutely nothing away from what it means to be integrated in all sorts of important ways: speaking the dominant language, being aware of the cultural and social norms, being educated sufficiently well to work and participate in the political institutions of one's country, and so on. Indeed, one can live one's entire life within a segregated neighborhood and in a number of crucial ways still be integrated. In Chapter 1 I referred to this as *integration by other means*. Integration as others envision it—some unspecified degree of spatial mixing—under the right kinds of conditions may indeed produce more self-respect and parity of participation. But to suggest that integration is the only or even the best solution to these widespread patterns is naive. Indeed, we might expect voluntary separation—in which the resources necessary for flourishing are present—to do what integration so much of the time fails to do.

Notes

Chapter 1

1. Researchers also use different measurements to indicate segregation indices, the most well known being the index of uneven distribution and the index of isolation. Neither is relevant for the purposes of my argument.
2. DiPrete et al. 2011, p. 1236.
3. Tatum 1997.
4. Bauman 1996, p. 40.
5. Walzer 1998, p. 72.
6. These causes include housing policy, real estate discrimination, economic forces, and the residential preferences of others.
7. Young 2000, p. 219.
8. In the social sciences there is a large quantity of literature on the meaning of groups that I will not canvass here. For the purposes of my argument it will suffice to say that a group refers to two or more persons who interact with each other on the basis of shared background characteristics, values, or interests.
9. "We conclude that in the field of public education, the doctrine of separate but equal has no place. Separate educational facilities are inherently unequal." *Brown v. Board of Education*, 347 US 483, 495.
10. Bell 1980; Samuels 2004.
11. Rousseau 1963, bk. 1, ch. 4.
12. Anderson 2010; Blum 2002; Massey & Denton 1993; Orfield 2007; Trappenburg 2003.
13. For an example of "inclusionism," see McCarthy et al. 2012.
14. I use *integration* rather than, say, *inclusion* or *incorporation*, because the term is most often contrasted with *segregation* and because of its well-rehearsed articulations in both housing and educational policy in many countries, including the countries I know best—namely, Belgium, the Netherlands, Canada, and the United States.
15. See Nightingale 2012.
16. Kymlicka 2001b, p. 155.
17. See Eisenberg & Spinner-Halev 2005.
18. Of course most of our socialization patterns conform to our parents' choices and habits, at least through childhood, followed by peer influence, and these have a long-term impact on our own preferences.

19. In the United Kingdom there is now a booming business for law firms that can provide "*shar'iah* services" to their legal clients.
20. Through secession once-vulnerable minority groups often become majorities, and new and complex issues of minority rights and protections emerge. For a seminal discussion on secession, see Buchanan 1991. Minorities who secede then become the new majority, and secession does not remove the existence of internal conflict or the rights claims of even smaller minorities in their midst.
21. Of course, paternalistic state interference does not always produce salutary outcomes, as the raids on the David Koresh compound in Waco, Texas, or the YFZ ranch of the polygamous Mormon sect strongly suggest.
22. New & Merry 2010, 2011; van Baar 2012.
23. See Kymlicka 2001, esp. pp. 160–161.
24. See Bonilla-Silva 2003; and Estlund 2003. Both authors correctly observe that social interactions outside of the workplace among persons of decidedly different backgrounds are usually fleeting and superficial. Bonilla-Silva argues that this is due chiefly to white racism, but there is no need to employ such a reductionist argument. See Estlund 2003, esp. p. 61.
25. Consider the neighborhoods surrounding Gallaudet University in Washington, DC.
26. Farrell 2011.

Chapter 2

1. Integrationist aspirations resonate particularly in Western societies, where centuries of colonization and de jure segregation continue to have pervasive lingering effects.
2. Jenkins 2008; Orfield 2005. But for recent evidence that segregation levels in the United States are improving, see H. El Nasser 2011; for the same in England, see Weekes-Bernard 2007.
3. For recent evidence from the United Kingdom, see Coldron et al. 2010; Goodhart 2013; Hellen 2013.
4. For two recent reports from the United Kingdom, see Finney & Simpson 2009; and Weekes-Bernard 2007.
5. Coldron et al. 2010; Vedder 2006.
6. In the United Kingdom, at least since Gordon Brown, integration of this sort has hesitatingly been dubbed "Britishness."
7. The full transcript of this speech is available at http://www.newstatesman.com/blogs/the-staggers/2011/02/terrorism-islam-ideology.
8. Notwithstanding centuries of segregation along social class, political, and religious lines, such verbiage has all but disappeared in the United Kingdom in recent years in favor of alternatives like social inclusion and labor market participation.
9. Anderson 2010, p. 2.
10. Bakker et al. 2010; Farley 1994; Krivo et al. 2009; Krysan 1998, 2002a; Merry 2005a; New & Merry 2010; Orfield & Lee 2005; Phillips 2010; Rothstein 2004; Sampson 2008; Sharkey 2008; Wilson 2009.

11. Bolt & Van Kempen 2010; Ladd & Fiske 2009; Musterd & Ostendorf 2009.
12. Clotfelter et al. 2006; Scafidi et al. 2007.
13. Yet even within what some consider the paradigm case of harmful segregation (i.e., the ghetto), the portrait of disadvantage is often needlessly totalizing. From her meticulous ethnographic work in South Chicago, Mary Patillo (1999, pp. 207–8) observes the following:

    > About half of the residents in the average high poverty neighborhood are not poor; most poor blacks do not live in high poverty neighborhoods; and most majority black neighborhoods are not poverty neighborhoods ... At least from a spatial perspective, there are opportunities for poor African American to interact with non-poor blacks at the neighborhood and community levels. But this impression is rarely conveyed in the urban poverty literature, where poor African American are portrayed as being nearly completely cut off from working role models ... The ghetto ... is not bereft of role models and institutions. What are missing are jobs that pay a decent wage, health care, decent affordable housing, and effective educations. These issues are raised in the urban poverty literature, but within a discussion of the social isolation of the black poor.

14. Anderson 2010, p. 4.
15. Ibid., p. 117.
16. Ibid., p. 186.
17. Some of what follows is drawn from my review of Elizabeth Anderson's book *The Imperative of Integration*, which appeared in *Theory and Research in Education* 11 (1): 101–6.
18. Anderson 2007, p. 597.
19. Anderson 2010, p. 120.
20. Anderson 1999, p. 326.
21. On general problems with sufficientarianism, see Casal 2007, and for a more focused critique of Anderson's use of it, see Brighouse & Swift 2009. Educational policy in liberal democracies is already geared toward thresholds of sufficiency (or adequacy), even if assessed crudely in terms of test scores. It is therefore unclear how Anderson's argument, as stated, moves us beyond standard appeals for educational equality.
22. Anderson 2007, p. 618; cf. Anderson 1999.
23. Ironic though it certainly is, this belief—shared by many white liberals—is implicitly racist.
24. Anderson 2010, pp. 130–131.
25. Williams 2003, p. 236.
26. For the *locus classicus*, see Allport 1954; and, more recently, Estlund 2003.
27. Anderson 2010, p. 183.
28. Ibid., p. 20.
29. Bader 2007, p. 185. Bader continues (p. 255): "Policies of forced spreading, to prevent self-segregation and to increase inter-communal encounters, often motivated by emancipatory concerns, tend to produce counterproductive

results, apart from the facts that they are morally and legally more than dubious (freedom of settlement) and extremely hard to realise."
30. Denessen et al. 2005; Ihlanfeldt & Scafidi 2002; Tatum 1997.
31. Conger 2005; Ireson & Hallam 2005; Lleras & Rangel 2009; Wells & Crain 1997; Wells & Roda 2009.
32. Contact between persons of different backgrounds during periods of political stability is rarely substantive, even in so-called mixed settings. See Blokland & Van Eijk 2010; Bonilla-Silva 2003; Estlund 2003; and Moody 2001.
33. Hochschild & Scovronick 2003; Holme 2002; Söderström & Uusitalo 2010.
34. The unfortunate wording in the *Brown* decision was that segregated schools were "inherently unequal."
35. Swift 2004, 327.
36. His favorite example is bedtime stories.
37. Clayton & Stevens 2004, p. 117.
38. Ibid.
39. Ibid., p. 118.
40. And, of course, there are other ways that a large bank account, higher social class position, or more educational attainment can work to one's favor, even without selecting expensive private education. For while elite private schools are the chief worry, opting out need not be limited to elite private schools; it may, for instance, include opting out to be home educated, to receive an education at a low-fee independent school, or even to move to a more homogenous school where fewer high-need pupils attend or where a higher concentration of more experienced teachers is retained.
41. Clotfelter 2004; Orfield 2007; Wells 2008.
42. See esp. Kahlenberg 2001.
43. Clotfelter 2004; LaMorte 2008; Orfield 2005. Over a twenty-year period nearly $2 billion was spent in Kansas City alone to bring about systematic change, with hardly any result.
44. Other approaches include preference lists, controlled choice schemes, weighted pupil funding, categorical grants, and weighted lottery. Court decisions in the United States weighing in on matters of "diversity" and integration have implications for higher education but very little application in K–12 education, largely because admissions to local schools are so often tied to residential patterns, whereas higher education is not. See a discussion of this in LaMorte 2008.
45. Satz 2011, p. 163.
46. Bekerman 2009, pp. 135–136. Bekerman's work has focused for many years on the Israeli context, where small but ambitious efforts have been undertaken to integrate Palestinian and Jewish children in schools with an integrated, bilingual staff. Despite these heroic efforts, Bekerman reports that the sociopolitical context does little to support the aims of the school; that children self-select friendships and social interactions on the basis of shared characteristics, background, and preferences (cf. Aboud 1988; Bakker et al. 2007; Nesdale et al. 2005; Verkuyten 2002; Verkuyten & Thijs 2001); and that, notwithstanding very conscious efforts to equalize the balance of power, these integrated

schools continue to manifest a rather asymmetrical power structure in favor of the dominant group (i.e., Jewish children and their families).
47. A recent article profiling the public school choices of well-to-do European couples living in New York City illustrates this very well. Many report favoring public schools in order to give their children "exposure" to children of different backgrounds. But we cannot be surprised to read that "affluent foreign-born New Yorkers tend to live in relatively well-to-do neighbourhoods, which often have better public schools." And to the myth that liberal-minded whites are prepared to pursue integration no matter what, one Danish parent candidly confesses: "There are areas where we would never send [our children] to public school." See Semple 2012, pp. A1, A3. Members of majority groups often define an environment as "mixed" when the presence of minorities approaches 15–20 percent, while minority groups are more likely to define it as being closer to a 50–50 ratio. See, for example, Krysan 2002b.
48. Blokland & van Eijk 2010; Butler 2003; Butler & Hamnett 2011; Coldron et al. 2010; Crozier et al. 2008; Reay 2007; Reay et al. 2007; Southerton 2002.
49. Bakker 2011; Hanuschek et al. 2009; Rivkin 2000; Schofield 1995. In the Netherlands, a recent comprehensive investigation into the school mix effect also does not support the integrationist hypothesis. Driessen 2007.
50. There are some exceptions. One appears to be the "back to scratch" movement to improve the quality of school meals. See "Schools restore fresh cooking to the cafeteria," *New York Times* (August 17, 2011): A1, A16.
51. Arthurson 2005; Ball 2003; Brantlinger 2003; Butler 2003; Coldron et al. 2010; Crozier et al. 2008; Fine 1993; Holme 2002; Lareau 2000; Lareau & Conley 2008; Power 2006; Reay 2001, 2007; Reay et al. 2007; Reay et al. 2011.
52. Bell 1980; Darity & Jolla 2010; Harry & Klingner 2006; Hilberth & Slate 2012.
53. Schiff et al. 2010, p. 202.
54. Andersen et al. 2010, p. 112.
55. Bunar 2010, p. 95.
56. See "Voorkom segregatie, zet jonge kinderen bij elkaar," *Trouw* (October 18, 2011); and "Tijd voor veelkleurige voorschoolse opvang," *Trouw* (November 11, 2011).
57. Contrary to the habit of some scholars picking only worst-case examples, this also is true in the American context. A large number of urban schools serving concentrations of poor children not only have higher per-pupil spending rates; many also receive extra funding through Title I and also through the Individuals with Disabilities Education Act (IDEA) and a variety of other categorical grants. That is not to say that monies allocated for the disadvantaged reach their intended targets (but that is true in other countries as well). The funding situation in the United States is, however, highly variable but often not in the way portrayed by those who wish to contrast urban and suburban per-pupil spending rates in absolute terms. See Hill 2008; and Rubenstein et al. 2009.
58. Newman 2009, p. 80.

59. Brooks 1996; Newman et al. 1989; Merry & New 2008; Perez & Socias 2007; Samuels 2004; Timar & Roza 2010; Williams 2005.
60. *Social desirability bias* refers to the habit of responding to questions about sensitive topics in such a way that one believes her answers will be viewed favorably by others. *Implicit bias* describes the phenomenon of holding consciously egalitarian assumptions or beliefs about other people (e.g., "I wouldn't base my decision about the school my child will attend on the ethnic composition of the school") while simultaneously holding contradictory beliefs at a subconscious level (e.g., "a high concentration of ethnic minorities in a school is a proxy for a bad school"). The literature on implicit bias argues that it is the assumptions and beliefs that operate in our subconscious minds—arguably beyond our cognizant detection—that most strongly influence how we think and behave.
61. Wells & Crain 1997; Wells & Roda 2009; Roda & Wells 2013.
62. Bakker et al. 2010; Denessen et al. 2010; Driessen 2007; Dronkers & van der Velden 2013; Ireson & Hallam 2001; Schofield 2010; Thrupp et al. 2002; Van Wijk & Sleegers 2010.
63. Tooley 2007.
64. Ball 2002; Brantlinger 2003. For further evidence of this habit in the Dutch context, see "Elite kiest een school met 'ons soort mensen,'" *Trouw* (December 15, 2010).
65. Power 2006, p. 28, emphasis added.
66. Coldron et al. 2010, p. 24.
67. Manley & van Ham 2011, p. 3,141. Also see Steinberg 2010.
68. For recent evidence that it has not worked at all in the Dutch context, where ambitious efforts were undertaken to restrict parental choices within specific municipalities for the purposes of promoting more integration, see "Scholen in Nijmegen nog altijd zwart-wit ondanks advies," *Trouw* (November 2, 2011).
69. For Du Bois (1935), sympathetic teachers, knowledge of self, and a quest for truth were to be valued over simply mixing schools.

Chapter 3

1. Pettit 1997.
2. Hume 1748.
3. Sen 2009.
4. Mill 1859/1978. Mill also sanctioned interference with liberty when the exercise thereof would occasion irreversible harm to others or oneself, such as selling oneself into slavery. For other articulations of paternalism, see Feinberg 1971; De Marneffe 2006; Dworkin 2005; and Schiffrin 2000.
5. Lomasky 1987; Narveson 1996; Nozick 1974.
6. Determining exactly what "harm" entails is a complicated matter that I will not pursue here.
7. For a thought-provoking quantitative comparative account between the United States and a number of European countries, see Baldwin 2009.

8. But even opponents of the redistribution of wealth through taxation do not complain when resources are used to benefit their own communities. Transportation infrastructure, unemployment insurance, police protection, disaster relief, public schools, parks and libraries, and so forth continue to receive broad political support even in the most libertarian constituencies.
9. See Glenn & de Groof 2002. For example, private education may exacerbate social inequality in one context while enhancing it in another. Its effects will depend on a number of institutional features and demographic variables.
10. I will not explore the interesting and intricate question here about whether parents have rights, prerogatives, or privileges to have and raise children and what the basis of each of those claims is. Let me only say this: regardless of how we morally or legally frame these issues, parents do not possess *irrevocable* entitlements to have or raise children, even if that is how most of us continue to think of it. Biology does not confer entitlement. Our relationship as parents to our own children is largely role dependent, which means that we are charged with duties to care for our own children, and states have duties to intervene when there is clear evidence of abuse or neglect. States, even liberal democratic ones, ascribe to themselves—legitimately or not—ultimate authority over the lives of citizens, and when parents fail to meet their basic duties to their children they effectively surrender their privileges. Accordingly, child protection services can remove abused or neglected children from their homes and place them in foster care. So states already possess the trump card. See Archard 2003 for a thorough examination of these issues.
11. Thomas 2005.
12. Rawls 2001.
13. Merry & De Ruyter 2011.
14. Sen 1981; Dworkin 1981; Van Parijs 1995; Cohen 1997; Macleod 1998; Anderson 1999; Arneson 2000.
15. Kateb 2011; Pogge 1989.
16. Kant 1998.
17. Margalit 1996.
18. Rawls 2001, p. 59.
19. Though Rawls (2001) concerns himself more with the social bases of self-respect rather than the attitude itself, there is no doubt that self-respect is a central feature of justice as fairness.
20. Sen 1992, p. 2.
21. Brighouse & Swift 2009; Gutmann 1999; Satz 2007.
22. For the purposes of my argument I ignore here the economic rationale for public education, the obvious effects of social and cultural capital, and the individual talent and effort that structure and mediate institutional opportunities such as schools.
23. Green 2007; Hirsch 1977.
24. Of course there is a difference between being available to all equally and attempting to "equalize," although the underlying values may be the same, and the former may also have an equalizing effect.

25. Jencks 1988; Mason 2001.
26. Aristotle 1984, bk. 8.1.
27. Macedo 2000, p. 43.
28. Galston 2005, p. 65.
29. Bader 2007; Barry 2001; Deveaux 2000; Kymlicka 1995; Kukathas 1998; Macedo 2000; Mason 2000; Nussbaum 2006; Okin 2002; Spinner-Halev 2000.
30. Fullinwider 1995, p. 498.
31. Gutmann 1999, p. 298.
32. Merry 2009.

Chapter 4

1. Though stigma has many applications and may be attached to many different groups, for convenience I focus here on minorities whose *visible* differences unavoidably lend themselves to stigma within a given context.
2. See Wilson 2009.
3. But see Kateb 2011 for a recent defense of human dignity.
3. Du Bois, p. 328.
4. See Berliner 2006.
5. Bader 2007; Short 2002; Spinner-Halev 2000.
6. Du Bois, p. 335.
7. Audi 2011, esp. pp. 134–36.
8. Putnam 2007.
9. Shapiro 1999; Brennan 2011.
10. One need not see these as having civic import but rather social or even moral import.
11. Merry & De Ruyter 2011.
12. Brooks 1996.
13. See Aytar & Rath 2012.
14. Bolt et al. 1998; Bolt & van Kempen 2003; Damm 2009; Merry 2010; Murdie & Ghosh 2010; Permentier et al. 2007; Phillips 2006, 2010.
15. Not all associational memberships are "spatialized."
16. In some societies, the self-organization of minority groups is even encouraged and supported through institutional structures. But as with all things political, the ability to effect political change will vary according to the size of demographic concentration, the issues on the political agenda, the dominant language used, and the way that electorate boundaries are drawn.
17. Bolt et al. 2009; Breton 1964; Fennema & Tillie 1999; Fischer 1975; Jacobs et al. 2004
18. This outcome is not automatic; much will depend on the available social networks, political structures, the personalities engaged in politics, and current levels of corruption, not to mention the fiscal challenges. Tamir (1997, p. 215) writes, "Some associations have the contradictory effect; they threaten social cohesion, erode the social capital, frustrate social equality and equal opportunity, and violate individual rights." For a discussion of a particularly pernicious

example of associational network—residential community associations—that work against civic virtue, see Bell 1997.
19. I put aside the empirical question of whether our socializations involve some coercion, or how socialization itself shapes our preferences.
20. But for an argument for voluntary separation even under *ideal* conditions, given the tendency of schools that address the needs of one group to do a better job protecting and reproducing the culture, history, and experience of minority groups, see Valls 2002.
21. Du Bois 1935, p. 335.
22. It is certainly not effortless for everyone. For example, gay and lesbian students—also victims of stigma—also may seek shelter away from the stresses of hetero norms and like ethnic and racial minorities also can be overwhelmed with the pressure to "be normal." Yet unlike most gay and lesbian students, the visible differences of most ethnic and racial minorities are inassimilable.
23. Anderson 2011, p. 35.
24. Kahlenberg 2001; Orfield & Lee 2005.
25. Dutch Minister of Education Maria van Bijsterveldt announced this in February 2011.
26. Freire 1970; hooks 2000; Merry 2008b.
27. See, for example, Kahlenberg 2001; Rury & Saatcioglu 2011; and Wells 2008.
28. For recent evidence from the Netherlands, see Dronkers & van der Velden 2013; Gijsberts 2006; Gijsberts & Dagevos 2005; Hornstra 2013; Overmaat & Ledoux 2001; Peetsma et al. 2006; Tazelaar et al. 1996; van Wijk & Sleegers 2010. These studies point to a positive correlation between a segregated class composition for minorities and their levels of motivation to learn.
29. Bakker et al. 2010; Bolt et al. 2002; Clotfelter 2004; Doughterty 2009; Harris 2010; Jenkins et al. 2008; Johnston et al. 2007; Musterd 2005; Musterd & van Kempen 2009; Phillips 2010; Taylor 2009. But for contradictory evidence that segregation levels in the United States are improving, see El Nasser 2011; for the same in England, see Weekes-Bernard 2007.
30. Golubeva & Austers 2010; Kymlicka 2001; Nedelcu et al. 2010.
31. The examples could easily be multiplied across continents, in virtually every society. But most examples of ethnic or religious strife are deeply complex and cannot simply be reduced to some version of "ethnocentrism." Most involve power struggles over resources, and both media and appointed officials often stoke rather than quell interethnic tensions.
32. This is precisely one of the problems presently besetting the European Union. The backlash against non-Western immigration on the one hand and top-down edicts from Brussels on the other has manifested in far-right populist movements in virtually every European country. In some countries, far-right parties enjoy a substantial portion of the vote.
33. Williams 2003, p. 208.
34. Consider the case of neighborhood schools. Even in consciously mixed neighborhoods, many whites are empty nesters, attend local private schools, avail themselves of magnet or "alternative" schools offering a selective curriculum,

or simply choose a school outside of the neighborhood. See Butler 2003; Nyden & Maly 1997; and Vedder 2006. More generally, see Flint 2010; Jackman & Muha 1984; Short 2002; Stephan 1997; and Sykes 2011.
35. Anderson & Pasheviciute 2006; Müller 2012; Pettigrew & Tropp 2006; Uslaner 2010.
36. Such superiority includes apartheid educational schemes in the former South Africa and persisting segregationist education in Serbia, Croatia, and Bosnia, where the curriculum, more than 15 years after bloody genocides, continues to denigrate the other groups.
37. Fordham & Ogbu 1986; Merry 2005a; Villalpando 2003.
38. Marks 2006; Regnerus 2003.
39. Young 2002, p. 6.
40. Weinstock 2005, p. 239.
41. Fraser 1996.
42. Anderson 2010. Anderson's argument focuses exclusively on the United States—and on blacks in particular—but her arguments for an integrated elite tend to downplay sharp cultural, political, and social class divisions among blacks in the United States. It is likely true that members of marginalized groups generally exhibit different legislative priorities than members of historically privileged groups. Even so, there is little reason to believe that elites from marginalized groups will be more responsive than others to the concerns of their society's more vulnerable and politically disenfranchised members. Also see Darby 2011. For stratification in the black community, see Moore 2008; Patillo 2007; and Robinson 2010.
43. Galston 2002.
44. By "reasonable," I mean efforts that involve the knowledgeable and willing consent of those affected and also efforts that do not place the burden of desegregation on those least advantaged. This would describe certain voluntary desegregation schemes.

Chapter 5

1. Joppke 2004; van Oers et al. 2010.
2. Penninx et al. 2004; Vasta 2007.
3. Berry et al. 2006; Bader 2012.
4. And in Europe, both explicit and implicit vestiges of Christianity continue to infuse the political culture as well as the identities and aims of its public institutions. Baldwin (2009, p. 170) writes, "The American observer of Europe is often puzzled at claims to secularism in the Old World, since displays of religion here are so frequent, so palpable, and so public, and yet—apparently—so taken for granted as to pass unnoticed." In the Netherlands, for instance, several of the prominent political parties are explicitly Christian, several Christian holidays are publicly recognized (Ascension Day, Pentecost, Easter, etc.), and Protestant or Catholic schools—which comprise some 60 percent of all schools—are funded by the state.
5. Spiecker & Steutel 2001.

6. "Black" (*zwart*) is indeed how schools with high concentrations of minorities are labelled in the Netherlands, though there is some discrepancy regarding exactly what percentage of minorities a school must have before it is labelled "black." A school also can be labelled "black" without actually having any black pupils, but as the label suggests, a black school is believed by many to be simply inferior.
7. CBS 2013.
8. Merry & Driessen 2013.
9. Driessen & Merry 2006.
10. Teunissen 1990.
11. Bloemberg & Nijhuis 1993; Driessen & Merry 2006; Merry & Driessen 2008; Roelsma-Somer 2008; Teunissen 1990.
12. Merry & Driessen 2012.
13. The frequency of inspections for most schools is only once every few years, while for Islamic schools the inspections have been more frequent given the concerns about educational quality.
14. Bloemberg & Nijhuis 1993; Roelsma-Somer 2008.
15. Kurien 2001, p. 289. Many ethnic churches and mosques operate as welfare and security institutions. See Penninx & Schrover 2001.
16. But for anecdotal evidence to the contrary, see Vink 2010.
17. Badawi 2005; Merry 2007.
18. Merry 2007.
19. Verkuyten & Thijs 2002.
20. Buijs 2009.
21. See "Ondergang van een Moslimschool," *HP De Tijd* (July 2, 2010), pp. 20–28.
22. See "Islamitisch onderwijs maakt sprong vooruit," *Trouw* (June 7, 2012).
23. Merry & Driessen 2012; Van Niekerk 2004.
24. This is according to comments I heard on several occasions from Dutch Hindu educators.
25. Ladson-Billings 2009; Sleeter & Cornbleth 2011.
26. About half of the children are from low-educated families.
27. Merry & Driessen 2012.
28. Merry & Driessen 2013.
29. Cf. Qur'an 33:35.
30. Kelly 1999; Zine 2008. Both references are from Canada, which, not incidentally, hosts a much higher educated Muslim population than the Netherlands.
31. Hermans 1995; Haw 1994. But for recent evidence of improvement for girls, see Crul & Holdaway 2009; and Crul & Schneider 2009.
32. See "Te weinig vrouwen bereiken de top" (February 17, 2011).
33. See Slaughter 2012.
34. Istanbouli 2000; Manji 2003; Zine 2008.
35. See Thompson 2011.
36. Karsten et al. 2006; Musterd & Ostendorf 2009; Vedder 2006.
37. Van Niekerk 2004, 2007; Verkuyten & Thijs 2002; Villalpando 2003.
38. The literature on multiculturalism is replete with examples, but for educational examples among the Maori in New Zealand, among First Nations tribes

in Canada, and with respect to Israeli-Palestinian bilingual education in Israel, see, respectively, Waitere & Court 2008; Haig-Brown & Hodson 2008; and Bekerman 2008.
39. Van Niekerk 2004.
40. Suriname was a Dutch colony until 1975.
41. Dagevos & Gijsberts 2007.
42. See "Schaamte staat als muur rond Marokkanen," *De Volkskra*nt (May 11, 2010); "Wat bezielt de Marokkaan?," *Elsevier* (May 8, 2010), pp. 24–28; and "Joden op de Vlucht," *De Telegraaf* (June 26, 2010).
43. See "Niets te Vrezen," *De Groene Amsterdamer* (February 18, 2010), pp. 26–28.
44. Istanbouli 2000, pp. 220–221. I use an American example for three reasons. First, unlike a number of other Western countries (notably, England, Canada, and the United States), only one Islamic secondary school in the Netherlands for the moment remains open. Second, what little available ethnographic material from Islamic high schools there is comes from North America. Third, and perhaps most important, the vast majority of pupils who attend Islamic primary schools leave to attend non-Islamic schools. The quotation, on the other hand, comes from an Islamic secondary school where kids arguably are more sheltered and yet where critical thinking on a range of issues is abundantly in evidence.
45. Clayton 2006; Dwyer 1998; Feinberg 1980; Gardner 1988; Macleod 2003.
46. Burtt 1994, 1996; De Ruyter & Merry 2009; Merry 2005b; Rosenblum 1998; Schinkel 2010; Swaine 2006.
47. Burtt 1994; Merry 2005c; Mills 2003; Schinkel 2010; Swaine 2006, 2009, 2010, 2012.
48. Brighouse 2006; White 2011.
49. But for evidence of changing attitudes, see "Moslims Vernederlandsen," *De Volkskrant* (March 24, 2011); and "Ik vertel over christenen en joden," *De Volkskrant* (April 16, 2010). For further evidence on changing attitudes about homosexuality, see Merry 2005d.
50. Merry & Karsten 2010.
51. De Ruyter & Merry 2009.
52. Given the way weighted pupil funding operates in the Netherlands, schools with higher concentrations of minorities—hence Hindu and Islamic schools—are more likely to have extra staff.
53. To the contrary, not only are conservative Christian political parties still represented in the Parliament; by far the most conservative religious schools in the Netherlands are to be found in the Christian Reformed tradition. Further, one of the main Dutch political parties, the SGP (*Staatkundig Gereformeerde Partij*), does not allow its female members to vote, and in the run up to the 2012 national elections, its party leader, Kees van der Staaij, was forced to defend his antiabortion remarks in late summer of 2012 that women had some natural mechanism for rejecting pregnancy after rape.
54. Baldwin (2009, p. 169) correctly reports figures from Switzerland, Austria, Germany, France, and the United Kingdom, where belief in the efficacy of

good luck charms, fortune telling, and astrology is exceptionally high. He writes, "In the most secular nations [of Europe] there seems to be belief in some higher power that is not captured by a simple question on a survey about faith in God."
55. Blokland & Van Eijk 2010; Dronkers & van der Velden 2013.
56. Merry & Driessen 2012; Spinner-Halev 2005.

Chapter 6

1. Kunjufu 2004.
2. West 1993.
3. African-centered schools can also be found in Canada—particularly in Toronto and Montreal.
4. Kunjufu 2004.
5. By *culture*, I mean the collective interaction of behavioral patterns, habits, attitudes, beliefs, and modes of interaction, all of which intermingle and inform a person's outlook. Culture informs how I experience the world and respond to phenomena. Culture provides us with systems of meaning from whence I derive some normative guidance concerning what I ought to believe and how I ought to behave and interact with others. Culture consciously or unconsciously structures our experiences and perception and is highly relevant to how I learn and understand and to how I relate to others and feel ourselves to be members of a single group or a variety of groups.
6. Akoto 1992; Asante 1991; Binder 2000; Giddings 2001; Lee 1994.
7. Adair 1984; Edwards 1996; Irvine & Irvine 1983; Rossell 1983; Siddle-Walker & Archung 2003.
8. Fultz 2004.
9. Faltz and Leake 1996, p. 246.
10. Rossell 1983.
11. Fordham 1988; Fordham and Ogbu 1986; Ogbu 2003; Polite 1993; Steele 1997.
12. Davis 2012; Eyler et al. 1983; Harry & Klingner 2006; Ladson-Billings and Tate 1995.
13. Faltz and Leake 1996, p. 231.
14. Clotfelter et al. 2011; Gill 1991; Hanuschek et al. 2004; Scafidi et al. 2007; Span 2002.
15. Comer 1997; Lee 1994; Pollard & Ajirotutu 2000; Ratteray 1992; Span 2002.
16. Binder 2000; Giddings 2001.
17. Ratteray 1992.
18. *Missouri v. Jenkins*, 495 US 33, 1990; *Freeman v. Pitts*, 503 US 467, 1992; *Grimes v. Cavazos*, 786 F. Supp. 1184, 1992. Rivkin (1994) shows that even if all US school districts had been perfectly integrated such that each school had the district share of all racial groups, housing patterns would still have led to large numbers of blacks having few white schoolmates. Also see Hanushek et al. 2009.
19. Brown 2000; Jarvis 1992; Neely 1994.

20. Brown 1993; Siegel 1996. No higher court has addressed this issue explicitly, but Clarence Thomas did offer his imprimatur for African-centered schools in his concurrence in the recent *Parents v. Seattle and Meredith v. Jefferson County Board of Education* case (127 S. Ct. 2738, 2007), in which the court struck down voluntary desegregation admissions schemes as unconstitutional.
21. Siddle-Walker 1996, 2000.
22. Leake & Leake 1992a; Pollard & Ajirotutu 2000.
23. Parents select African-centered schools today for many of the same reasons that others choose different types of community-based schools. Chiefly, they desire a strong culturally based education, one centered on the values and principles of ACP. Yet they also care about academic excellence, safety, discipline, a perceived lack of values or sense of community in their neighborhood public schools, and a desire to see a greater correspondence between the values of the home and those of the school. See Pollard & Ajirotutu 2000; and Ratteray & Shujaa 1987.
24. Binder 2000; Kifano 1996; Pollard and Ajirotutu 2000; Span 2002; Teicher 2006.
25. Irvine 2000; Kunjufu 2004; Lee 1992; Lynn 2006.
26. Takaki 1993.
27. Mandara 2006.
28. Asante 2001; Dei 1995; Traoré 2003.
29. Murrell 2002, p. xxxv.
30. Akoto 1992; Asante 1991; Karenga 1995; Kunjufu 2004; Lee 1994.
31. Boateng 1990, p. 73.
32. Akoto 1992; Diop 1981.
33. Phinney 2003.
34. Alston 2005, pp. 206–207.
35. Kifano 1996.
36. There is, in fact, important literature that contends that black children in general do not suffer from low self-esteem. See Fine 1991; Irvine 1990, 2000; and Mickelson 1990. Others argue that self-esteem derives from academic success and not the other way around. See Kohn 1994.
37. Clotfelter et al. 2006; Hanushek et al. 2000; Hanuschek et al. 2004; Player 2010.
38. Clotfelter et al. 2007; Jackson 2009; Vandenberghe & Huberman 1999.
39. Jackson 2009, p. 214.
40. Clotfelter et al. 2011.
41. However, schools serving children with high needs often receive considerable additional resources to compensate for poverty effects. See Hill 2008; Rubenstein et al. 2009. How the resources are in fact used is admittedly difficult to ascertain, but it is important to note that while extra resources often do not reduce staff turnover rates, they can make a difference—for example, in terms of number of staff present and reduced class size. Even so, one major report in the United States concluded, "There was no evidence [found] that the efforts to target compensatory dollars on segregated inner city schools had produced substantial gains for the minority students." Morantz 1994, p. i.
42. Elmore 2000; Newmann et al. 1989; Timar & Roza 2010.

43. Entrance requirements to magnet schools are also highly competitive and often cater to suburban demands rather than local need. Further, while the average magnet school does not increase stratification, they do not appear to do very much to reduce it either. Blacks in particular appear to benefit very little from magnet schools as compared with whites and Latinos. See Conger 2005; and Davis 2012.
44. Anderson 2010, pp. 233–234.
45. It should also be remembered that VS has less to do with public versus private status and more to do with its organizational features. Further, whether there is a per-pupil figure below which it is impossible to provide a child with a quality education is unsettled. Evidence suggests that the problem with per-pupil spending is with how inefficiently it is used and not what the amount is in absolute terms. See, for example, Hill 2007.
46. Dei 1994, p. 17.
47. Akoto 1994, p. 320.
48. Carmichael & Hamilton 1992/1967.
49. Gutmann 1999.
50. Estlund 2003.
51. Asante 1991; Dei 1994.
52. Leake & Leake 1992b.
53. Gates 1996; hooks 1995; Irvine 2000; Ransby & Matthews 1993; West 1993.
54. Chowdhury 1997.
55. hooks 1995, pp. 243–244.
56. Asante and Abarry 1996, p. 257.
57. Asante 2005, p. 215.
58. Collins 2006, p. 118.
59. Herzfeld 2005.
60. West 1993.
61. Collins 2006, p. 97.
62. Chowdhury 1997.
63. Ladson-Billings 2000, p. 193.
64. Hall et al. 1972; Jackson 1976; Sherif & Sherif 1970; Tatum 1997.
65. Jackson referred to four distinct stages: (1) passive acceptance, in which blacks unwittingly accept white norms, including assumptions about black people; (2) active resistance, which normally entails a complete rejection of all things white; (3) redirection, in which it is recognized that energy spent reacting to white racism is energy wasted—rather, a person's energies are reoriented to focus on positive goals, values, traditions, and behaviors; and (4) internalization, in which black individuals integrate their sense of blackness with other aspects of themselves, including sexuality, role identities, and spirituality. The fourth of these stages represents a deeper understanding of self that requires no validation from others for one's feelings, thoughts, or actions. Internalization also entails a move toward coalition building with others committed to fighting oppression in all forms. See Jackson 1976, pp. 28–45.

66. Gingwright 2004; Ladson-Billings 2009.
67. Collins 2006, pp. 119–20.
68. hooks 1995, p. 244.
69. Carruthers 1994; Woodson 1933/1998.
70. Binder 2000; Kifano 1996; Pollard & Ajirotutu 2000; Span 2002; Teicher 2006.

Chapter 7

1. England is the *specific* focus of this case study, but Great Britain (encompassing England, Northern Ireland, Scotland, and Wales) provides the more general backdrop to research on working-class communities.
2. "Working class" is a fluid and open construction subject to varied interpretation based on several factors, including income, occupation, educational attainment, attitudes, preferences, and social status. Working-class status also—like any other—need not be a fixed status, and persons who decidedly identify with middle-class attitudes and preferences may nevertheless be poor in terms of income and wealth. While many continue to talk about a "respectable working class," increasingly the line is blurred between what it means to be working class and what it means to be simply white, poor, and excluded. However, in this chapter I use the term very broadly to capture persons whose occupations describe old and new forms of manual labor.

    As a category, however, working class continues to be problematic. Those who self-identify as working class are far more likely to be white, male, 35 and older, and living in the Midlands or the North, with only high school educational attainment or less. See Surridge 2007. If we include not only traditional manual labor but also the entire service industry, then close to 50 percent of Britain's population is working class. See Reay 2012. However, owing to dramatic changes in the economy in the last thirty years, an inevitable slippage occurs between the labels *working class* and *working poor*. The percentage of the working class that has entered what one can call the working poor has grown exponentially. Meanwhile, the term *underclass* has long since entered the lexicon, and many of the socially excluded are referred to with this term, though it remains a contested category. See Buckingham 1999; and Welshman 2005.
3. Here I have in mind cities like Bradford, Middlesbrough, and Stoke-on-Trent, where entire industries were decimated and never restored; large remaining pockets of Birmingham, Manchester, and Newcastle; and areas lying southwest of Leeds. However, there is no reason to limit the focus to larger cities or to the North. Clusters of white poverty can be found throughout the United Kingdom.
4. Radio 4 Interview, http://www.digitaltoast.co.uk/great-white-hopes-david-gillborn.
5. For the full transcript of Powell's "Rivers of Blood" speech, see http://www.telegraph.co.uk/comment/3643823/Enoch-Powells-Rivers-of-Blood-speech.html.

6. While Cameron's sentiments were to echo Angela Merkel and others in heralding the "failure of multiculturalism," many municipalities continue to be decidedly mixed in composition, even if impenetrable pockets of ethnic and social class concentration are the norm. Inevitably, interethnic relationships have become far more common than thirty years ago, particularly in places like Leicester and many of London's boroughs, and this is perhaps even more so the case among the working class. Yet while interethnic tensions should not be hyperbolized, as I have demonstrated in earlier chapters, facts about spatial mixing also do not tell us very much about social trust or mutual understanding. In any case, a more "multicultural Britain" has not altered the crisis facing the white working class.
7. This calls to mind the comment of bell hooks (2000, p. 111): "Assailed and assaulted by privileged white folks, [poor whites] transferred their rage and class hatred onto the bodies of black people."
8. The BNP did well in 2009 European elections, securing two seats, and in some council elections at about the same time. Subsequently, support seems to have waned, and they did not do well in the last general election.
9. Buckingham 1999; Skeggs 1997. Skeggs argues that members of the working class increasingly self-identify according to what they are *not* (i.e., an underclass). Also see the Iain Duncan Smith report, "Breakthrough Britain" (2007), which refers to an "underclass" and highlights the breakdown of British society on many levels (available at http://www.centreforsocialjustice.org.uk/publications/breakthrough-britain-chairmans-overview).
10. Haylett 2001, p. 358.
11. Ibid., p. 353.
12. Hanley 2007; Jones 2012. The television program hosted by Jeremy Kyle routinely brings on guests believed to represent the abhorrent "white trash," much like Jerry Springer's program in the United States had done many years before.
13. Bonnett 1998; Jones 2012; Lawler 2012; Reay 2011.
14. Lawler 2012, p. 418.
15. Dunne & Gazeley 2008; Ingram 2009.
16. "Poor pupils fail to make the grade," *Times* (December 12, 2008), p. 25; "White boys on free meals fall further behind in GCSEs," *Guardian* (December 12, 2008), pp. 20–21; "Social class affects white pupils' exam results more than those of ethnic minorities," *Guardian* (September 3, 2010), http://www.guardian.co.uk/education/2010/sep/03/social-class-achievement-school.
17. Though persons who participated in the looting, arson, and public disorder during the 2011 riots did not come from just one group (whites, blacks, and Asians were all involved), a rather conservative response was certainly to be expected in many of the comments of Prime Minister Cameron in August 2011. The destructive riots in a dozen British cities, he insisted, came down to bad attitudes, behavior, and choices. They signaled a "moral collapse" of communities "out of control" and a general absence of personal responsibility. Working hard and playing by the rules, he added, would allow almost anyone to succeed. Though very few questioned opportunistic hooliganism and brash

criminality in the riots that year, a mantra repeated by many at the time was that parents had failed to do their job and that there was a need to promote a stronger sense of citizenship and common values.

18. The tendency to find fault with the cultural and home environment of poor whites bears striking resemblance to cultural deprivation theory, which was in circulation at the end of the 1960s and was used to explain how certain disadvantaged groups lack the relevant enabling conditions and cultural resources necessary for succeeding in school and beyond. Cultural deficit was soon thereafter repudiated and replaced by cultural difference theory. Its advocates' aim was to avoid stigmatizing or blaming vulnerable groups. They argued that different cultures produce difference forms of capital and that one is not better than the other but that some more closely correspond to expectations in school and society. Finally, social reproduction theory was to argue that schools not only do not value the cultural capital of certain minority groups but also serve to reproduce social class divisions in the labor market and society. Working-class children, then, receive differentiated instruction according to their "probable destines." Speech patterns, clothing styles, behavioral problems, and other unrecognized cultural traits combine with labeling practices, curricular silence, lowered expectations, and few role models to produce failure. Exceptions to the general pattern shine through, but the main aspirations of upward social mobility, to the extent that such mobility exists, are leveled by the institutional sorting and selection practices in which schools engage. Anyon 1981, 1997; Bernstein 1975; Bourdieu & Passerson 1977; Bowles & Gintis 1976; Fine 1991; Macleod 1987; Rothstein 2004; Stevenson & Ellsworth 2005; Valenzuela 1999; Weis 1990.
19. Blair's speech, "The Duty to Integrate: Shared British Values," is available at http://www.vigile.net/The-Duty-to-Integrate-Shared.
20. Beadle 2005.
21. Brighouse 2003, p. 167.
22. "Poll reveals middle class most likely to say they are left wing," *Guardian* (October 27, 2012), p. 14.
23. Ball 2003; Butler 2003; Butler & Hamlett 2011; Crozier et al. 2008; Reay 2006, 2007; Reay, Crozier, & James 2011; Reay et al. 2007; Vowden 2012; Willis 1977.
24. Harry & Klingner 2006; Merry 2008a.
25. Reay 2006, p. 298.
26. Ibid., p. 294.
27. Macleod 1995; Reay 2001, 2006; Weis 1990; Willis 1977.
28. Gillborn 2010, p. 4.
29. Gillborn 2000, p. 272.
30. Cf. Rosenblum 1998.
31. Haylett 2001, p. 360.
32. Jones 2012.
33. Brighouse 2003, p. 167.
34. Marx 1938, p. 12.
35. Bonnett 1998, p. 336.

36. Reay 2012, p. 593; cf. Reay 2011.
37. Ingram 2009, p. 423.
38. Freire 1970, p. 31.
39. Cf. Giroux 1983.
40. Macleod 1995, p. 15.
41. Diane Reay, personal communication; Tim Butler, personal communication.
42. Morris 2011.
43. Cf. Bader 2012.

Afterword Notes

1. Kateb 1997, p. 36.
2. Soja 2010, p. 55.
3. Blum 2002, p. 384.
4. Brooks 1996, p. 214.
5. Charles Glenn's example from Germany illustrates this clearly enough. He observes, "Even many parents whose views are on the Left, and who strongly support the integration of Turkish pupils, find ways to send their own children to schools with few of them; Catholic schools are used by many non-Catholics for the same reason" (1996, p. 345). These behaviors call to mind the following observation of George Orwell: "All left-wing parties in the highly industrialized countries are at bottom a sham, because they make it their business to fight against something which they do not really wish to destroy" (1981, p. 120).
6. For a recent example of this, see Roda & Wells 2013.
7. Young 2000, p. 217.
8. The full "I Have a Dream" speech can be accessed at http://abcnews.go.com/Politics/martin-luther-kings-speech-dream-full-text/story?id=14358231.
9. Shapiro 2004.
10. Bell 1980; Samuels 2004. Samuels adds, "*Brown's* status as a cultural icon makes it difficult to criticize objectively. Once an idea achieves this status, any notions that appear to be contrary to the established view must bring to bear an enormous array of evidence simply to be heard. Those challenged with giving the unorthodox idea a fair hearing have difficulty doing so because of the latent static of unchallenged assumptions from which they proceed" (p. 12).
11. Carmichael & Hamilton 1967.
12. Baldwin 1962, p. 127.
13. Kleinfeld 2012.

References

Aboud, F. 1988. *Children and Prejudice*. Oxford: Blackwell.
Adair, A. 1984. *Desegregation: The Illusion of Black Progress*. Lanham, MD: University of Maryland Press.
Akoto, A. 1992. *Nationbuilding: Theory and Practice in Afrikan Centered Education*. Washington, DC: Pan Afrikan World Institute.
Alston, K. 2005. "Knowing Blackness, Becoming Blackness, Valuing Blackness," in George Yancy, ed., *White on White/Black on Black*, New York: Bowman & Littlefield.
Andersen, S., et al. 2010. "School Segregation in Danish Public Schools," in Bakker, J., Denessen, E., Peters, D., & Walraven, G., eds., *International Perspectives on Countering School Segregation* (pp. 99–113), Antwerp: Garant.
Anderson, E. 1999. "What is the Point of Equality?" *Ethics* 109: 287–337.
Anderson, E. 2007. "Fair Equality of Opportunity: A Democratic Equality Perspective." *Ethics* 117: 595–622.
Anderson, E. 2010. *The Imperative of Integration*. Princeton: Princeton University Press.
Anderson, C. J., & Pasheviciute, A. 2006. "How Ethnic and Linguistic Heterogeneity Influence Prospects for Civil Society: A Comparative Study of Citizenship Behaviour." *Journal of Politics* 68 (4): 783–802.
Anyon, J. 1981. "Social Class and School Knowledge." *Curriculum Inquiry* 11: 3–42.
Anyon, J. 1997. *Ghetto Schooling*. New York: Teachers College Press.
Aristotle. 1984. *The Complete Works of Aristotle*, trans. B. Jowet. Princeton: Princeton University Press.
Arthurson, K. 2005. "Social Mix and the Cities." *Urban Policy and Research* 23 (4): 519–523.
Asante, M. 1991. "The Afrocentric Idea in Education." *Journal of Negro Education* 60 (2): 170–180.
Asante, M. 2001. *African-American History: A Journey of Liberation*. Saddle Brook, NJ: Peoples.
Asante, M., & A. Abarry, eds. 1996. *African Intellectual Heritage: A Book of Sources*. Philadelphia: Temple University Press.
Audi, R. 2010. *Democratic Authority and the Separation of Church and State*. Oxford: Oxford University Press.
Aytar, V., & Rath, J. 2012. *Selling Ethnic Neighbourhoods: The Rise of Neighbourhoods as Places of Leisure and Consumption*. New York: Routledge.

Badawi, H. 2005. "Parental Reasons for School Choice: A Case Study of an Islamic School in the USA." PhD dissertation, University of Minnesota.

Bader, V. 2007. *Secularism or Democracy? Associational Governance of Religious Diversity*. Amsterdam: University of Amsterdam Press.

Bader, V. 2012. "Associational Governance of Ethno-Religious Diversity in Europe. The Dutch Case," in Smith, R., ed., *Citizenship, Borders, and Human Needs* (pp. 273–297), Philadelphia: University of Pennsylvania Press.

Bakker, J. 2011. "Mengen moet, maar waarom doen we het ook alweer? Over de 'framing' van een maatschappelijke vraagstuk." Presented at the Landelijke Pedagogendag (May 25), University of Amsterdam.

Bakker, J., et al. 2007. "De houding jegens klasgenoten: etnisch gekleurd?" *Pedagogiek* 27 (3): 201–219.

Bakker, J., et al., eds. 2010. *International Perspectives on Countering School Segregation*. Antwerp: Garant.

Baldwin, J. 1962. *The Fire Next Time*. New York: Dell.

Baldwin, P. 2009. *The Narcissism of Minor Differences: How Europe and America Are Alike*. Princeton: Princeton University Press.

Ball, S. 2003. *Class Strategies and the Education Market: The Middle Classes and Social Advantage*. London: Routledge.

Bauman, G. 1996. *Contesting Culture: Discourses of Identity in Multi-Ethnic London*. Cambridge: Cambridge University Press.

Baysu, G., & Valk, H. 2012. "Navigating the School System in Sweden, Belgium, Austria and Germany: School Segregation and Second Generation School Trajectories." *Ethnicities* 12 (6): 776–799.

Beadle, P. 2005. "Working Class Zeros." *Guardian* (December 13). http://www.guardian.co.uk/world/2005/dec/13/race.teaching?INTCMP=SRCH.

Bekerman, Z. 2008. "On Their Way Somewhere: Integrated Bilingual Palestinian-Jewish Education in Israel," in P. Woods & G. Woods, eds., *Alternative Education for the 21st Century: Philosophies, Approaches, Visions* (pp. 123–138), New York: Palgrave Macmillan.

Bell, D. 1997. "Civic Society versus Civic Virtue," in A. Gutmann, ed., *Freedom of Association* (pp. 239–272), Princeton: Princeton University Press.

Bell, D. 1980. "*Brown v. Board of Education* and the Interest Convergence Dilemma." *Harvard Law Review* 93: 518–533.

Berliner, D. 2006. "Our Impoverished View of Educational Reform." *Teachers College Record* 108 (6): 949–995.

Bernstein, B. 1975. *Class Codes and Control*. London: Routledge.

Berry, J., et al. 2006. "Immigrant Youth: Acculturation, Identity and Adaptation." *Applied Psychology* 55 (3): 303–332.

Bhabha, H. 1999. "Liberalism's Sacred Cow," in S. Okin, ed., *Is Multiculturalism Bad for Women?* (pp. 79–84), Princeton: Princeton University Press.

Binder, A. 2000. "Why Do Some Curricular Challenges Work While Others Do Not? The Case of Three Afrocentric Challenges." *Sociology of Education* 73 (2): 69–91.

Bloemberg, L., & Nijhuis, D. 1993. "Hindoescholen in Nederland." *Migrantenstudies* 9 (3): 35–52.

Blokland, T., & van Eijk, G. 2010. "Do People who Like Diversity Practice Diversity in Neighborhood Life? Neighborhood Use and the Social Networks of 'Diversity Seekers' in a Mixed Neighborhood in the Netherlands." *Ethnic and Migration Studies* 36 (2): 313–332.

Blum, L. 2002. "The Promise of Racial Integration in a Multicultural Age," in S. Macedo & Y. Tamir, eds., *Nomos XLIII: Moral and Political Education* (pp. 383–424), New York: New York University Press.

Boateng, F. 1990. "Combatting Deculturalization of the African-American Child in the Public School System: A Multicultural Approach," in K. Lomotey, ed., *Going to School: The African-American Experience*, Albany, NY: SUNY Press.

Bolt, G., et al. 1998. "On the Social Significance of Spatial Location: Special Segregation and Social Inclusion," *Netherlands Journal of Housing and the Built Environment* 13 (1): 83–95.

Bolt, G., et al. 2002. "Ethnic Segregation in the Netherlands: New Patterns, New Policies?" *Tijdschrift voor Economische en Sociale Geografie* 93 (2): 214–220.

Bolt, G., et al. 2009. "After Urban Restructuring: Relocations and Segregation in Dutch Cities." *Tijdschrift voor Economische en Sociale Geografie* 100 (4): 502–518.

Bolt, G., & van Kempen, G. 2003. "Escaping Poverty Neighbourhoods in the Netherlands." *Housing, Theory and Society* 20 (4): 209–222.

Bolt, G., & van Kempen, R. 2010. "Ethnic Segregation and Residential Mobility: Relocations of Minority Ethnic Groups in the Netherlands." *Ethnic and Migration Studies* 36 (2): 333–354.

Bonilla-Silva, E. 2003. *Racism without Racists: Color-Blind Racism and the Persistence of Racial Inequality in the United States*. Lanham, MD: Rowman & Littlefield.

Bonnett, A. 1998. "How the British Working Class Become White: The Symbolic (Re)formation of Racialized Capitalism." *Historical Sociology* 11 (3): 316–340.

Bourdieu, P., & Passerson, J. 1977. *Reproduction in Society, Education and Culture*. London: Sage.

Brantlinger, E. 2003. *Dividing Classes: How the Middle-Class Negotiates and Rationalizes School Advantage*. New York: Routledge.

Brennan, J. 2011. *The Ethics of Voting*. Princeton: Princeton University Press.

Breton, R. 1964. "Institutional Completeness of Ethnic Communities and the Personal Relations of Immigrants." *American Journal of Sociology* 70 (2): 193–205.

Brighouse, H. 2003. "Should We Teach Patriotic History?" in W. Feinberg & K. McDonough, eds., *Citizenship and Education in Liberal-Democratic Societies* (pp. 157–175), Oxford: Oxford University Press.

Brighouse, H. 2006. *On Education*. London: Routledge.

Brighouse, H., & Swift, A. 2009. "Educational Equality versus Educational Adequacy: A Critique of Anderson and Satz." *Journal of Applied Philosophy* 26 (2): 117–128.

Brink, M., et al. 2010. *Tegengaan segregatie in het basisonderwijs; monitoring van de OCW-pilots*. Amsterdam: Regioplan.

Brooks, R. 1996. *Integration or Separation? A Strategy for Racial Equality*. Cambridge: Harvard University Press.

Brown, E. 2000. "Black Like Me? Gangsta Culture, Clarence Thomas and Afrocentric Academies." *New York University Law Review* 75: 308–352.

Brown, K. 1993. "Do African-Americans Need Immersion Schools? The Paradox Created by Legal Conceptualization of Race and Public Education." *Iowa Law Review* 78 (4): 813–882.

Bryk, A., et al. 2010. *Organizing Schools for Improvement: Lessons from Chicago*. Chicago: University of Chicago Press.

Buchanan, A. *Secession: The Morality of Political Divorce from Fort Sumter to Lithuania and Quebec*. Boulder, CO: Westview Press, 1991.

Buckingham, A. 1999. "Is There an Underclass in Britain?" *British Journal of Sociology* 50 (1): 49–75.

Buijs, F. 2009. "Muslims in the Netherlands: Social and Political Developments after 9/11." *Ethnic and Migration Studies* 35 (3): 421–438.

Bunar, N. 2010. "Segregation, Education and Urban Policy in Sweden," in Bakker, J., Denessen, E., Peters, D., & Walraven, G., eds., *International Perspectives on Countering School Segregation* (pp. 83–98), Antwerp: Garant.

Burtt, S. 1994. "Religious Parents, Secular Schools: A Liberal Defense of an Illiberal Education." *Review of Politics* 56 (1): 51–70.

Burtt, S. 1996. "In Defense of Yoder: Parental Authority and the Public Schools," in I. Shapiro & R. Hardin eds., *Nomos 38: Political Order* (pp. 412–437), New York: NYU Press.

Butler, T. 2003. "Living in the Bubble: Gentrification and its 'Others' in North London." *Urban Studies* 40 (12): 2469–2486.

Butler, T., & Hamlett, C. 2011. *Ethnicity, Class and Aspiration: Understanding London's New East End*. London: Policy Press.

Carmichael, S., & Hamilton, C. 1992/1967. *Black Power: The Politics of Liberation*. New York: Vintage.

Carruthers, J. 1994. "Black Intellectuals and the Crisis in Black Education," in Mwalimu Shujaa, ed., *Too Much Schooling, Too Little Education: A Paradox of Black Life in White Societies*, Trenton, NJ: Africa World.

Casal, P. 2007. "Why Sufficiency is Not Enough." *Ethics* 119: 296–326.

Cavanaugh, M. 2002. *Against Equality of Opportunity*. Oxford: Oxford University Press.

CBS 2013. Centraal Bureau voor de Statistiek. http://www.cbs.nl/nl-NL/menu/home/default.htm.

Chowdhury, K. 1997. "Afrocentric Voices: Constructing Identities, (Dis)placing Difference." *College Literature* 24 (2): 35–56.

Clayton, M. 2006. *Justice and Legitimacy in Upbringing*. Oxford: Oxford University Press.

Clotfelter, C. 2004. *After Brown: The Rise and Retreat of School Desegregation*. Princeton: Princeton University Press.

Clotfelter, C., et al. 2006. "Teacher-Student Matching and the Assessment of Teacher Effectiveness." *Journal of Human Resources* 61 (4): 778–820.

Clotfelter, C., et al. 2007. "High Poverty Schools and the Distribution of Teachers and Principals." *North Carolina Law Review* 85: 1345–1380.

Clotfelter, C., et al. 2009. "Are Teacher Absences Worth Worrying About in the United States?" *Education Finance and Policy* 4 (2): 115–149.

Clotfelter, C., et al. 2011. "Teacher Mobility, School Segregation, and Pay-Based Policies to Level the Playing Field." *Education Finance and Policy* 6 (3): 399–438.

Coldron, J., et al. 2010. "Why Are English Secondary Schools Socially Segregated?" *Journal of Education Policy* 25 (1): 10–35.

Collins, P. H. 2006. *From Black Power to Hip Hop: Racism, Nationalism and Feminism*. Philadelphia: Temple University Press.

Comer, J. 1997. *Waiting for a Miracle: Why Schools Can't Solve Our Problems—and How We Can*. New York: Dutton.

Conger, D. 2005. "Within-School Segregation in an Urban District." *Educational Evaluation and Policy Analysis* 27 (3): 225–244.

Crozier, G., et al. 2008. "White Middle-Class Parents, Identities, Educational Choice and the Urban Comprehensive School: Dilemmas, Ambivalence and Moral Ambiguity." *British Journal of Sociology of Education* 29 (3): 261–272.

Crul, M., & Holdaway, J. 2009. "Children of Immigrants in Schools in New York and Amsterdam: The Factors Shaping Attainment." *Teachers College Record* 111 (6): 1476–1507.

Crul, M., & Schneider, J. 2009. "Children of Turkish Immigrants in Germany and the Netherlands: The Impact of Difference in Vocational and Academic Tracking Systems." *Teachers College Record* 111 (6): 1508–1527.

Dagevos, J., & Gijsberts, M. 2007. "Integration Report 2007. Summary," in J. Dagevos & M. Gijsberts, eds., *Jaarraport integratie* (pp. 311–326), Den Haag, The Netherlands: SCP.

Damm, A. P. 2009. "Ethnic Enclaves and Immigrant Labour Market Outcomes: Quasi-Experimental Evidence." *Labor Market Economics* 27 (2): 281–314.

Darby, D. 2011. "Adequacy, Inequality and Cash for Grades." *Theory and Research in Education* 9 (3): 209–232.

Darity, W., & Jolla, A. 2010. "Desegregated Schools with Segregated Education," in C. Harman & G. Squires, eds., *The Integration Debate: Competing Futures for American Cities* (pp. 99–118), New York: Routledge.

Davis, T. 2012. "School Choice and Segregation: 'Tracking' Racial Equity in Magnet Schools." *Education and Urban Society* (pp. 1–35). Online early. http://eus.sagepub.com/search/results?fulltext=school+choice&submit=yes&journal_set=speus&src=selected&andorexactfulltext=and&x=8&y=7.

Dei, G. 1995. "Examining the Case for 'African-Centred' Schools in Ontario." *McGill Journal of Education* 30 (2): 179–198.

De Marneffe, P. 2006. "Avoiding Paternalism." *Philosophy and Public Affairs* 34 (1): 68–94.

Denessen, E., et al. 2005. "Segregation by Choice? A Study of Group-Specific Reasons for School Choice." *Journal of Education Policy* 20 (3): 347–368.

Denessen, E., et al. 2010. "School and Classroom Diversity Effects on Cognitive and Non-Cognitive Students Outcomes." *Journal of Education Research* 4 (2): 1–13.

De Ruyter, D. & Merry, M.S. 2009. "Why Education in Public Schools Should Include Religious Ideals." *Studies in Philosophy and Education* 28 (4): 295–311.
Diop, C. 1981. *The African Origin of Civilization: Myth or Reality*. Chicago: Lawrence Hill.
DiPrete, T., et al. 2011. "Segregation in Social Networks Based on Acquaintanceship and Trust." *American Journal of Sociology* 116 (4): 1234–1283.
Dougherty, J., et al. 2009. "School Choice in Suburbia: Test Scores, Race and Housing Markets." *American Journal of Education* 115 (4): 523–548.
Driessen, G. 2007. *Peer Group Effects on Educational Achievement: An International Review of Effects, Explanations and Theoretical and Methodological Considerations*. Nijmegen, The Netherlands: ITS.
Driessen, G. 2008. "De verwachtingen waargemaakt? Twee decennia islamitische basisscholen." *Mens en Maatschappij* 83 (20): 168–189.
Driessen, G., & Merry, M. S. 2011. "The Effects of Integration and Generation of Immigrants on Language and Numeracy Achievement." *Educational Studies* 37 (5): 581–592.
Dronkers, J., & van der Velden, R. 2013. "Positive but Also Negative Effects of Ethnic Diversity in Schools on Educational Achievement? An Empirical Test with Cross-National Pisa-Data," in M. Windzio, ed., *Integration and Inequality in Educational Institutions* (pp. 71–98), London, New York: Springer.
Du Bois, W. E. B. 1935. "Does the Negro Need Separate Schools?" *Journal of Negro Education* 4: 328–335.
Du Bois, W. E. B. 1986. *Writings*. New York: Library of America.
Dunne, M., & Gazeley, L. 2008. "Teachers, Social Class and Underachievement." *British Journal of Sociology of Education* 29 (5): 451–463.
Dworkin, G. 2005. "Moral Paternalism." *Law and Philosophy* 24: 305–319.
Dwyer, J. 1998. *Religious Schools vs. Children's Rights*. Ithaca: Cornell.
Edwards, P. 1996. "Before and After Desegregation: African American Parents' Involvement in Schools," in Mwalimu J. Shujaa, ed., *Beyond Desegregation: The Politics of Quality in African American Schooling*, Thousand Oaks, CA: Corwin.
Elmore, R. 2000. *Building a Structure for New School Leadership*. Washington, DC: Albert Shanker Institute.
"Elite kiest een school met 'ons soort mensen.'" *Trouw* (December 15, 2010).
El Nasr, H. 2011. "Blacks' Flight to Suburbia Hastens Desegregation." *USA Today* (December 8), 1A–2A.
Estlund, C. 2003. *Working Together: How Workplace Bonds Strengthen a Diverse Democracy*. Oxford: Oxford University Press.
Eyler, J., et al. 1983. "Resegregation: Segregation within Desegregated Schools," in Christine H. Rossell & Willis D. Hawley, eds., *The Consequences of School Desegregation*, Philadelphia: Temple University Press.
Farley, R., et al. 1994. "Stereotypes and Segregation: Neighborhoods in the Detroit Area." *American Journal of Sociology* 100 (3): 750–780.
Faltz, C., & Leake, D. 1996. "The All-Black School: Inherently Unequal or a Culture-Based Alternative?" in Mwalimu J. Shujaa, ed., *Beyond Desegregation: The Politics of Quality in African American Schooling*, Thousand Oaks, CA: Corwin.

Farrell, A. 2011. *Fat Shame: Stigma and the Fat Body in American Culture.* New York: NYU Press.
Feinberg, J. 1971. "Legal Paternalism." *Canadian Journal of Philosophy* 1 (1): 105–124.
Feinberg, J. 1980. "A Child's Right to an Open Future," in W. Aiken & H. LaFollette, eds., *Whose Child? Parental Rights, Parental Authority and State Power* (124–153), Totowa, NJ: Littlefield, Adams.
Fennema, M., & Tillie, J. 1999. "Political Participation and Political Trust in Amsterdam: Civic Communities and Ethnic Networks." *Ethnic and Migration Studies* 25 (4): 703–726.
Fine, M. 1991. *Framing Dropouts: Notes on the Politics of an Urban High School.* Albany, NY: SUNY Press.
Fine, M. 1993. "(Ap)parent Involvement: Reflections on Parents, Power and Urban Public Schools." *Teachers College Record* 94 (4): 682–729.
Finney, N., & Simpson, L. 2009. *'Sleepwalking to Segregation'? Challenging Myths about Race and Migration.* Bristol: Policy Press.
Fischer, C. S. 1975. "Toward a Subcultural Theory of Urbanism." *American Journal of Sociology* 80 (6): 1319–1341.
Flint, J. 2010. "Faith and Housing in England: Promoting Community Cohesion or Contributing to Urban Segregation?" *Ethnic and Migration Studies* 36 (2): 257–274.
Fordham, S. 1988. "Racelessness as a Factor in Black Students' School Success: Pragmatic Strategy or Pyrrhic Victory?" *Harvard Educational Review* 58 (1): 54–84.
Fordham, S., & Ogbu, J. 1986. "Black Students' School Success: Coping with the Burden of 'Acting White.'" *Urban Review* 18 (3): 176–206.
Fraser, N. 1996. *Justice Interruptus: Critical Reflections on the "Postsocialist" Condition.* New York: Routledge.
Freire, P. 1993/1970. *Pedagogy of the Oppressed.* New York: Continuum.
Fullinwider, R. 1995. "Citizenship, Individualism, and Democratic Politics." *Ethics* 105 (3): 497–515.
Fultz, M. 2004. "The Displacement of Black Educators Post-Brown: An Overview and Analysis." *History of Education Quarterly* 44 (1): 11–45.
Galston, W. 2002. *Liberal Pluralism.* Cambridge: Cambridge University Press.
Galston, W. 2005. *The Practice of Liberal Pluralism.* Cambridge: Cambridge University Press.
Gardner, P. 1988. "Religious Upbringing and the Liberal Ideal of Religious Autonomy." *Journal of Journal of Philosophy of Education* 22 (1): 89–105.
Gates, H. L. 1996. "The Parable of the Talents," in H. L. Gates Jr. & Cornel West, eds., *The Future of the Race,* New York: Vintage.
Giddings, G. J. 2001. "Infusion of Afrocentric Content into the School Curriculum: Toward an Effective Movement." *Journal of Black Studies* 31 (4): 462–482.
Gijsberts, M. 2006. "De afnemende invloed van etnische concentratie op schoolprestaties in het basisonderwijs 1988–2002." *Sociologie* 2: 157–177.
Gijsberts, M., & Dagevos, J. 2005. *Uit elkaars buurt. De invloed van etnische concentratie op integratie en beeldvorming.* Den Haag, The Netherlands: Sociaal en Cultureel Planbureau.

Gillborn, D. 2000. "White Heat: Racism, under-Achievement and White Working-Class Boys." *International Journal of Inclusive Education* 4 (4): 271–288.

Gillborn, D. 2010. "The White Working Class, Racism and Respectability: Victims, Degenerates and Interest-Convergence." *British Journal of Educational Studies* 58 (1): 3–25.

Gingwright, S. 2004. *Black in School: Afrocentric Reform, Urban Youth and the Promise of Hip-Hop Culture.* New York: Teachers College Press.

Giroux, H. 1983. *Theory and Resistance in Education.* London: Heinemann.

Glenn, C. 1996. *Educating Immigrant Children: Schools and Minorities in Twelve Nations.* New York: Garland.

Golubeva, M., & Austers, I. 2010. "Alternative Civil Enculturation: Political Disenchantment and Civic Attitudes in Minority Schools in Estonia, Latvia, and Slovakia." *European Education* 42 (4): 49–68.

Golubeva, M., et al. 2010. "Separate Schooling of Minorities in Eastern and Southern Europe: Is There a Way to Overcome the Negative Effects of Segregation?" In Bakker et al., eds., *International Perspectives on Countering School Segregation* (pp. 239–247), Antwerp: Garant.

Goodhart, D. 2013. "White Flight? Britain's New Problem—Segregation." *Prospect* (February 2013): 30–31.

Green, T. 2007. "The Law of Zero-Correlation," in R. Curren, ed., *Journal of Journal of Philosophy of Education: An Anthology* (pp. 230–235), Oxford: Blackwell Press.

Gutmann, A. 1999. *Democratic Education*, 2nd ed. Princeton: Princeton University Press.

Haig-Brown, C., & Hodson, J. 2008. "Starting with the Land: Toward Indigenous Thought in Canadian Education," in P. Woods & G. Woods, eds., *Alternative Education for the 21st Century: Philosophies, Approaches, Visions* (pp. 167–187), New York: Palgrave Macmillan.

Hall, W. S., et al. 1972. "Stages in the Development of a Black Awareness: An Exploratory Investigation," in R. L. Jones, ed., *Black Psychology*, New York: Harper & Row.

Hanley, L. 2007. *Estates: An Intimate History.* London: Granta.

Hanuschek, E., et al. 2000. "School Desegregation, Academic Attainment, and Earnings." *Journal of Human Resources* 35 (2): 333–346.

Hanuschek, E., et al. 2004. "Why Public Schools Lose Teachers." *Journal of Human Resources* 39 (2): 326–354.

Hanuschek, E., et al. 2009. "New Evidence about *Brown v. Board of Education*: The Complex Effects of School Racial Composition on Achievement." *Journal of Labor Economics* 27 (3): 349–383.

Harry, B., & Klingner, J. K. 2006. *Why Are So Many Minority Students in Special Education? Understanding Race and Disability in Schools.* New York: Teachers College Press.

Haw, K. 1994. "Muslim Girls' Schools—A Conflict of Interests?" *Gender and Education* 6 (1): 63–76.

Haylett, C. 2001. "Illegitimate Subjects? Abject Whites, Neoliberal Modernisation, and Middle-Class Multiculturalism." *Environment and Planning D: Society and Space* 19: 351–370.

Hellen, N. 2013. "Britons 'Self-Segregate' as White Flight Soars." *Sunday Times* (January 27, 2013), p. 15.
Hermans, P. 1995. "Moroccan Immigrants and School Success." *International Journal of Educational Research* 23 (1): 33-43.
Herzfeld, M. 2005. *Cultural Intimacy*. New York: Routledge.
Hilberth, M., & Slate, J. 2012. "Middle School Black and White Student Assignment to Disciplinary Consequences: A Clear Lack of Equity." *Education and Urban Society* (pp. 1–17). Online early.
Hill, P. 2008. "Spending Money When It Is Not Clear What Works." *Peabody Journal of Education* 83 (2): 238–258.
Hirsch, F. 1977. *Social Limits to Growth*. London: Taylor & Francis.
Hochschild, J., & Scovronick, N. 2003. *The American Dream and the Public Schools*. Oxford: Oxford University Press.
Holme, J. J. 2002. "Buying Homes, Buying Schools: Schools Choice and the Social Construction of Equality." *Harvard Educational Review* 72 (2): 181–205.
hooks, b. 1995. *Killing Rage: Ending Racism*. New York: Henry Holt.
hooks, b. 2000. *Where We Stand: Class Matters*. New York: Routledge.
Hornstra, L. 2013. "Motivational Developments in Primary School: Group Specific Differences in Various Learning Contexts." PhD dissertation, University of Amsterdam.
Ihlanfeldt, K., & Scafidi, B. 2002. "Black Self-Segregation as a Cause of Housing Segregation: Evidence from a Multi-City Study of Urban Inequality." *Journal of Urban Economics* 51 (2): 366–390.
"Ik vertel over christenen en joden." *De Volkskrant* (April 16, 2010).
Ingram, N. 2009. "Working-Class Boys, Educational Success and the Misrecognition of Working-Class Culture." *British Journal of Sociology of Education* 30 (4): 421–434.
Ireson, J., & Hallam, S. 2005. "'Pupils' Liking for School: Ability Grouping, Self-Concept and Perceptions of Teaching." *British Journal of Educational Psychology* 75 (2): 297–311.
Irvine, J. 1990. *Black Students and School Failure: Policies, Practices and Prescriptions*. Westport, CT: Greenwood.
Irvine, J. 2000. "Afrocentric Education: Critical Questions for Further Considerations," in Diane S. Pollard & Cheryl Ajirotutu, eds., *African-Centered Schooling in Theory and Practice*, Westport, CT: Bergin & Garvey.
Irvine, R. W., and J. J. Irvine. 1983. "The Impact of the Desegregation Process on the Education Process of Black Students." *Journal of Negro Education* 52 (4): 410–422.
"Islamitisch onderwijs maakt sprong vooruit." *Trouw* (June 7, 2012).
Istanbouli, M. 2000. "An Exploratory Case Study of Religio-Cultural in an Islamic School: Implications for Socialization and Inculturation." PhD dissertation, Loyola University.
Jackman, M. R., & Muha, M. 1984. "Education and Intergroup Attitudes: Moral Enlightenment, Superficial Democratic Commitment, or Ideological Refinement?" *American Sociological Review* 49 (6): 751–769.
Jackson III, B. W., 1976. "The Function of a Black Identity Development Theory in Achieving Relevance in Education for Black Students." PhD dissertation, University of Massachussetts at Amherst.

Jackson, C. K. 2009. "Student Demographics, Teacher Sorting, and Teacher Quality: Evidence from the End of School Desegregation." *Journal of Labor Economics* 27 (2): 213–256.

Jacobs, D., et al. 2004. "Associational Membership and Political Involvement among Ethnic Minority Groups in Brussels." *Journal for Ethnic and Migration Studies* 30 (3): 543–559.

Jarvis, S. 1992. "*Brown* and the Afrocentric Curriculum." *Yale Law Journal* 101: 1285–1304.

Jenkins, S., et al. 2008. "Social Segregation in Secondary Schools: How Does England Compare with Other Countries?" *Oxford Review of Education* 34 (1): 21–37.

Jencks, C. 1988. "Whom Must We Treat Equally for Educational Opportunity to be Equal?" *Ethics* 98 (3): 518–533.

"Joden op de Vlucht." *De Telegraaf* (June 26, 2010).

Johnston, R., et al. 2007. "The Geography of Ethnic Residential Segregation: A Comparative Study in Five Countries." *Annals of the Association of American Geographers* 97 (4): 713–738.

Jones, O. 2011. *Chavs: The Demonization of the Working Class.* London: Verso.

Joppke, C. 2004. "The Retreat of Multiculturalism in the Liberal State: Theory and Policy." *The British Journal of Sociology* 55 (2): 237–257.

Kahlenberg, R. 2001. *All Together Now: Creating Middle-Class Schools through Public School Choice.* Washington: Brookings Institution.

Kant, I. 1998. *Groundwork of the Metaphysics of Morals.* Trans. Mary J. Gregor. Cambridge: Cambridge University Press.

Karenga, M. 1995. "Afrocentricity and Multicultural Education: Concept, Challenge and Contribution," in Bowser, B. P., T. Jones, & G. Young, eds., *Toward the Multicultural University*, Westport, CT: Praeger.

Karsten, S., et al. 2006. "Choosing Segregation or Integration? The Extent and Effects of Ethnic Segregation in Dutch Cities." *Education and Urban Society* 38 (2): 228–247.

Kateb, G. 1997. "The Value of Association," in A. Gutmann, ed., *Freedom of Association* (pp. 35–62), Princeton: Princeton University Press.

Kateb, G. 2011. *Human Dignity.* Cambridge: Harvard University Press.

Kelly, P. 1999. "Integration and Identity in Muslim Schools: Britain, United States and Montreal." *Islam and Christian-Muslim Relations* 10 (2): 197–217.

Kifano, S. 1996. "Afrocentric Education in Supplementary Schools: Paradigm and Practice at the Mary McLeod Bethune Institute." *Journal of Negro Education* 65 (2): 209–218.

Kleinfeld, N. R. 2012. "Why Don't We Have Any White Kids?" *New York Times* (May 11).

Kohn, A. 1994. "The Truth about Self-Esteem." *Phi Delta Kappan* 76 (4): 272–283.

Krivo, L., et al. 2009. "Segregation, Racial Structure and Neighborhood Violent Crime." *American Journal of Sociology* 114 (6): 1765–1802.

Krysan, M. 1998. "Privacy and the Expression of White Racial Attitudes: A Comparison across Three Contexts." *Public Opinion Quarterly* 62 (4): 506–544.

Krysan, M. 2002a. "Whites Who Say They'd Leave: Who They Are, and Why Would They Leave?" *Demography* 39 (4): 675–696.

Krysan, M. 2002b. "Community Undesirability in Black and White: Examining Racial Residential Preferences through Community Perceptions." *Social Problems* 49 (4): 521–543.

Kukathas, C. 1998. "Liberalism and Multiculturalism: The Politics of Indifference," *Political Theory* 26 (5): 686–699.

Kunjufu, J. 2004. *Solutions for Black America*. Chicago: African American Images.

Kurien, P. 2001. "Religion, Ethnicity and Politics: Hindu and Muslim Indian Immigrants in the United States." *Ethnic and Racial Studies* 24 (2): 263–293.

Kymlicka, W. 2001a. *Can Liberal Pluralism Be Exported? Western Political Theory and Ethnic Relations in Eastern Europe*. Oxford: Oxford University Press.

Kymlicka, W. 2001b. *Politics in the Vernacular: Nationalism, Multiculturalism and Citizenship*. Oxford: Oxford University Press.

Ladd, H., & Fiske, H. 2009. "The Dutch Experience with Weighted Student Funding: Some Lessons for the U.S." Working papers, Sanford School of Public Policy.

Ladson-Billings, G. 2000. "Culturally Relevant Pedagogy in African-Centered Schools: Possibilities for Progressive Educational Reform," in D. S. Pollard & C. Ajirotutu, eds., *African-Centered Schooling in Theory and Practice*, Westport, CT: Bergin & Garvey.

Ladson-Billings, G. 2009. *The Dream-Keepers: Successful Teachers of African-American Children*, 2nd ed. San Francisco, CA: Jossey-Bass.

Ladson-Billings, G. & Tate, W. 1995. "Toward a Critical Race Theory of Education." *Teachers College Record* 97 (1): 47–68.

LaMorte, M. 2008. *School Law: Cases and Concepts*, 9th ed. Boston: Pearson.

Lareau, A., & Conley, D., eds. 2008. *Social Class: How Does It Work?* New York: Russell Sage.

Lawler, S. 2012. "White Like Them: Whiteness and Anachronistic Space in Representations of the English White Working Class." *Ethnicities* 12 (4): 409–426.

Leake D., & Faltz, C. 1993. "Do We Need to Desegregate All of Our Black Schools?" *Journal of Education Policy* 7 (3): 373–387.

Leake, D., & Leake, B. 1992. "African-American Immersion Schools in Milwaukee: A View from the Inside." *Phi Delta Kappan* 73 (10): 783–785.

Lee, C. 1992. "Profile of an Independent Black Institution: African-Centered Education at Work." *Journal of Negro Education* 61 (2): 160–177.

Lee, C. 1994. "African-Centered Pedagogy: Complexities and Possibilities," in Mwalimu Shujaa, ed., *Too Much Schooling, Too Little Education: A Paradox of Black Life in White Societies*, Trenton, NJ: Africa World.

Lleras, C., & Rangel, C. 2009. "Ability Grouping Practices in Elementary School and African-American / Hispanic Achievement." *American Journal of Education* 115 (2): 279–304.

Lynn, M. 2006. "Education for the Community: Exploring the Culturally Relevant Practices of Black Male Teachers." *Teachers College Record* 108 (12): 2497–2522.

Macedo, S. 2000. *Diversity and Distrust: Civic Education in a Multicultural Democracy*. Cambridge: Vard.

Macleod, C. 2003. "Shaping Children's Convictions." *Theory and Research in Education* 3 (1): 315–330.

Macleod, J. 1995. *Ain't No Makin' It: Aspirations and Attainment in a Low-Income Neighbourhood.* London: Westview Press.

Mandara, J. 2006. "The Impact of Family Functioning on African American Males' Academic Achievement: A Review and Clarification of the Empirical Literature." *Teachers College Record* 108 (2): 206–223.

Manji, I. 2003. *The Trouble with Islam Today.* New York: St. Martin's.

Manley, D., & van Ham, M. 2011. "Choice-Based Letting, Ethnicity and Segregation in England." *Urban Studies* 48 (14): 3125–3143.

Margalit, A. 1996. *The Decent Society.* Cambridge: Harvard University Press.

Marks, L. 2006. "Religion and Family Relational Health: An Overview and Conceptual Model." *Journal of Religion and Health* 45 (4): 603–618.

Marx, K. 1938. *Critique of the Gotha Programme.* New York: International Publishers.

Mason, A. 2001. "Equality of Opportunity, Old and New." *Ethics* 111 (4): 760–781.

Massey, D., & Denton, N. 1993. *American Apartheid.* Cambridge: Harvard University Press.

Merry, M. S. 2005a. "Social Exclusion of Muslim Minority Youth in Flemish- and French-Speaking Belgian Schools." *Comparative Education Review* 49 (1): 1–22.

Merry, M. S. 2005b. "Cultural Coherence and the Schooling for Identity Maintenance." *Journal of Philosophy of Education* (39) 3: 477–497.

Merry, M. S. 2005c. "Indoctrination, Moral Instruction and Non-Rational Beliefs: A Place for Autonomy?" *Educational Theory* 55 (4): 399–420.

Merry, M. S. 2005d. "Should Educators Accommodate Intolerance? Mark Halstead, Homosexuality, and the Islamic Case." *Journal of Moral Education* 34 (1): 19–36.

Merry, M. S. 2007. *Culture, Identity and Islamic Schooling: A Philosophical Approach.* New York: Palgrave Macmillan.

Merry, M. S. 2008a. "Educational Justice and the Gifted." *Theory and Research in Education* 6 (1): 47–70.

Merry, M. S. 2008b. "How Schools Inhibit the Autonomy of the Middle Class," in B. Stengel, ed., *Journal of Philosophy of Education Proceedings 2007* (pp. 517–520), Normal, IL: Philosophy of Education Society.

Merry, M. S., 2009. "Patriotism, History and the Legitimate Aims of American Education." *Educational Philosophy and Theory* 41 (4): 378–398.

Merry, M. S. 2010. "Does Segregation Matter?" in J. Bakker, E. Denessen, G. Walvaren, & D. Peters, eds., *International Perspectives on Countering School Segregation* (pp. 253–265), Antwerp: Garant.

Merry, M. S., & De Ruyter, D. 2011. "The Relevance of Cosmopolitanism for Moral Education." *Journal of Moral Education* 40 (1): 1–18.

Merry, M. S., & Driessen, G. 2012. "Equality on Different Terms: The Case of Dutch Hindu Schools." *Education and Urban Society* 44 (5): 632–648

Merry, M. S., & Driessen, G. 2013. "On The Right Track? Islamic Schools in the Netherlands after an Era of Turmoil." *Ethnicities*, in press.

Merry, M. S., & Karsten, S. 2010. "Restricted Liberty, Parental Choice and Homeschooling." *Journal of Philosophy of Education* 44 (4): 497–514.

Merry, M. S., & New, W. 2008. "Constructing an Authentic Self: The Challenges and Promise of African-Centered Pedagogy." *American Journal of Education* 115 (1): 35–64.

Mickelson, R. 1990. "The Attitude-Achievement Paradox among Black Adolescents." *Sociology of Education* 6 (3): 44–61.

Mill, J. S. 1978/1879. *On Liberty*. Indianapolis: Hackett.

Mills, C. 2003. "The Child's Right to an Open Future?" *Journal of Social Philosophy* 34 (4): 499–509.

Modood, T. 2010. "Multiculturalism in the West and Muslim Identity," in M. S. Merry & J. Milligan, eds., *Citizenship, Identity and Education in Muslim Communities: Essays on Attachment and Obligation* (pp. 63–84), New York: Palgrave Macmillan.

Moody, J. 2001. "Race, School Integration and Friendship Segregation in America." *American Journal of Sociology* 107 (3): 679–716.

Moore, K. 2008. "Class Formations: Competing Forms of Black Middle-Class Identity." *Ethnicities* 8 (4): 492–517.

Morantz, A. 1994. *Money, Choice and Equity in Kansas City: Major Investments with Modest Returns*. The Harvard Project on School Desegregation. Cambridge: Harvard University Press.

Morris, S. 2011. "School Academy Rises to the Challenge of the Young, White Working Class." *Guardian* (September 23). http://www.guardian.co.uk/education/2011/sep/23/school-academy-challenge-white-working-class.

"Moslims Vernederlandsen." *De Volkskrant* (March 24, 2011).

Müller, F. 2012. "Making Contact: Generating Interethnic Contact for Multicultural Integration and Tolerance in Amsterdam." *Race, Ethnicity and Education* 15 (3): 425–440.

Murdie, R., & Ghosh, S. 2010. "Does Spatial Concentration Always Mean a Lack of Integration? Exploring Ethnic Concentration and Integration in Toronto." *Ethnic and Migration Studies* 36 (2): 293–311.

Murrell, P. 2002. *African-Centered Pedagogy: Developing Schools of Achievement for African American Children*. Albany, NY: SUNY Press.

Musterd, S. 2005. "Social and Ethnic Segregation in Europe: Levels, Causes, and Effects." *Journal of Urban Affairs* 27 (3): 331–348.

Musterd, S., & Ostendorf, W. 2009. "Residential Segregation and Integration in the Netherlands." *Ethnic and Migration Studies* 35 (9): 1515–1532.

Musterd, S., & van Kempen, R. 2009. "Segregation and Housing of Minority Ethnic Groups in Western European Cities." *Tijdschrift voor Economische en Sociale Geografie* 100 (4): 559–566.

Nedelcu, A., et al. 2010. "Students' Perceptions of the 'Others' in Ethnic Separated School Systems." *European Education* 42 (4): 69–86.

Neely, D. 1994. "Pedagogy of Culturally Biased Curriculum in Public Education: An Emancipatory Paradigm for Afrocentric Educational Initiatives." *Capital University Law Review* 23: 131–150.

Nesdale, D., et al. 2005. "Threat, Group Identification, and Children's Ethnic Prejudice." *Social Development* 14: 189–205.

New, W., & Merry, M. S. 2010. "Solving the 'Gypsy Problem': D. H. and Others v. Czech Republic." *Comparative Education Review* (54) 3: 393–414.

New, W., & Merry, M. S. 2011. "Learning Who They 'Really' Are: From Stigmatization to Opportunities to Learn in Greek Romani Education," in Z. Bekerman & T. Geisler, eds., *International Handbook of Migration, Minorities and Education: Understanding Cultural and Social Differences in Processes of Learning* (pp. 623–640), Dordrecht, The Netherlands: Springer.

Newman, A. 2009. "All Together Now? Some Egalitarian Concerns about Deliberation and Journal of Education Policy-Making." *Theory and Research in Education* 7 (1): 65–87.

Newmann, F., et al. 1989. "Organizational Factors that Affect School Sense of Efficacy, Community and Expectations." *Sociology of Education* 62 (4): 221–238.

"Niets te Vrezen." *De Groene Amsterdamer* (February 18, 2010).

Nightingale, C. 2012. *Segregation: A Global History of Divided Cities*. Chicago: University of Chicago Press.

Noguera, P. 2003. *City Schools and the American Dream: Reclaiming the Promise of Public Education*. New York: Teachers College Press.

Nussbaum, M. 2006. *Frontiers of Justice: Disability, Nationality, Species Membership*. Cambridge: Harvard University Press.

Nyden, P., & Maly, M. 1997. The Emergence of Stable Racially and Ethnically Diverse Urban Communities: A Case Study of Nine US Cities." *House Policy Debate* 8 (2): 491–534.

Ogbu, J. 2003. *Black American Students in an Affluent Suburb: A Study of Academic Disengagement*. Mahwah, NJ: Erlbaum.

O'Hair, M., et al. 2008. "The K20 Model for Systemic Educational Change and Sustainability: Addressing Social Justice in Rural Schools and Implications for Educators in All Contexts," in P. Woods & G. Woods, eds., *Alternative Education for the 21st Century: Philosophies, Approaches, Visions* (pp. 15–28), New York: Palgrave Macmillan.

"Ondergang van een Moslimschool." *HP De Tijd* (July 2, 2010): 20–28.

Orfield, G. 2005. *School Resegregation: Must the South Turn Back?* Durham: University of North Carolina Press.

Orfield, G. 2007. *Lessons in Integration: Realizing the Promise of Racial Diversity in America's Public Schools*. Richmond: University of Virginia Press.

Orfield, G., & Lee, C. 2005. "Why Segregation Matters: Poverty and Educational Inequality." *The Civil Rights Project*. Cambridge: Harvard University.

Orwell, G. 1981. *A Collection of Essays*. London: Harvest.

Overmaat, M., & Ledoux, G. 2001. "Een toezocht naar succesfactoren op zwarte basisscholen." *Pedagogiek* 21: 359–371.

Patillo, M. 1999. *Black Picket Fences: Privilege and Peril among the Black Middle Class*. Chicago: University of Chicago Press.

Patillo, M. 2007. *Black on the Block: The Politics of Race and Class in the City*. Chicago: University of Chicago Press.

Pearce, M., et al. 2003. "Religiousness and Depressive Symptoms among Adolescents." *Clinical Child and Adolescent* 32 (2): 267–276.

Peetsma, T., et al. 2006. "Class Composition Influences on Pupils' Cognitive Development." *School Effectiveness and School Improvement* 17 (3): 275–302.
Penninx, R., et al. 2004. *Citizenship in European Cities: Immigrants, Local Politics and Integration Policies*. Aldershot, England: Ashgate.
Penninx, R., & Schrover, M. 2001. *Bastion of bindmiddel? Organisaties van immigranten in historisch perspectief*. Amsterdam: Aksant.
Perez, M., & Socias, M. 2003. "Highly Successful Schools: What Do They Do Differently and at What Cost?" *Education Finance and Policy* 3 (1): 90–108.
Permentier, M., et al. 2007. "Behavioural Responses to Neighbourhood Reputations." *Housing and the Built Environment* 22 (2): 199–213.
Pettigrew, T. F., & Tropp, L. R. 2006. "A Meta-Analytic Test of Intergroup Contact Theory." *Personality and Social Psychology* 90 (5): 751–783.
Pettit, P. 1997. *Republicanism: A Theory of Freedom and Government*. Oxford: Clarendon Press.
Phillips, D. 2006. "Parallel Lives? Challenging Discourses of British Muslim Self-Segregation." *Environment and Planning: Society and Space* 24 (1): 25–40.
Phillips, D. 2010. "Minority Ethnic Segregation, Integration and Citizenship: A European Perspective." *Ethnic and Migration Studies* 36 (2): 209–225.
Phinney, J. 2003. "Ethnic Identity and Acculturation," in K. Chun, P. B. Organista, & G. Marin, eds., *Acculturation: Advances in Theory, Measurement, and Applied Research*, Washington, DC: American Psychological Association.
Player, D. 2010. "Nonmonetary Compensation in the Public Teacher Labor Market." *Education Finance and Policy* 5 (1): 82–103.
Pogge, T. 1989. *Realizing Rawls*. Ithaca, NY: Cornell University Press.
Polite, V. 1993. "If Only We Knew Then What We Know Now: Foiled Opportunities to Learn in Suburbia." *Journal of Negro Education* 62 (3): 337–354.
Pollard, D., & Ajirotutu, S., eds. 2000. *African-Centered Schooling in Theory and Practice*. Westport, CT: Bergin & Garvey.
Power, S. 2006. "Comments on 'How Not to Be a Hypocrite.'" *Theory and Research in Education* 2 (1): 23–29.
Putnam, R. 2007. "*E Pluribus Unum*: Diversity and Community in the Twenty-First Century." *Scandinavian Political Studies* 30 (2): 137–174.
Ransby, B., & T. Matthews. 1993. "Black Popular Culture and the Transcendence of Patriarchal Illusions." *Race and Class* 35 (1): 57–68.
Ratteray, J. D. 1992. "Independent Neighborhood Schools: A Framework for the Education of African Americans." *Journal of Negro Education* 61 (2): 138–147.
Ratteray, J. D., and Shujaa, M. 1987. *Dare to Choose: Parental Choice at Independent Neighborhood Schools*. Washington, DC: Institute for Independent Education.
Rawls, J. 2001. *Justice as Fairness: A Restatement*. Cambridge: Cambridge University Press.
Reay, D. 2001. "Finding or Losing Yourself? Working-Class Relationships to Education." *Journal of Education Policy* 16 (4): 333–346.
Reay, D. 2006. "The Zombie Stalking English Schools: Social Class and Educational Inequality." *British Journal of Educational Studies* 54 (3): 288–307.

Reay, D. 2007. "'Unruly Places': Inner-City Comprehensives, Middle-Class Imaginaries and Working Class Children." *Urban Studies* 44 (7): 1191–1201.

Reay, D. 2012. "What Would a Socially Just Education System Look Like? Saving the Minnows from the Pike." *Journal of Education Policy* 27 (5): 587–599.

Reay, D., et al. 2007. "'A Darker Shade of Pale?' Whiteness, the Middle Classes and Multi-Ethnic Inner City Schooling." *Sociology* 41 (6): 1041–1060.

Regnerus, M. 2003. "Religion and Positive Adolescent Outcomes: A Review of Research and Theory." *Review of Religious Research* 44 (4), 394–413.

Rhodes, J. 2010. "White Backlash, 'Unfairness' and Justifications of British National Party (BNP) Support." *Ethnicities* 10 (1): 77–99.

Rivkin, S. 1994. "Residential Segregation and School Integration." *Sociology of Education* 67 (4): 279–292.

Rivkin, S. 2000. "School Desegregation, Academic Attainment, and Earnings." *Journal of Human Resources* 35 (2): 333–346.

Robinson, E. 2010. *Disintegration: The Splintering of Black America*. New York: Anchor Books.

Roda, A., & Stuart Wells, A. 2013. "School Choice Policies and Racial Segregation: Where White Parents' Good Intentions, Anxiety and Privilege Collide." *American Journal of Education* 119: 261–293.

Roelsma-Somer, S. 2008. "De kwaliteit van hindoescholen." PhD dissertation, University of Tilburg.

Rossell, C., & Hawley, W. 1983. *The Consequences of School Desegregation*. Philadelphia: Temple University Press.

Rosenblum, N. 1998. *Membership and Morals: The Personal Uses of Pluralism in America*. Princeton: Princeton University Press.

Rothstein, R. 2004. *Class and Schools*. Washington: Economic Policy Institute.

Rousseau, J. J. 1963. *The Social Contract and Discourses*. London: Dent.

Rubenstein, R., et al. 2009. "Spending, Size, and Grade Span in K–8 Schools." *Education and Finance Policy* 4 (1): 60–88.

Rury, J., & Saatcioglu, A. 2011. "Suburban Advantage: Opportunity Hoarding and Secondary Attainment in the Postwar Metropolitan North." *American Journal of Education* 117 (3): 307–342.

Satz, D. 2011. "Unequal Chances: Race, Class and Schooling." *Theory and Research in Education* 10 (2): 155–170.

Schapiro, I. 1999. *Democratic Justice*. New Haven: Yale University Press.

Saiger, A. 1999. Disestablishing Local School Districts as a Remedy for Educational Inadequacy. *Columbia Law Review* 99 (7): 1830–1870.

Sampson, R. 2008. "Moving to Inequality: Neighbourhood Effects and Experiments Meet Social Structure." *American Journal of Sociology* 114 (1): 191–233.

Samuels, A. 2004. *Is Separate Unequal? Black Colleges and the Challenge to Desegregation*. Lawrence: University of Kansas Press.

Scafidi, B., et al. 2007. "Race, Poverty and Teacher Mobility." *Economics of Education Review* 26 (2): 145–159.

"Schaamte staat als muur rond Marokkanen." *De Volkskrant* (May 11, 2010).

Schiff, C., et al. 2010. "Combating School Segregation: The Case of France," in J. Bakker, E. Denessen, G. Walvaren, & D. Peters, eds., *International Perspectives on Countering School Segregation* (pp. 189–204), Antwerp: Garant.

Schiffrin, S. 2000. "Paternalism, Unconsciounability Doctrine, and Accommodation." *Philosophy and Public Affairs* 29 (3): 205–250.

Schinkel, A. 2010. "Compulsory Autonomy Promoting Education." *Educational Theory* 60 (1): 97–116.

Schofield, J. 1995. "Review of Research on School Desegregation's Impact on Elementary and Secondary School Students," in James A. Banks & Cherry A. McGee Banks, eds. *Handbook of Research on Multicultural Education* (pp. 597–616), New York: Palgrave Macmillan.

Schofield, J. 2010. "International Evidence on Ability Grouping with Curriculum Differentiation and the Achievement Gap in Secondary Schools." *Teachers College Record* 112 (5): 8–9.

"Scholen in Nijmegen nog altijd zwart-wit ondanks advies." *Trouw* (November 2, 2011).

"Schools Restore Fresh Cooking to the Cafeteria." *New York Times* (August 17, 2011), A1, A16.

Semple, K. 2012. "Born Abroad, Well Off and Using Public Schools." *New York Times* (Feb. 15, 2012), A1, A3

Sen, A. 1992. *Inequality Reexamined*. Cambridge: Harvard University Press.

Sen, A. 2009. *The Idea of Justice*. Cambridge: Harvard University Press.

Shapiro, I. 1999. *Democratic Justice*. New Haven: Yale University Press.

Shapiro, T. 2004. *The Hidden Cost of Being African-American: How Wealth Perpetuates Inequality*. Oxford: Oxford University Press.

Sharkey, P. 2008. "The Intergenerational Transmission of Context." *American Journal of Sociology* 113 (4): 931–969.

Sherif, M., & Sherif, C. 1970. "Black Unrest as a Social Movement toward an Emerging Self-Identity." *Social and Behavioral Sciences* 15: 41–52.

Short, G. 2002. "Faith-Based Schools: A Threat to Social Cohesion?" *Journal of Philosophy of Education* 36 (2): 559–572.

Siddle-Walker, V. 1996. *Their Highest Potential: An African School Community in the Segregated South*. Chapel Hill: University of North Carolina Press.

Siddle-Walker, V. 2000. "Value-Segregated Schools for African American Children in the South, 1935–1969: A Review of Common Themes and Characteristics." *Review of Educational Research* 70 (3): 253–285.

Siddle-Walker, V., & Archung, K. N. 2003. "The Segregated Schooling of Blacks in the Southern United States and South Africa." *Comparative Education Review* 47 (1): 21–40.

Siegel, S. 1996. "Ethnocentric Public School Curricula in a Multicultural Nation: Proposed Standards for Judicial Review." *New York University Law Review* 40: 311–361.

Skeggs, B. 1997. *Formations of Class and Gender: Becoming Respectable*. London: Sage.

Slaughter, A. M. 2012. "Why Women Still Can't Have It All." *The Atlantic* (July/August): 85–102.

Sleeter, C., & Cornbleth, C. 2011. *Teaching with Vision: Culturally-Responsive Teaching in Standards-Based Classrooms*. New York: Teachers College Press.

Söderström, M., & Uusitalo, R. 2010. "School Choice and Segregation: Evidence from an Admission Reform." *Scandinavian Journal of Economics* 112 (1): 55–76.

Soja, E. 2010. *Seeking Spatial Justice*. Minneapolis: University of Minnesota Press.

Southerton, D. 2002. "Boundaries of 'Us' and 'Them': Class, Mobility and Identification in a New Town." *Sociology* 36 (1): 171–193.

Span, C. 2002. "Black Milwaukee's Challenge to the Cycle of Urban Miseducation: Milwaukee's African American Immersion Schools." *Urban Education* 37 (5): 610–630.

Spiecker, B., & Steutel, J. 2001. "Multiculturalism, Pillarization and Liberal Civic Education in the Netherlands." *International Journal of Educational Research* 35 (3): 293–304.

Spinner-Halev, J. 2000. *Surviving Diversity: Religion and Democratic Citizenship*. Baltimore: Johns Hopkins University Press.

Spinner-Halev, J. 2005. "Hinduism, Christianity, and Liberal Religious Toleration." *Political Theory* 33 (1), 28–57.

Steele, C. 1997. "A Threat in the Air: How Stereotypes Shape Intellectual Identity and Performance." *American Psychologist* 52: 613–629.

Steinberg, S. 2010. "The Myth of Concentrated Poverty," in Harman, C., & Squires, G., eds., *The Integration Debate: Competing Futures for American Cities* (pp. 213–228), New York: Routledge.

Stephan, W. G. 1997. *Reducing Prejudice and Stereotyping in Schools*. New York: Teachers College Press.

Stevenson, R., & Ellsworth, J. 2005. "Dropouts and the Silencing of Critical Voices," in L. Weis & M. Fine, eds., *Beyond Silenced Voices: Class, Race and Gender in the United States*, Albany: SUNY Press.

Surridge, P. 2007. "Class Belonging: A Quantitative Exploration of Identity and Consciousness." *The British Journal of Sociology* 58 (2): 207–226.

Swaine, L. 2006. *The Liberal Conscience: Politics and Principle in a World of Religious Pluralism*. New York: Columbia University Press.

Swaine, L. 2009. "Deliberate and Free: Heteronomy in the Public Sphere." *Philosophy and Social Criticism* 35 (1-2): 83–113.

Swaine, L. 2010. "Heteronomous Citizenship: Civic Virtue and the Chains of Autonomy." *Educational Philosophy and Theory* 42 (1): 73–93.

Swaine, L. 2012. "The False Right to Autonomy in Education." *Educational Theory* 62 (1): 107–124.

Sykes, B. 2011. "Spatial Order and Social Position: Neighbourhoods, Schools and Educational Inequality." PhD dissertation, University of Amsterdam.

Takaki, R. 1993. *A Different Mirror: A History of Multicultural America*. Boston: Little Brown.

Tamir, Y. 1997. "Revisiting the Civic Sphere," in A. Gutmann, ed., *Freedom of Association* (pp. 214–238), Princeton: Princeton University Press.

Tatum, B. 1997. *Why Are All the Black Kids Sitting Together in the Cafeteria?* New York: Basic.
Taylor, C. 2009. "Choice, Competition, and Segregation in a United Kingdom Urban Education Market." *American Journal of Education* 115 (4): 549–568.
Tazelaar, C., et al. 1996. *Kleur van de school. Etnische segregatie in het onderwijs.* Houten/Diegem: Bohn Stafleu van Loghum.
Teicher, S. 2006. "An African-Centered Success Story." *Christian Science Monitor* (June 8), 14–15.
Teunissen, J. 1990. "Basisscholen op islamitische en hindoeïstische grondslag." *Migrantenstudies* 6 (2): 45–57.
"Te weinig vrouwen bereiken de top" (February 17, 2011). http://www.nu.nl/werk-en-prive/2449419/weinig-vrouwen-bereiken-top.html.
Thomas, L. 2005. *The Family and the Political Self.* Cambridge: Cambridge University Press.
Thompson, R. 2011. "Faith Schools Fragment Communities." *Guardian* (June 13). http://www.guardian.co.uk/commentisfree/belief/2011/jun/13/faith-schools-fragment-communities.
Thrupp, M., et al. 2002. "School Composition and Peer Effects." *International Journal of Educational Research* 37 (5): 483–504.
"Tijd voor veelkleurige voorschoolse opvang." *Trouw* (November 11, 2011).
Timar, T., & Roza, M. 2010. "'A False Dilemma': Should Decisions about Education Resource Use Be Made at the State or Local Level?" *American Journal of Education* 116: 397–422.
Tooley, J. 2007. "From Adam Smith to Adam Swift: How the 'Invisible Hand' Overcomes Middle-Class Hypocrisy." *Journal of Philosophy of Education* 41 (4): 727–741.
Traoré, R. 2003. "African Students in America: Reconstructing New Meanings of 'African American' in Urban Education." *Intercultural Education* 14 (3): 243–254.
Trappenburg, M. 2003. "Against Segregation: Ethnic Mixing in Liberal States." *Journal of Political Philosophy* 11 (3): 295–319.
Uslaner, E. 2010. "Segregation, Mistrust and Minorities." *Ethnicities* 10 (4): 415–434.
Valenzuela, A. 1999. *Subtractive Schooling: U.S. Mexican Youth and the Politics of Caring.* Albany: SUNY Press.
Valls, A. 2002. "The Broken Promise of Racial Integration," in S. Macedo & Y. Tamir, eds., *Nomos XLIII: Moral and Political Education* (pp. 456–474), New York: New York University Press.
van Baar, H. 2012. "The European Roma. Minority Representation, Memory and the Limits of Transnational Governmentality." PhD dissertation, University of Amsterdam.
Vanderberghe, R., & Huberman, M. 1999. *Understanding and Preventing Teacher Burnout.* Cambridge: Cambridge University Press.
Vanderbilt-Adriance, E., & Shaw, D. 2008. "Conceptualizing and Re-Evaluating Resilience Across Levels of Risk, Time, and Domains of Competence." *Clinical Child Family Psychological Review* 11 (1–2): 30–58.

Van Niekerk, M. (2004). "Afro-Caribbeans and Indo-Caribbeans in the Netherlands: Premigration Legacies and Social Mobility." *International Migration Review* 38 (1): 158–183.

van Oers, R., et al. 2010. *A Re-Definition of Belonging? Language and Integration Tests in Western Europe.* Leiden, The Netherlands: Brill.

van Wijk, R., & Sleegers, P. 2010. "Ethnic Minorities and School Achievement," presented at AERA (April 30–May 4), Denver, CO.

Vasta, E. 2007. "From Ethnic Minorities to Ethnic Majority Policy: Multiculturalism and the Shift to Assimilationism in the Netherlands." *Ethnic and Racial Studies* 30 (5): 713–740.

Vedder, P. 2006. "Black and White Schools in the Netherlands." *European Education* 38 (2): 36–49.

Verkuyten, M. 2002. "Attitudes among Minority and Majority Children: The Role of Ethnic Identification, Peer Group Victimization and Parents." *Social Development* 11: 558–570.

Verkuyten, M., & Thijs, J. 2001. "Ethnic and Gender Bias among Dutch and Turkish Children in Late Childhood: The Role of Social Context." *Infant and Children Development* 10: 203–217.

Verkuyten, M., & Thijs, J. 2002. "Racist Victimization among Children in the Netherlands: The Effect of Ethnic Group and School." *Ethnic and Racial Studies* 25: 310–331.

Villalpando, O. 2003. "Self-Segregation or Self-Preservation? A Critical Race Theory and Latina / o Critical Theory Analysis of a Study of Chicana / o College Students. *International Journal of Qualitative Studies in Education* 16 (5): 619–646.

Vink, A. 2010. *Witte Zwanen, Zwarte Zwanen: de mythe van de zwarte school.* Amsterdam: Meulenhoff.

"Voorkom segregatie, zet jonge kinderen bij elkaar." *Trouw* (October 18, 2011).

Vowden, K. J. 2012. "Safety in Numbers? Middle-Class Parents and Social Mix in London Primary Schools." *Journal of Education Policy* 27 (6): 731–745.

Waitere, H., & Court, M. 2008. "'Alternative' Maori Education? Talking Back / Talking through Hegemonic Sites of Power," in P. Woods & G. Woods, eds., *Alternative Education for the 21st Century: Philosophies, Approaches, Visions* (pp. 139–166), New York: Palgrave Macmillan.

Walzer, M. 1983. *Spheres of Justice: A Defense of Pluralism and Equality.* New York: Basic Books.

Walzer, M. 1998. "On Involuntary Association," in A. Gutmann, ed., *Freedom of Association* (pp. 64–74), Princeton: Princeton University Press.

"Wat bezielt de Marokkaan?" *Elsevier* (May 8, 2010), 24–28.

Weinstock, D. 2005. "Beyond Exit Rights: Reframing the Debate," in A. Eisenberg & J. Spinner-Halev, eds., *Minorities within Minorities: Equality, Rights and Diversity* (pp. 227–247), Cambridge: Cambridge University Press.

Weekes-Barnard, D. 2007. *School Choice and Ethnic Segregation.* London: Runnymeade Trust.

Weis, L. 1990. *Working Class without Work: High School Students in a De-Industrializing Economy.* New York: Routledge.

Wells, A. S. 2008. *Both Sides Now: The Story of School Desegregation's Graduates.* Berkeley: University of California Press.

Wells, A. S., & Crain, R. 1997. *Stepping Over the Color Line: African American Students in White Suburban Schools.* New Haven: Yale University Press.

Wells, A. S., & Roda, A. 2009. *White Parents, Diversity and School Choice Policies: Where Good Intentions, Anxiety, and Privilege Collide.* Nashville: National Center on School Choice, Vanderbilt University. http://www.vanderbilt.edu/schoolchoice/search/publication.php?id=80.

Welshman, J. 2005. *Underclass: A History of the Excluded 1880–2000.* London: Bloomsbury.

West, C. 1993. *Race Matters.* Boston: Beacon.

White, J. 2011. *Exploring Wellbeing in Schools: A Guide to Making Children's Lives More Fulfilling.* London: Routledge.

Williams, M. 2003. "Citizenship as Identity, Citizenship as Shared Fate, and the Functions of Multicultural Education," in K. McDonough & W. Feinberg, eds., *Citizenship and Education in Liberal Democratic Societies: Teaching for Cosmopolitan Values and Collective Identities* (pp. 208–246). Oxford: Oxford University Press.

Williams, T. et al. 2005. *Similar Students, Different Results: Why Do Some Schools Do Better?* Mountain View, CA: EdSource.

Willis, P. 1977. *Learning to Labour: How Working Class Children Get Working Class Jobs.* Farnborough, UK: Saxon House.

Wilson, W. J. 2009. *More than Just Race: Being Black and Poor in the Inner City.* Chicago: University of Chicago Press.

Woodson, C. 1933/1998. *The Mis-Education of the Negro*, 10th printing. Trenton, NJ: Africa World.

Young, I. M. 2000. *Inclusion and Democracy.* Oxford: Oxford University Press.

Young, I. M. 2002. "Equality of Whom? Social Groups and Judgments of Injustice." *Journal of Political Philosophy* 9 (1): 1–18.

Zine, J. 2008. *Canadian Islamic Schools: Unraveling the Politics of Faith, Gender, Knowledge and Identity.* Toronto: University of Toronto Press.

Index

African-centered pedagogy, 117–38
autonomy / self-determination
　group, 96
　personal, 26, 69, 71, 87, 109–11, 157
　political, 12

British National Party (BNP), 144,
　153–54, 187
Brown decision, 5, 118–21, 168

civic virtue, 18–20, 33–34, 61–62,
　64–69, 72–85, 87–90, 100, 106,
　109, 113, 115–16, 130, 138–40,
　156–59, 163–64, 178
cults, 69, 84

deaf persons/culture, 16, 78
deliberation, 18, 25, 29, 43, 68, 78, 80,
　86–88, 111

English Defence League (EDL), 144,
　153
essentialism
　cultural, 19, 103, 118, 132–37
　social class, 154, 159
ethnocentrism, 9, 54, 63–64, 68–69, 80,
　83–84, 105, 111, 113, 130–31, 150,
　154, 179
European Court of Justice, 12

gangs, 34, 69, 84, 100, 117, 134, 144,
　146, 158
ghettos, 34, 105, 173

Hindus, 95, 101–2, 106–7, 115, 142,
　160

homophily principle, 11

implicit bias, 43, 166–67, 176
inclusion, 7–8
indoctrination, 111, 135
involuntary memberships, 50, 63
involuntary segregation / conditions,
　2–4, 7, 18, 22, 26, 39, 67–68, 70,
　76–80, 83, 87, 106, 121, 128–29,
　144, 158, 163–64

Jews, 11, 78, 97, 107, 170, 174

Muslims, 11, 16, 87, 95, 101, 105, 107–
　8, 113, 115–16, 142, 147, 160

partiality, 6, 17–18, 35–38, 45, 48, 52–
　54, 57, 60, 65–66, 111–13, 151
Plessy decision, 4, 119, 168
poverty, 12, 24, 26, 34, 39, 40, 58, 76,
　80–83, 122, 126–28, 139, 145, 148,
　151–52, 158, 164, 167–68, 173,
　184, 186
preferences (adapted or distorted), 3,
　128, 169

school choice, 35–39, 111, 175
secession, 12–13, 85, 172
self-respect, 18–20, 26–27, 33, 43, 46,
　48, 54–56, 60, 67–72, 78–79, 81–
　82, 85–86, 89–90, 100, 102–3, 113,
　115, 122, 126, 128–29, 138–40,
　144–45, 149, 156, 163–65, 169–70,
　177
sexism, 132–33, 137
shared fate, 30, 33, 37, 83, 86, 89, 130

social desirability bias, 43, 166, 176
stigma, 1–2, 6, 14–17, 19, 25–27, 31, 33, 70–72, 76, 78–80, 89, 102, 109, 121, 126, 137, 139–40, 145–47, 149, 151, 153, 159–60, 163, 178
stratification, 39, 68, 80, 120, 173
sufficientarianism, 28, 173

teachers
    effects, 70

incentives, 38, 40, 58, 127, 153

violence, 9–10, 22, 26, 34, 50, 63, 70, 84, 87, 107, 117, 126, 131, 134, 143–44, 158

well-being, 12, 50, 53, 69, 71, 73, 85, 100, 103, 110–14, 123, 125, 128
whiteness, 123, 133, 136, 139, 145, 154–56, 160

Printed and bound by CPI Group (UK) Ltd, Croydon, CR0 4YY